Market forces are never absen<!-- obscured --> <!-- obscured -->stated objectives. What is int<!-- obscured --> <!-- obscured -->Supply and demand are always <!-- obscured -->erty rights as they have emerge<!-- obscured --> <!-- obscured -->an informative and readable nar<!-- obscured --> <!-- obscured --> …pply to modern Chinese urban development. R<!-- obscured --> …… development and rapid urbanization, on scales never before seen, make this discussion valuable and poignant. The book offers a wonderful summary of how markets, especially urban land markets, function in today's China. The book is rich in factual detail, clearly written, and well-grounded in relevant property rights theory. It is informative as well as a pleasure to read.

—*Peter Gordon, Professor Emeritus, School of Public Policy, University of Southern California, USA*

Jieming Zhu has a clear understanding of the nuances of land rights and 'markets' in China and of their evolution since 1978. He depicts how these evolving and convoluted sets of rights affected behavior in land markets, the evolution of the spatial structure of cities, and inequality. I urge researchers on land markets in China to read this informative scholarly work and to carefully consider its informed perspectives.

—*Vernon Henderson, Professor, London School of Economics and Political Science, UK*

This book (re)examines China's urban and rural development through the unique lens of land rights and helps us understand China's development after the establishment of People's Republic of China and the dynamic changes in China's urban and rural regions. Scholars, students, and professionals of planning, geography, urban studies, and so on will definitely enjoy the profound insights and originality of what this book offers.

—*Zhigang Li, Professor, School of Urban Design, Wuhan University, China*

Zhu describes in depth a 'growth machine with Chinese characteristics'. Here the interests of the national and local state sometimes converge but often conflict, land is publicly owned but city officials depend on revenues from developers to finance local services, fortunes are being made from speculative building and everyone is jockeying for a share of it, while the migrants whose growing numbers support the system are mostly excluded from its benefits.

—*John R. Logan, Professor of Sociology, Brown University, USA*

Jieming Zhu's new book viewing China's urban development through the lens of changing land rights is an important addition to the literature on China's march toward urbanization. By tracing the evolution of urban versus rural land rights from before and after the Economic Reforms of 1978, Professor Zhu provides

unique understanding of how the dual land market impacts the built environment. His impressive scholarship gives readers new insight into why suburban areas are characterized by low density while urban centers are overly compact as well as why unequal land rights cause rural villages to often bear the burden of unfettered urban development.
—*Richard Peiser, Michael D. Spear Professor of Real Estate Development, Harvard University, USA*

As a young British soldier performing compulsory National Service in 1950, I was posted to Hong Kong and a camp at Lo Wu, in the shadow of the low range of hills dividing the then British colony from the newly established Chinese People's Republic. An occasional soldiery duty was to climb to an observation post to spend 48 hours observing and reporting on activities across the border on the Chinese side. There was customarily little to report as happening across the wide but quiet view, largely of paddy fields reaching to the horizon and traversed only by the then closed railway line to Canton, now Guangzhou. In 1950, it could not be foreseen that centuries of rice production and peasant would be displaced by the megacity and modern industrial economy of Shenzhen, forming just a part of China's exceptional and unique program of urbanization.

Western planners were thought that by their earlier experience of planning new towns – albeit on much lesser scale, as in the UK – they had lessons to teach for developing countries. The complexity of land issues as described by Zhu in China shows how different its conditions and experience have been to that of the UK, where attempts to reform legislation for land assembly since 1945 have so repeatedly failed to bring an equitable balance between public and private interests. The balance and outcomes in China may be argued over, but the scale of what has been done is beyond compare and Zhu's account a very important record documenting the experience.
—*Urlan Wannop, Professor Emeritus, previously British new town and regional planner, UK*

Jieming Zhu, a well-established scholar on China land, provides a systematic treatment of changing land institution in China. The book describes the change from land as a means of production to land as assets, highlighting complex relationship between land rent and land rights. The book is full of fresh insights and fascinating cases and has made a great contribution to China urban studies.
—*Fulong Wu, Bartlett Professor of Planning, University College London, UK*

Urban Development in China under the Institution of Land Rights

How have the development and redevelopment of China's cities since the early 1950s transformed the settlements and fortunes of a fifth of the world's population? Rapid urbanization since the 1980s has changed the nation from a rural society to an urban one, marking it as one of the most significant transformations in history. As a country with severe land scarcity, land resources are intensively contested for during urbanization under the new regime of marketization. This book focuses on the impact of the institution of land rights that have transitioned from private ownership to socialist state ownership, and subsequently to public land leasing in the urban domain, and to collective ownership in rural areas.

In the context of defining the relationship between the state and the market, the gradualist transition of land rights gives rise to intriguing processes of place-making. The elaboration of these processes will engage several revealing conceptual notions: land as a means of production, land commodification, ambiguous land rights, incomplete land rights, trading land use rights for land development rights, institutional uncertainty, land rent seeking and dissipating, local developmental state, *danwei*-enterprises, and more. The newly created landed interests are embedded intricately within the urban spatial structure.

This book will be of interest to scholars interested in developmental economics, urban planning, geography, public policies, public management, and sociology, and also practitioners focusing on development and planning.

Jieming Zhu (FAcSS) is Distinguished Professor in Urban Planning, Tongji University, China. His researches are in institutional analysis of urban development, planning of high-density low-income Asian cities, and lately, inclusive urbanization in China.

Routledge Advances in Regional Economics, Science and Policy

Creative Ageing Cities
Place Design with Older People in Asian Cities
Edited Keng Hua Chong and Mihye Cho

Competitiveness and Knowledge
An International Comparison of Traditional Firms
Knut Ingar Westeren, Hanas Cader, Maria de Fátima Sales, Jan Ole Similä and Jefferson Staduto

Gastronomy and Local Development
The Quality of Products, Places and Experiences
Edited by Nicola Bellini, Cécile Clergeau and Olivier Etcheverria

The Geography of Scientific Collaboration
Agnieszka Olechnicka, Adam Ploszaj and Dorota Celińska-Janowicz

The Canada-U.S. Border in the 21st Century
Trade, Immigration and Security in the Age of Trump
John B. Sutcliffe and William P. Anderson

Economic Clusters and Globalization
Diversity and Resilience
Edited by Francisco Puig and Berrbizne Urzelai

Transnational Regions in Historical Perspective
Edited by Marten Boon, Hein A.M. Klemann and Ben Wubs

Urban Development in China under the Institution of Land Rights
Jieming Zhu

For more information about this series, please visit www.routledge.com/series/RAIRESP

Urban Development in China under the Institution of Land Rights

Jieming Zhu

LONDON AND NEW YORK

First published 2020
by Routledge
2 Park Square, Milton Park, Abingdon, Oxon OX14 4RN

and by Routledge
52 Vanderbilt Avenue, New York, NY 10017

Routledge is an imprint of the Taylor & Francis Group, an informa business

First issued in paperback 2021

© 2020 Jieming Zhu

The right of Jieming Zhu to be identified as author of this work has been asserted by him in accordance with sections 77 and 78 of the Copyright, Designs and Patents Act 1988.

All rights reserved. No part of this book may be reprinted or reproduced or utilised in any form or by any electronic, mechanical, or other means, now known or hereafter invented, including photocopying and recording, or in any information storage or retrieval system, without permission in writing from the publishers.

Trademark notice: Product or corporate names may be trademarks or registered trademarks, and are used only for identification and explanation without intent to infringe.

British Library Cataloguing-in-Publication Data
A catalogue record for this book is available from the British Library

Library of Congress Cataloging-in-Publication Data
A catalog record has been requested for this book

ISBN: 978-0-367-35803-7 (hbk)
ISBN: 978-1-03-208943-0 (pbk)
ISBN: 978-0-429-34185-4 (ebk)

Typeset in Galliard
by codeMantra

Visit the eResources: www.routledge.com/9780367358037

To all those great thinkers who advocate liberalism and globalism fiercely

Contents

	List of figures	xi
	List of tables	xiii
	Acknowledgements	xv
1	Land rights as an institution for urban development	1
2	Land as a means of production: urban and rural changes without market mechanisms prior to 1978	23
3	Restoration of land as assets: genesis of a market of land leasehold	51
4	Land markets in the making: a dual land market and land rent seeking	71
5	Urban restructuring along with a transitional institution of land development right	97
6	Bottom-up rural spatial changes under an uncertain institution of collective land rights	126
7	From rural fragmentation to urban integration: governance over spatial change	167
8	Conclusion: land rights and sustainable urbanization in the future	199
	Index	207

Figures

2.1	Three categories of cities to be industrialized, 1952	25
2.2	Three categories of cities to be industrialized, 1954	26
2.3	Locations of 156 Soviet-assisted manufacturing projects	27
2.4	Treaty port consumer cities	29
2.5	Slums and shacks in Shanghai, 1949	34
2.6	Layout of Caoyang Workers' New Village	35
2.7	A typical *lilong* residential quarter for the working class (L) and that for the high-income class (R), Shanghai	36
2.8	The floor plans of Workers' New Village housing	38
2.9	Stock of shacks in Shanghai, 1949–1978	39
2.10	Location of ten industrial zones in the urban peripheries and seven industrial towns in the suburbs of Shanghai	43
4.1	Spatial layout of *zhajidi* housing in Shipai *chengzhongcun*, 2015	87
4.2	Spatial layout of Luohu before redevelopment, 1988	88
4.3	Spatial layout of Luohu after redevelopment, 1998	89
5.1	Shanghai's urban districts and prime office locations, 1990s	112
5.2	Shanghai's strategic planning, 1980s	114
5.3	Land uses along Huaihai Road East, 1979	115
5.4	Land uses along Huaihai Road East, 2012	115
5.5	Land uses along Nanjing Road, 1980	116
5.6	Land uses along Nanjing Road, 2012	116
6.1	Correlation between nonagricultural economies and rural GDP per capita in Jiangsu province, 2014	128
6.2	Nonagricultural sectors as a percentage of the county's economies at the provincial level, 2000	130
6.3	Nonagricultural sectors as a percentage of the county's economies at the provincial level, 2010	131
6.4	Beiqijia in Beijing municipality	134
6.5	Agricultural and nonagricultural land uses in 21 villages, Beiqijia township	136
6.6	Kunshan in the Yangtze River Delta	137
6.7	Built-up areas in Kunshan, 1989 (L) and 2010 (R)	138
6.8	Location of Nanhai in the Pearl River Delta	139

xii *Figures*

6.9 Development of the built-up areas in Nanhai, 1990–2008   140
6.10 Urban built-up areas in Guangzhou Metropolitan Region,
     1996 and 2004   144
6.11 Panyu district in the Pearl River Delta   144
6.12 Agricultural and nonagricultural land uses in Panyu district   145
6.13 State-sponsored and collective-initiated land development in Panyu   146
6.14 Extensive mixture of residential and industrial land uses in
     Panyu. A full-color version of this image can be found at
     http:// www.routledge.com/9780367358037   155
6.15 Potential spillover of externalities from a crowded village into a
     planned housing estate, Panyu   157
6.16 Two kinds of governance: open village settlement versus gated
     housing estate   158
6.17 Gated super-housing-estates in Panyu district   160
7.1 A high-plot-ratio with low-site-coverage housing estate   169
7.2 A low-plot-ratio with high-site-coverage street block   170
7.3 Plan of Shipai urbanizing village, Guangzhou, China   171
7.4 Vicious cycle in the land development market leading to
     unsustainable urban forms   173
7.5 Industrial agglomeration from rural factories to industrial zones   191

Tables

1.1	Growth of urban population (million)	13
1.2	Expansion of urban built-up areas (square kilometer)	13
2.1	Categorization of cities to be industrialized, 1952	25
2.2	Categorization of cities to be industrialized, 1954	26
2.3	Numbers of urban population in the EKICs and five coastal cities (thousands)	27
2.4	State investment in capital construction (%)	31
2.5	WNV housing in Shanghai, 1949–1979	36
2.6	Structure of urban land uses: comparison between market cities (Japanese and Paris) and planned cities (Chinese and Moscow) (% of total built-up areas)	37
2.7	Population density in selected Chinese cities (1,000 per sq km, 1983)	38
2.8	Urban investment as percentage of GDP	41
2.9	Population growth and construction of the built environment, Shanghai, 1949–1979	41
2.10	Change in the size of built-up area of selected Chinese cities (1949–1957, square kilometer)	42
2.11	Industrial towns of Shanghai	44
2.12	Farmland holdings in *Kaihsienkung* Village, 1935	45
2.13	Distribution of landholdings between the rural social strata prior to the land reform	46
2.14	Distribution of landholdings between the rural social strata after land reforms	46
3.1	Shenzhen GDP and population, 1979–2016	59
3.2	Shenzhen property stocks, 1985–1999 (million square meters)	59
3.3	Changes in property price indexes	60
3.4	Property transactions in the primary markets, Nanshan district, Shenzhen	61
3.5	Capital Construction Investment by source (%)	62
3.6	Property development and Capital Construction Investment by period	63
4.1	Subsidized land lease in Shenzhen	72
4.2	Land supply by leasing modes, 1987–2016	72

5.1	Housing transactions in the secondary market, Shanghai	99
5.2	Private housing price and office rental indexes, Shanghai	100
5.3	Hierarchy of socialist land users	101
5.4	Dual land acquisition in Jing'an district, Shanghai (1992–2000)	102
5.5	Land redevelopment under LDR in Jing'an district, Shanghai, 1992–2000	105
5.6	Comparison of the quality of office property developments	108
5.7	Development of buildings in floor space, on average per year (million square meters)	109
5.8	Investment in housing in three periods, Shanghai	110
5.9	Expansion of building stocks from 1949 to 2016, Shanghai (millions square meters)	110
5.10	Distribution of office stock (million square meters) in districts and increase of office stock over periods 1985–1991 and 1993–2002 (%)	113
5.11	Distribution of office stock in districts (%)	113
5.12	Investment in fixed assets by SOEs as percentage of total in five cities	119
5.13	Commoditization of building development in Shanghai	120
5.14	Regional disparities in economic growth and marketization, 2000	120
6.1	Nonagricultural jobs as a percentage of rural population in China's five regions, 1987, 1996, and 2011	129
6.2	The shares of agricultural outputs, labors, and population in the national total	131
6.3	Agricultural outputs and rural population as % of Kunshan's total	131
6.4	Land uses in Beiqijia township, 2002	135
6.5	Economic, social, and physical changes over the period 1970–2010, Kunshan	137
6.6	Land development by the two competitors in Beiqijia	150
6.7	Fragmentation of urban and rural housing and industrial land uses in Panyu	155
6.8	Patch analysis of industrial and agricultural land uses in the six-township area	156
6.9	Gated super-housing-estates in Panyu	160
7.1	Statistical characteristics of the total collective income and land rental income of 162 villages, Kunshan, 2012 (¥ thousand)	177
7.2	Demographic structure by the residence status in Nanhai, 1982–2010	177
7.3	Demographic structure by the residence status in Kunshan, 1980–2010	177
7.4	Statistical characteristics of township's industrial output as % of total municipal industrial output, 1995 and 2011	186
7.5	Agglomerated industrial jobs and dispersed rural industrial workers	192

Acknowledgements

This book cannot be accomplished without generous helps from those former students and collaborators: Dr. Yan GUO, Dr. Xuan LIU, and Ms. Tingting HU. Their contributions are gratefully recognized. Wonderful cartographic works done by Peiyu ZHAN, Muwen ZHU and Zhao ZHU are greatly appreciated. The professionalism demonstrated by the editorial team led by Yongling LAM and Samantha PHUA at Routledge is excellent, which goes through from initiation of the manuscript to its completion. I am indebted to the project manager Jeanine FURINO and her team at codeMantra for the meticulous copyediting.

1 Land rights as an institution for urban development

Although cities as a form of civilization have been in existence for more than 5,000 years, and more than half of the world population live in cities by now, understanding of the production of those entities is far from adequate. Cities are built on land as an essential factor, and land rights as institutions are closely linked to economic systems and social norms. Land rights can be assigned by the state, transacted through the market, and maintained by the communities according to public, private, and social interests. Land rights have a profound impact on the urban built environment, exemplified by informal settlements, gated communities, and diverse community spaces. The socioeconomic transition from the central planning to market orientation provides a great opportunity to understand the formation of China's cities in the context of institutional change to land rights.

Land as natural resources and economic assets

Being an essential natural resource, land serves humanity for its survival and prosperity by maintaining an ecosystem with biodiversity, through which food, water, and minerals are provided so that economic, social, and cultural activities can be carried out. However, with a burgeoning population, the living environment is increasingly under pressure with competitive demands for land from pursing higher quality of life, eradicating poverty in the developing countries, and maintaining healthy and ecological lives. The Intergovernmental Science-Policy Platform on Biodiversity and Ecosystem Services (IPBES) warns recently that biodiversity continues to decline globally, drastically reducing nature's capacity to serve people's well-being, based on the four regional investigations of ecosystem services covering the Americas, Asia and the Pacific, Africa, Europe, and Central Asia (https://www.ipbes.net/, accessed March 25, 2018). Excessive farming, fishing, and felling of trees make economies, livelihoods, food security, and the quality of life of people in the world increasingly unsustainable.

Finite supply and unlimited demand inevitably make land resources scarce. Scarcity makes land resources valuable assets and thereby entails competition. Competition over land resources occurs between human communities and natural reservations. Those lands used by human communities are further categorized as urban and rural. Distributed among various jurisdictions, land resources are under pressure at different degrees determined by the local territorial factors. These factors include the climate, number of habitants, economic status, social values, and cultural attitudes. Competition gives rise to mechanisms for allocation of scarce land resources between users. Those mechanisms used in history include indigenous traditional negotiation, coercive appropriation, or transaction based on bilaterally agreed rules. Creating a market for land, granting power to the state, and relying on community traditions as mechanisms for allocation seem the mainstreams in the modern times.

Mechanisms for land assignment: state, market, and community

Economic systems are decentralized if decisions are made mainly at bottom levels, whereas they are centralized if decisions are made at top levels. Mechanisms for coordinating decision-making reveal the dichotomy between market and plan. A planned economy is the one in which production units are coordinated by directives from central authorities. Economic activities are guided by plans formulated by the state. A market economy is the system coordinated by voluntary and autonomous demand and supply. The basic decision of production in a market economy is in the domain of consumer sovereignty, whereas decisions are made according to planners' preferences in a planned economy (Gregory and Stuart, 1992). The market economic system seems to have triumphed over the planned economic system since the fundamental political changes in the former east-European socialist countries and gradual economic changes in China and Vietnam in Asia.

The social transformation, spearheaded by the economic reforms, has also changed the state from one engaged in socialist, centrally planned provision to a state searching for its position in a new economy that has yet to take shape. According to Block (1994: 691), there is a single continuum regarding the state's role in the economy:

> [at] one end of this continuum is the minimalist 'night watchman state' of classical liberalism; at the other end is a society in which the state has absorbed the basic tasks of economic production and distribution, largely eliminating the possibility for market transactions.

Five 'ideal types' of the state are identified, ranking from the lowest to the highest degree of state control over the economy: public goods state, macroeconomic stabilization state, social rights state, developmental state, and socialist state. This categorization is, nevertheless, deemed the old paradigm. The new paradigm recognizes that "state action *always* plays a major role in constituting economies" and emphasizes "qualitative differences in state activities" (*ibid.*: 696, original emphasis). Thus, the debate on the issue of state versus market should be developed in the context of the state *constructing* the market.

The market stresses both the social and the economic importance of individual initiatives, choices, and freedom. Pro-market schools of thought believe that the market is "a system of economic freedom and a necessary condition for political freedom" (Friedman and Friedman, 1979: ix). It is claimed that transactions beneficial to two parties in exchange occur only when the exchange is voluntary. Freedom to choose enables individuals to cooperate with one another for collective benefits. A competitive market powerfully facilitates efficient use of resources, and unrestrained demand-supply equilibrium mediated by free price mechanisms is an effective means of coordination for efficient production. Through the 'invisible hand', free markets can maximize both individual and collective benefits, and coordinate a multitude of individual actors with complex priorities.

However, there are market failures, and the market is not perfectly competitive. Factors like negative externalities, business cycles, and socially inequitable distribution are classic examples of market problems. Nonrival and nonexcludable public goods, though desired and valued, would not be provided by the market because of the free-rider problem. Olson (1965: 2) asserts that "unless there is coercion or some other special device to make individuals act in their common interest, rational, self-interested individuals will not act to achieve their common or group interests". Coordination of conflicting social groups and provision of rules to the public are as important public goods as social and physical infrastructure to the workings of the market. Economic well-being and social welfare thus cannot be secured by private, free transactions only. They also depend on public goods, law enforcement, and infrastructure provided by the state (Heertje, 1989). Galbraith (1977) in *The Age of Uncertainty* regarded state governance and intervention as essential for maintaining economic stability and efficiency and achieving social equity in view of deficiencies of the market. Rules, i.e. regulations, provide regularity with which a predictable and transparent system can reduce transaction costs and therefore make market exchanges efficient. It is the failures of markets that prompt the legitimate coercion of the state (Popkin, 1988; Dunford, 1990; World Bank, 1992).

Nevertheless, state intervention is not without its problems and negative implications. Though the state is the institutionalization of sovereignty and authority, which is empowered to enforce laws and attain social goals (Nettl, 1968), it provides the ground for potential rent-seeking (Krueger, 1974; Wolf, 1993). By regulating the market, the state likely generates rent. Regulations create opportunities for rent-seeking. Rent-seeking and rent-extracting are wasteful, which make the market inefficient. At this juncture, market advocates claim that only free market forces should be able to enhance the welfare of society efficiently (Lal, 1983), and the state should be kept to its minimal role of protecting private property rights, enforcing private contracts, and providing defense, order, and justice (Buchanan, Tollison, and Tullock, 1980).

The ideal type of *laissez-faire* market guided by Adam Smith's 'invisible hand' does not exist in reality because it is hampered by market failures. Because of free-rider problems, markets without state involvement would produce an inadequate amount of noncompetitive and nonexcludable public goods. Public goods, such as infrastructure, open space, and public parks, are necessary for the functional well-being of the city. Provision of public goods goes beyond the physical facet to the institutional dimension. With law and order, functioning of the land market is maintained and facilitated by an institutional structure that defines property rights over land assets and guarantees contracts for transactions (Buchanan, 1977; Olson, 1982). Therefore, without proper order that is provided through law and property rights, freedom to choose alone does not enable individuals to cooperate with one another for collective benefits. The state and market are the two paramount factors in the organization of economies. There is still a long-running debate on the relationship between the state and the market, which has an ideological inclination as well as a practical dimension. In spite of the debate, the state's role in shaping institutions for the land market is widely considered both crucial and essential.

John Turner, a British architect, argued forcefully in the 1970s that autonomy in the built environment, particularly building the habitats for the poor, should be superior to both the state and the market (Turner, 1976). Self-help housing and self-management of neighborhoods were strongly advocated as they were better than "those built through government programs or large corporations" (Turner and Fichter, 1972: front cover page). Local autonomy seems usual in many developing as well as developed countries. It is a common practice that dwellings are built by people themselves in villages and probably in small towns as well, using local materials and observing local customs. Traditional villages are often spontaneously and organically built up. In this circumstance, autonomously built housing must be the most suitable and affordable accommodation. Some aesthetically appeasing traditional villages have become cultural assets. Social order for the homogeneous rural communities can probably be established through community's autonomous self-management, based on mutual trust and tacit knowledge shared within the community, and thus collective actions derived from unwritten rules can be obtained without a coercive state.

Rapid industrialization and urbanization are relatively recent phenomena in Asian developing countries. While the economies and settlements are urbanized, some rural institutions are more or less in place, managing the society that is transforming. Community management as a way of rural life continues its usefulness as a transitory means of controls in the newly formed urban settlements. Autonomous land development based on rural traditions occurs because zoning as an urban institution has not set its roots in urban governance. Indonesia is used herewith as an example in illustration (Zhu and Simarmata, 2015). Indonesia's Basic Agrarian Law of 1960 states that the land ownership follows *adat*[1] philosophy (Wallace, Parlindungan, and Hutagalung, 2000). Because of the colonization, Indonesia has two systems of land laws: the Western law, installed by the Dutch colonizers; and the *adat*, indigenous customary law. Land with the *girik* (literally meaning tax receipts) title signifies that the holder should have the land tax receipts which suggest the landholder pays land tax regularly and become the proof of customary ownership. *Girik* land has full property rights similar to freehold ownership. Ownership under *garapan* (use right) is based on transfer agreements between individuals, a weaker claim than *girik* (Winayanti and Lang, 2004).

Lands with formal titles are surrounded by a vast territory held under indigenous rights. Leaf (1993: 484) reckons that "the majority of lands which comprise *kampung*[2] neighborhoods in Jakarta are unregistered". Land management in Jakarta remains largely based on *adat* laws. A survey of nine Indonesian cities (Jakarta, Bandung, Yogyakarta, Serang, Medan, Bandar Lampung, Jambi, Balikpapan, and Kupang) showed a similar pattern of land rights: 63 percent unregistered titles and 37 percent registered titles (Struyk, Hoffman, and Katsura, 1990: 93).

Though indigenous governance is socially effective and inclusive to the community members with neither the coercive state nor the competitive market, urban development managed by autonomous communities could be problematic as dynamic urban communities are heterogeneous, and collective actions are hard to be coordinated because community members become diverse and individualistic. Those are the different characteristics between *gemeinschaft* and *gesellschaft*. When collectivistic social relations and tacit agreements do not exist within the ever-changing urban community, coordination of conflicting social groups and provision of rules to urban societies as community goods become extremely challenging.

Property rights: the rules of the game

Coordination of economic activities, whether by the market, by the state, or by the community, can be encapsulated as that who owns the rights over the said object. Property rights are a bundle of rights that link an economic system with a political structure and a legal regime, and property rights are primarily rights of ownership. Property rights are defined by prevailing legal opinions (Bazelon, 1963) and are concerned with economic efficiency and distributive justice, which places limits on the actions of individuals and governments (Paul, Miller, and Paul, 1994). On an individual level, property rights affect peoples' freedom and well-being (Denman, 1978). According to Roman law, which specifies several categories of property rights, ownership consists the right to use an asset (*usus*), the right to capture benefits from an asset (*ususfructus*), the right to change its form and substance (*abusus*), and the right to transfer all or some of the rights specified above to others at a mutually agreed price (Pejovich, 1990: 27–28). Property rights are an institution devised by society to shape human interaction (North, 1990). In the same vein, land rights are composed of the right to use, the right to rent, the right to develop, and the right to sell the land in question.

Societies and economies are bound by institutions that are "the humanly devised constraints that structure political, economic, and social interactions" (North, 1991: 97). A society is deemed an organized community because individuals living together as group members share the same rules and customs that regulate their social behaviors. Institutions thus provide "regularities in behavior which are agreed to by all members of a society and which specify behavior in specific recurrent situations" (Schotter, 1981: 9). In the economic domain, institutions are deemed "sets of rights and obligations affecting people in their economic lives" (Matthews, 1986: 905). The functioning of an economic system depends on a whole set of institutional conditions. As institutions determine an incentive structure for the market, an efficient market should be shaped by institutions which minimize transaction costs and encourage competition through price and quality (North, 1998). Uncertainty in the interactions or transactions is effectively mitigated by institutions that limit the set of choices and increase the predictability of social behavior. On a pragmatic note, the World Bank (2002) defines institutions as rules, enforcement mechanisms, and organizations. Organizations, whether they are political, economic, or social, behave and perform as collective actors within a framework defined by institutions (Knight, 1992; Weimer, 1997).

Institutions are composed of both formal rules such as constitutions, regulations, and laws, and informal constraints, such as conventions, moral rules, and social norms. Formal institutions are explicitly enforced by the state, while informal institutions are maintained by the community. Neo-classical economists have faith in the premise that clearly defined property rights should achieve Pareto efficiency in a market system. Exclusivity and transferability, secured by well-defined property rights, generate powerful incentives for owners to pursue the highest-valued use for their resources and for resources to seek the most productive owners to achieve the highest productivity (Alchian, 1961; Posner, 1973). The Coase Theorem specifies that free exchange with costless transaction tends to move resources to the highest valued uses, independent of prior assignment of rights (Coase, 1960). However, in reality, transaction costs are always positive. Thus, the assignment of property rights matters for the achievement of efficiency.

Land rights as an institution for urbanization: zoning

Demsetz (1967) points out that one of the economic functions of property rights is to internalize externalities in the competitive use of resources. The structure of land rights determines the mode of land development and thus has direct impacts on the form of the resultant built environment. Land rent is the value of land appropriated in economic transactions, as the market price of land is interpreted as capitalized land rent in perpetuity. The rental value of a land plot is largely determined by the equilibrium of demand for and supply of land as commodity in its use designated by zoning (agricultural, residential, commercial, and so on). The potential land rent represents the amount of rent that can be capitalized under the 'highest and best use'. The gap between the potential land rent and actual land rent capitalized under the present land use is the land-rent differential (Smith, 1979). Capture of land-rent differentials gives landowners sufficient incentive to redevelop lands for the 'highest and best' uses. Because of various restrictions, and thus attenuations of property rights, the land market is not a construct of absolutely free interplay between demand and supply. Land rent is appropriated under a framework of property rights. Property rights are initially formulated to manage social cooperation in the use of scarce resources (Becker, 1977). The subject of land transactions is not land *per se* but, essentially, interests in rights over the land. Property rights are thus deemed essential in the governance of land markets (Fischel, 1985; Webster and Lai, 2003).

Market failures are marked and inherent in the land market because of heterogeneity, low liquidity, high transaction cost, and location fixity in relation to land parcels. Externalities because of interdependence between land sites are pronounced, and market mechanisms alone are not able to internalize the costs/benefits of negative/positive externalities in the pricing of land plots.[3] The adverse effects of negative externalities are not automatically compensated for through a market process and are difficult to internalize without a third party to intervene; subsequently, the community will bear the consequences (World Bank, 1992). Land use and development rights are therefore defined by land use planning in order to internalize externalities. Zoning or planning controls, which attenuate private land rights by the state's control over use and development rights, are regarded as positive in making the land market efficient and equitable (Pigou, 1932; Nelson, 1977; Brabant, 1991; Lai, 1999). Zoning is deemed as community rights to safeguard the collective interests (Fischel, 1985). As an essential factor shaping the land market, land use planning stabilizes the land market through enhanced certainty with respect to the future character of a place (Jud, 1980). By assigning rights and liabilities, the state may play a supportive role in making urban built environment sustainable. Serious land scarcity in China is prone to create externalities which generate enormous social costs. The structure of land rights must be conducive to the achievement of sustainable urban forms.

Informality as the commons versus rights to the stakeholders for diversity

The value of an asset to its owner is determined by how secure the owner's property rights are. If property rights are not perfectly delineated, some attributes will be in the open domain and, hence, subject to unrestricted access (Barzel, 1989). If land rights are defined ambiguously and incompletely to owners, land rent will be appropriated – openly or covertly. As a result, land rent dissipates. Some matters in relation to land rights are significantly formative in the process of urbanization. Informality prevails as a way of life in many developing countries (Roy and AlSayyad, 2004). The informal economy emerges in the circumstance of influx of migrants into cities, mainly driven by the rural poverty, and the formal economy cannot provide sufficient number of jobs to those newcomers. "[T]he lower the level of development of a country, the larger its informal sector" (Charmes, 1990: 17). In parallel to the informal economy, informal housing predominates in the same vein (Hall and Pfeiffer, 2000). Rapid urbanization driven by the rural poverty has resulted in sprawling slums and squatter settlements in the cities. Urbanization in South America has created highly polarized cities, where informal housing settlements have been ever growing to accommodate poor migrants (Gilbert, 2004; Perlman, 2004). Urban informality results from residents' spontaneous bottom-up response to the incapacity of the state and its formal sectors (De Soto, 1989). When people's basic needs are not satisfactorily met within the formal framework managed by the state and the market, informality emerges and becomes a mode of urban life.

Self-built housing constructed without obtaining planning permits (zoning controls) is known as informal housing, or termed euphemistically as popular housing (Janoschka and Norsdorf, 2006). It is estimated that a substantial number of inhabitants in the developing countries live in informal shelter (United Nations Centre for Human Settlement, 1987). Ostrom (1990) advocates management of common pool resources with neither centralized government control nor privatization. Nevertheless, contextual variables, such as the relative scarcity of the resource and the size of the collective involved, are emphasized as critical for effective collective self-governance (Ostrom, 2000). High population density and land scarcity challenge collective governance over urban public spaces which are held as common resources. Modes of housing construction do not remain static in the course of industrialization and urbanization. Two prominent factors have to be considered for the developing countries: continuous, unabated rural-urban migration until arrival of a matured level of urbanization, and thus rising residential density because of acute land scarcity. Accommodating new migrants is as important and demanding as solving housing problems for the existing urban residents. However, the informal housing discourse has been only concerned with the latter, ignoring the fact that the former are in a graver situation.

Because of primitive construction and low building technologies, informal housing is usually low-rise, and thus utilization of scarce land resources is far from optimal. Though low-cost, informal housing is affordable to low-income social groups initially, urban land becomes increasingly scarcer all the time as demand from new migrants outstrip supply of additional land (Benjamin, Arifin, and Sarjana, 1985). As a result, density in informal settlements increases progressively as more newcomers arrive. Rapid net increase of population aggravates the scarcity of urban land resources, and great land scarcity generates intensive competition over access to land use. Optimal land utilization to maximize provision of building spaces and urban facilities becomes a critical issue for the urban planning agendas of Asian cities. Informal housing builders always try to maximize the housing floor areas without planning regulations, and thus imposing negative externalities on the neighborhood. Individual gains (maximization of housing floor areas) lead to neighborhood losses (loss of open and green spaces). The damaging effects of negative externalities on the neighborhood are costless to the inflictor initially, which then gives incentives to all house builders to follow suit. Negative externalities are aggregated, and neighborhood environment deteriorates.

The neighborhood becomes *the commons*, a property rights situation where environmental amenities are overconsumed and land utilization becomes suboptimal. The commons is the case of open access to resources. Individuals seeking personal gains without restriction leads to depletion of resources as a result of overconsumption and underinvestment, which harm the collective benefit, resulting in the so-called 'tragedy of the commons' (Hardin, 1968). Uncontrollable urban sprawl goes further, and more open space and agricultural land are encroached upon. Collective action, rather than individual decisions, is imperative in this case to achieve the goal of sustainable land use. However, coordination for dealing with conflicts between social groups and provision of rules to urban societies as public goods become extremely challenging, because "rational, self-interested individuals will not act to achieve their common or group interests" (Olson, 1965: 2). Substandard, inferior, and deteriorating habitations ensue.

When the state is incapable of administering quality urban governance, the market will take its place by providing alternatives. It is usually the declining quality of municipal services in the developed cities that gives rise to self-governance for the well-off neighborhoods, with the private provision of residential facilities and amenities (Webster, 2002; Atkinson and Blandy, 2006). Judd (1995: 155) states that a common-interest residential development is "a community in which the residents own or control common areas or shared amenities" and which "carries with it reciprocal rights and obligations enforced by a private governing body". An absence of public zoning gives rise to private exclusionary zoning. In the setting of developing cities with rising population density and land scarcity, gated communities emerge in response to state incapacity, as private neighborhoods provide civic goods and services, which are not provided by the municipal government. The dichotomy between informal settlements and gated communities is a prevalent phenomenon in many developing countries. It occurs when urbanization has attracted an influx of poor migrants and created an emerging middle class and a rising middle class' demand for decent housing has to be fulfilled in the gated communities as informal settlements are mainly for the poor. The juxtaposition of the commons and exclusionary private zoning results from state incapacity and ineffective governance over the process of land development. Social polarization is exacerbated by the spatial segregation as a result of informal settlement – gated-community symbiosis.

There is widespread criticism against new towns as being physically and socially homogenous. But if land rights granted are exercised by a collection of diverse stakeholders, which is not the case for new town development, diversity is imbedded in the development of the built environment. Stakeholders in a locality are naturally concerned with how the locality would be remolded. Urbanization has created places that are usually shared by people living disparate lifestyles and believing in diverse values. The evolution of planning theories from comprehensive physical planning to public participation, communicative planning, and further to collaborative planning reflects that the process of shaping local environments should take a wide range of stakeholders into consideration (Healey, 1997). Diversity has become one of the principal guidelines for today's urban planning. Fainstein (2005: 4) proclaims that "diversity attracts human capital, encourages innovation, and ensures fairness and equal access to a variety of groups". Public participation assures the involvement of groups and individuals with diverse interests in the planning process, yet diverse opinions and NIMBYism ('not in my backyard') render planning devoid of actions. This is the property rights situation known as *the anticommons*, or practically known as 'hold-out' problems, where multiple owners have effective rights excluding each other from efficient utilization of resources (Heller, 1998; Buchanan and Yoon, 2000). Though full of bargains and negotiations and thus high transaction costs, communicative planning and collaborative planning aim at positive consensus building among different viewpoints (Innes, 1995; Healey, 1997). "Collaborative approaches ... are focused explicitly on the task of building up links across disparate networks, to forge new relational capacity across the diversity of relations which coexist these days in places" (Healey, 1997: 61).

The practices of public participation and consensus building are procedural rather than substantive in nature. Fainstein (2000: 464) observes that "if one visits the world's planned new towns and downtown redevelopment projects, even those built with commitment to diversity and community, one is struck by their physical and social homogeneity". Jane Jacobs, a critic of modern town planning, quips that new towns "were really very nice towns if you were docile and had no plans of your own and did not mind spending your life among others with no plans of their own" (1966: 102). It is not necessary that urban planning should create homogenous towns. Planning alone is just a constraint imposed upon land use right and development right, while many choices and decisions still rest entirely with landowners. The alleged homogeneity occurs only when a new town is mostly built by a single developer who owns a large proportion, if not all, of land before subdivided land plots are sold to residents. Many new towns are built in such a manner. The comprehensively planned new towns of Columbia (Maryland, USA) and Reston (Virginia, USA) were built in such a manner (http://www.columbiaassociation.com/; http://www.reston.org/).

A developer's commitment to a comprehensive master plan does not yield a planned new town without extensive landownership prior to land development. Jacobs (1961) believes that good urban design (mixed land uses, small street blocks, conservation of historic buildings, and high density) could generate or maintain diversity in the built form. I believe that diversity in places should be secured by a diverse structure of land rights. If property rights over land and buildings are granted to and exercised by a collection of diverse actors, diversity is imbedded in the development of the built environment. The old town's charm is to a great extent attributed to its diversity and pluralism, which results from numerous individual landowners' free decisions over time. The planned new towns, claimed as monotonous, are often created by a homogeneous structure of property rights or by a too dominant state in the management of land development. The rhetoric of procedural public participation can easily be annulled by the substantive land rights regime.

Development and redevelopment of *Niucheshui*, Singapore, is a case enlightening the effect of land rights on the built environment (Zhu, Sim, and Liu,

2007). Though there was no formal land use planning for *Niucheshui*, simple guidelines were provided for the area to be built in conformity with the building codes. By the end of the 1950s, most street blocks in *Niucheshui* were divided by individual landowners into strips. A so-called 'shophouse' was built on each strip. Shophouses were mostly two or three stories high, with a shop on the ground floor and a residence above the shop. As the majority of Chinese immigrants came from the southeastern coastal provinces of China, the architecture of early *Niucheshui* shophouses was strongly influenced by that of southern China (URA, 1995). Identified by the ethnic Chinese as the center for their communities, *Niucheshui* became a place prolific with community goods such as temples (*Fuk Tak Chi* by Hakka and Cantonese, *Thian Hock Keng* by Hokkien); parks (*Hong Lim* Green provided by a Hokkien community leader Cheng Hong Lim); clan associations (*huikuans*) organized along the lines of locality, dialect, surname, or trade; and Chinese schools (*Yueng Ching* School, *Chong Hock* Girl's School) (Cheng, 1990).

Niucheshui was built by the local communities and was the product of community initiatives prior to the 1950s. Nevertheless, those players have faded from the scene since the 1960s, and the redevelopment of *Niucheshui* has been the product of state management facilitated by the government-controlled property rights system in the forms of compulsory land acquisition, rent control, land leasing, and conservation of historical buildings. The free market for land redevelopment is reined in heavily by the state. Otherwise, fragmented landownership would have made land assembly difficult. From the perspective of property rights as an institution in land (re)development, if cultural pluralism and diversity are the values for the city which strives to be 'a thriving world class city', various stakeholders' rights should be recognized and incorporated into the property rights system. A tripartite partnership between the state, market, and stakeholders may have to replace the bipartite one between the state and the market.

China's institutional change in land rights in the context of rapid urbanization

The socialist revolution in 1949 gave birth to the People's Republic of China, which subsequently jettisoned the capitalist market economy. Capitalism was considered exploitative, and it was the system where capitalists suppressed the workers and peasants. The centrally controlled economy was soon established, so as to build a new China. The new socialist economy was based on the state ownership, and urban land was nationalized and treated as a means of production only, rather than an economic asset. Urbanization was pursued without participation of land markets. Socialist cities were planned and constructed based on the 'productive sectors', and the legacy of 'bourgeois consumer cities' had to be transformed to 'proletarian producer cities'. Socialist land use rights played a key role in building ostensibly equal cities.

Ownership of the means of production (including land) constitutes the mode of production. Capitalism is an economic system where the means of production are owned privately, so are the surplus profits, whereas socialism advocates social ownership of the means of production and the surplus profits are retained by society in general. Private ownership of the means of production creates classes. The bourgeoisie as the capitalist class are able to derive rents and profits from the means of production owned. In contrast, the proletariat as the working class have to sell their labor power for wages due to an absence of control over the means of production. Marxism believes that land as a natural resource, nonproduced and finite in supply, generates unearned ground-rent that is transformed from surplus profit as a payment for land use appropriated by the landowners. Private land ownership becomes a part and parcel of capitalism that generates class oppression. Socialist revolution makes land as a means for production for all people, instead of economic assets for some people.

Significant changes with a single goal of developing the national economy have been initiated since 1978, symbolized by formal integration of the Four Modernization (agriculture, industry, science, and defense) into the new Constitution. Endorsed by the Fifth National People's Congress in March 1978 and then by the Third Plenum of the Eleventh Central Committee of the Chinese Communist Party in December 1978, a social transformation spearheaded by the economic reforms was launched aiming at a grand goal of national advancement. The rigid central-controlled system was to be reformed in order to build vigor into the economies that were mostly state-owned. The economic reforms were expected to stimulate the inactive economies which had been, as believed, stifled by the central planning regime. The new policies called for a shift of strategy from overemphasized self-reliance to participation in the world market, and from inward self-sufficient production to outward trading in the context of globalization.

It is understood that old institutions, which used to play a principal role in the old planning system, are still the determinants for the reforms (Chen, 1992). Old politico-economic forces are still at work. The reform process turns out to be a result of ideological battles rather than a matter of economic rationality. In this context, it is understandable that there has been no blueprint to guide the unprecedented transformation. The liberals try to push the reforms forward, while the conservatives intend to hold the existing system. Nevertheless, a desire to build a strong economy has given liberals a powerful mandate and forced to unite politicians of the two extremes on the political spectrum. Pragmatism has prevailed as a result. Pragmatism and political rhetoric determine an approach of trial-and-error for the implementation. "Crossing the river by groping stones" (*mozhe shitou guohe*) is a succinct adage revealing the underlined philosophy. The economic reforms as institutional change are gradualist and incremental.

Being a very poor agricultural country where urbanites only accounted for 10.6 percent of the total population in 1949, China was still dominated by the agricultural production in 1978, when urban population only represented 17.9 percent of the total. The rate of urban population reached drastically at 57.4 percent in 2016. Over the period (1978–2016), 620.5 million people were urbanized (NBSC, 2017, see Table 1.1). China's economic reforms have brought about tremendous changes to the country. Market orientation and opening up to the world are the two key factors underpinning the economic miracle. Economic growth leads to physical change. China's cities have experienced a drastic transformation in the course of economic reforms. An emerging land market has been structured by newly evolved institutions which are responsible, to a large extent, for the phenomenon of rapid spatial change. The drastic turn occurred in 1988, when public land leasing replaced the socialist free land allocation. Between 1981 and 2016, 46,041.3 square kilometers of land were converted to urban uses (see Table 1.2).

Land as natural and scarce resources should be used efficiently. Though ground-rent is a sort of economic rent accruing to owners as a result of the exclusive ownership privilege, free land use breeds social inequality and political corruption. Ricardo ([1821] 1951) demonstrated that rent for the more fertile land is derived from its advantage over the less fertile land, and thus land rent is determined by the fertility differential. Von Thünen ([1826] 1966) developed the theory of land rent further based on location differential, suggesting that land rent should increase with the accessibility of land. Accessibility replaces fertility

Table 1.1 Growth of urban population (million)

Year	1949	1978	1988	2016
Total population	541.7	962.6	1,110.3	1,382.7
Percent of urban population in total population	10.6	17.9	25.8	57.4
Urban population	57.7	172.5	286.6	793.0
Net increase of urban population		114.8	114.1	506.4

Note: Statistics do not include Taiwan, Hong Kong, and Macau.
Source: NBSC, 2017.

Table 1.2 Expansion of urban built-up areas (square kilometer)

Year	1981	1986	2016
Urban built-up areas	6,720.0	10,127.3	52,761.3
Net increase of urban built-up areas		3,407.3	42,634.0

Source: www.ceicdata.com/zh-hans/china/urban-area/area-of-city-construction (accessed October 4, 2018) for 2016 data.

14 *Land rights as urban development*

as the determinant of land rent, which yields the bid rent function in the urban context. The gap between the potential land rent based on the 'highest and best use' and the actual land rent capitalized under the present land use constitutes the land rent differential.

Land commoditization and marketization generate explicit land rent, and competition for land rent ensues. In the context of gradualist and incremental reforms, the transition from land being 'a means of production' to land leasehold hatches out land rights in a variety of forms that impose impact on the process of land development and subsequent spatial patterns of urban formation and reformation. During the transition, rural community land rights, *danwei*'s[4] and people's socialist land use rights, ambiguous collective land rights emerge, and their respective impacts are clearly shown on the transformation of the built-up environment. As more than half of the population are urbanized together with rapid economic growth, inclusive urban-rural integrated urbanization is now keenly pursued so as to tackle ambiguous land rights. The prolonged gradualist reforms from socialist central planning to socialist market orientation have generated numerous transitional institutions that give rise to various forms of the built environment. This book endeavors to throw light on the mechanisms through which changing land rights impact on China's urbanization.

Uncertainty and ambiguity: generation of land rent

Uncertainty prevails in the real world, because of the complexity of human relationships and a lack of knowledge of the human world. Knowledge and uncertainty are mutually exclusive (Shackle, 1961). As human beings have gained much control over the physical world, uncertainty derived from human interactions has increased tremendously, resulting from the gap between human competence and difficulties in the real world (Heiner, 1983). Scarcity also complicates problems in human relationships (Commons, 1934), though neoclassical economists believe that scarce resources should be used efficiently if market forces are unshackled so as to drive the market toward a long-term equilibrium of demand and supply. When uncertainty occurs, it prevents individuals from making rational and the most appropriate decisions because causality is unknown. Following patterns and thus rigidity and inflexibility of behavior is a way to cope with the capricious real world: "the flexibility of behavior to react ... is constrained to smaller behavioral repertoires that can be reliably administered" (Heiner, 1983: 585).

Certainty is therefore created by regular and predictable patterns of behavior and cooperation between community members (Elster, 1989). Formation of rules thus aims to reduce complexity and uncertainty caused by actors' limited ability to gather information and also to lower transaction costs (Williamson, 1985). Transaction costs refer to the effort, time, and expense necessary to obtain sufficient information to make, negotiate, and enforce an exchange. Transactions are not costless, owing to expensively acquired knowledge. Hayek (1973) distinguishes between two types of order: organization and spontaneous order.

The former is formed consciously by human design, and the latter is shaped through an evolutionary process of social selection. Alternatively, order can be regarded as institutions which are considered as 'rules of the game', structuring and binding social interactions and market transactions. North (1991) suggests that institutions should be composed of both informal constraints such as sanctions, taboos, customs, traditions, and codes of conduct and formal rules like constitutions, regulations, and laws. Therefore, institutions, either formal or informal, are generated in the context of pervasive uncertainty in human interactions, and institutions "reduce uncertainty by providing a structure to everyday life" (North, 1990: 3). Institutions are fundamental to mitigating uncertainty, as social norms make human behavior more predictable by bounding individuals and providing regularity (Cornell and Kalt, 1997).

Institutions are evolving constantly, driven by socioeconomic and technological changes. In North's (1990) and Eggertsson's (1994) views, institutional change is made marginal, incremental, and path dependent by an immense stock of social capital in the form of an institutional matrix. Institutional change is related to social choices, and choices are constrained by cultural norms. Socially deeply embedded institutions of the status quo – both formal, which are sanctioned, maintained, and enforced by the state, and informal, which are controlled by the community and social network – will not be terminated immediately. Those strong institutions determine the path of change and are often themselves transformed, along with the change, into a new strain with much bearing on the past. The interests of the status quo should play a significant role in maintaining order and thus certainty in an evolutionary process of institutional change. A vacuum will be created when the institutions of the status quo are weakened and new institutions are yet to be established, and thus institutional change can generate uncertainty.

Institutional uncertainty during China's economic reforms and social transformation since 1978 has been well pronounced. Gradualism for socioeconomic change has been chosen because of political constraints, which brings in an approach of trial and error in the implementation of new initiatives. Without a clear chart to guide the change, gradualism leads to dualism, which means a coexistence of new and old systems. Institutional uncertainty during the institutional change is characterized by a vacuum of governance between the two systems, while old institutions are being phased out and new institutions are being phased in (Nee, 1991; Walder, 1992; Shirk, 1993; Sachs and Woo, 1994; Wang, 1995; Huang, 1996; Oi, 1996), which results in rampant arbitrage between the two systems. A lack of rules and institutions results in the absence of a predictable and transparent environment that is essential for social and economic activities (World Bank, 1992). Other examples such as increasingly significant sustainability and city capacity building in the global competition also point to the critical role of governance as institutions (Cowell and Owens, 2006; Benneworth and Dauncey, 2010).

In the sphere of China's urbanization and related land development, emerging market forces are at work, but new institutions managing market-driven land development are not fully established yet. Arising from the absence of formal governance, uncertainty can induce disorderly short-term behavior and thus unsustainable land development. Land rent dissipation occurs, in terms of land economics. Alternatively, uncertain circumstances can push for further institutional change to mend uncertainty. Examples are schemes such as farming cooperatives and insurance that were invented to spread risks in face of uncertainty (Schotter, 1981). During the transition, the formal governance over the rural land development is explicitly weak. When state governance is weak in maintaining order and managing interactions, private governance may emerge to fill the void. Disordered land rent competition is one of the key factors responsible for a spatially fragmented and disorganized intense mix of agricultural and nonagricultural land uses. Uncontrolled externalities accumulate and worsen the quality of social and ecological environments (Zhu and Guo, 2014).

Two spatial domains may possibly appear subsequently: one is where state governance is not in control, and the other is where private governance is in force. This institutional change is undesirable, and probably problematic, as the two domains would exacerbate social segregation. In the setting of high population density and rapid urbanization, this direction of institutional change can be damaging, locking social segregation in its spatial form. While developing rapidly to accommodate an influx of rural-urban migrants, high-density settlements without effective governance will easily slip into a worsening state due to uncontrolled negative externalities. A deteriorating place highlights its failed state governance, which strengthens the tendency toward private governance. Spatial polarization sets in. According to Barzel (1997), there are two aspects of property rights: economic rights and legal rights. Legal rights are those defined by the state and recognized by law. Economic rights are the ability of individuals to exercise their controls over a property. The value of a property is determined by how secure one's property rights are. Capture of attributes in the public domain is not costless when economic rights do not coincide with legal entitlements. The resources spent by competing parties are in proportion to the dissipated value of property. Moreover, these assets are not secure as the protection and full transfer of rights are either prohibitively costly or nonexistent. Ambiguous land rights induce disorderly competition for land rent and thus disorganized land development.

Structure of the book

Chapter 1 is about land rights that create and define land markets, upon which urbanization and urban development are unfolding. Informality and diversity are created under certain land rights. China's institutional change in land rights gives rise to rapid urban change as well as land rent that is derived from prevalent uncertainty and ambiguity. **Chapter 2** elaborates urbanization under the centrally planned regime (1949–1978), where land was regarded as a means of production. Centrally controlled urbanization was carried out without mechanisms of land markets, which subsequently gave rise to 'socialist' urban structures, where 'productive sectors' were prioritized over 'nonproductive sectors'. Socialist cities with ostensible equality and unique features were built as a result. Agrarian land reforms of 'land to the tillers' were implemented in the countryside, and rural land has finally been converted to collective ownership. **Chapter 3** tells a story of Shenzhen as a pioneer for market-driven land development that phases out free land utilization. Urban physical development and a new generation of developers based on the market equilibrium of demand and supply are brought up from this crucial experiment. It is the city built with land markets. Continuous institutional change gives rise to land leasehold. The nature of gradualism in reforms creates a dual land market and resultant arbitrage opportunities. Transformation of housing provision is successfully achieved from public welfare housing to private commercial housing.

While Shenzhen is a new town built on green fields, existing cities built in the central planning era, when land is a means of production, are to be refashioned under the new institution of land rights. **Chapter 4** discusses the nature of gradual reforms that determines the path-dependent incremental change to land rights. Gradualism and dualism, though politically sensible, worsen the problems of emerging principal-agent relations, leading to ambiguous delineation of land rights. The two new local agents of the local developmental state and *danwei*-enterprises have developed an informal local growth coalition, and land rent derived from the dual land market is used for strengthening local government-enterprise coalitions and by the local developmental state as instrument for intervention. As a result, the state as the third party for market mediation is absent. Land rent seeking and grabbing are rampant, evidenced by the impact on the resultant built environment. **Chapter 5** discusses the socialist land use right, which has become a unique institution incorporated in the building of socialist cities. Lacking a market of transactions, it hampered spatial restructuring of the built-up areas. The land development right is invented as a transitional institution to phase out the socialist land use right. Drastic urban restructuring ensued, as well as land rent seeking and dissipating. Rapid urban redevelopment ensues and gives rise to a new pattern of central business districts. Path-dependent institutional change goes on with organizational changes, along with regional disparities.

Rural industrialization has been a critical movement for rural development in China. *In situ* urbanization becomes phenomenal as rural nonagriculturalizaion takes hold in the two dynamic regions of Yangtze River Delta and Pearl River Delta. **Chapter 6** elaborates bottom-up rural nonagricultural development that shows intriguing patterns of intensive mixture of agricultural and nonagricultural land uses, suggesting highly fragmented *in situ* urbanization. The collective land rights that are conducive to farming become problematic when the villages are urbanizing as the accentuated land rent differentials are contested between the urban state as a *de jure* owner and the rural collective as a *de facto* land holder. The absence of the state in the land development market generates symmetric and interrelated land rights situations of the anticommons and commons, leading to locked-in unsustainable urban forms. **Chapter 7** focuses on villages as basic agricultural units that are autonomous and self-contained. Significant rural-rural inequality between villages and between peasant migrants and local villagers are created by land rent enhanced by urbanization besides the long-existent rural-urban divide. Autonomous villages in the urbanizing suburbs become a rentier class. The Renewal and Refurbishment Program implemented in the Pearl River Delta unveils that the collective has been entrenched amid the urbanized metropolis so as to extract land rent perpetually. Whereas township-led rural development in the Yangtze River Delta shows a promising trajectory toward industrial advancement, ecological integrity, and rural equality. According to the subsidiarity principles, the coordination level for high density urbanization should be appropriately chosen.

Chapter 8 concludes that China's rapid urbanization since the 1980s has been facilitated by institutional changes in land rights, which also have profoundly impacted the resultant urban physical forms. An initial land market regulated by the explicit land rights of leasehold is formulated as a result of three types of land rent dissipation, which leads to symmetric low-density suburban sprawl and overcompact central cities. It further complicates the future urban change by the fundamental issues of fairness and efficiency embedded in the spatial structure of land uses.

Notes

1 *Adat*, an Indonesian word, means traditional in English.
2 *Kampung* is an Indonesian word, meaning village.
3 For instance, beautification of one's garden does not receive pecuniary benefits from neighbors though there is an enhancement to the values of their houses, while deteriorated and derelict buildings without the voluntary maintenance from the owners would depress property values in the neighborhood.
4 State-owned units in socialist countries, or *danwei* in China, are a link in social redistribution chains. The *danwei*, literally meaning work unit in English, is a profound socialist institution which used to be essential and is, to certain extent, still important to Chinese urban residents. The functions of *danwei* are more than just organizing required production. They are a mechanism through which the state distributes socialist welfare to workers, social policies are implemented, and political campaigns are carried out (Li, 1993).

References

Alchian, A. A. (1961) *Some economics of property*. RAND P-2316, Santa Monica, CA: RAND Corporation.
Atkinson, R. & Blandy, S. (eds.) (2006) *Gated communities*. London: Routledge.
Barzel, Y. (1989) *Economic analysis of property rights*. Cambridge: Cambridge University Press.
Barzel, Y. (1997) *Economic analysis of property rights*, 2nd edition. Cambridge: Cambridge University Press.
Bazelon, D. T. (1963) *The paper economy*. New York: Random House.
Becker, L. C. (1977) *Property rights – philosophic foundations*. London: Routledge & Kegan Paul.
Benjamin, S., Arifin, M. A. & Sarjana, F. P. (1985) The housing costs of low-income Kampung dwellers – a study of product and process in Indonesian cities. *Habitat International*, 9(1): 91–110.

Benneworth, P. & Dauncey, H. (2010) International urban festivals as a catalyst for governance capacity building. *Environment and Planning C: Government and Policy*, 28: 1083–1100.

Block, F. (1994) The role of the state in the economy, in N. J. Smelser and R. Swedberg (eds.), *The handbook of economic sociology*, 691–710. Princeton, NJ: Princeton University Press.

Brabant, J. M. (1991) Property rights' reform, macroeconomic performance, and welfare, in H. Blommestein and M. Marrese (eds.) *Transformation of planned economies: property rights reform and macroeconomic stability*, 29–49. Paris: OECD.

Buchanan, J. M. (1977) *Freedom in constitutional contract: perspectives of a political economist*. College Station: Texas A & M University Press.

Buchanan, J. M., Tollison, R. D. & Tullock, G. (eds.) (1980) *Toward a theory of the rent-seeking society*. College Station: Texas A & M University Press.

Buchanan, J. M. & Yoon, Y. J. (2000) Symmetric tragedies: commons and anticommons. *Journal of Law and Economics*, 43: 1–13.

Charmes, J. (1990) A critical review of concepts, definitions and studies in the informal sector, in D. Turnham, B. Salome & A. Schwarz (eds.) *The informal sector revisited*, 10–48. Paris: OECD.

Chen, K. (1992) *Crossing the river while groping for planted stones: a public choice analysis of China's economic reform*. Unpublished staff seminar paper no. 21. Department of Economics and Statistics, National University of Singapore, Singapore.

Cheng, L. K. (1990) Reflections on the changing roles of Chinese clan associations in Singapore. *Asian Culture*, 14: 57–71.

Coase, R. H. (1960) The problem of social cost. *The Journal of Law & Economics*, 3: 1–44.

Commons, J. R. (1934) *Institutional economics: Its place in political economy*. New York: Macmillan.

Cornell, S. & Kalt, J. P. (1997) Cultural evolution and constitutional public choice: Institutional diversity and economic performance on American Indian reservations, in J. R. Lott, Jr (ed.) *Uncertainty and economic evolution*, 116–142. London: Routledge.

Cowell, R. & Owens, S. (2006) Governing space: Planning reform and the politics of sustainability. *Environment and Planning C: Government and Policy*, 24: 403–421.

Demsetz, H. (1967) Toward a theory of property rights. *The American Economic Review*, 57(2): 347–359.

Denman, D. (1978) *The place of property – a new recognition of the function and form of property rights in land*. Berkhamsted: Geographical Publications.

De Soto, H. (1989) *The other path: The invisible revolution in the third world*. London: I. B. Taurus.

Dunford, M. (1990) Theories of regulation. *Environment and Planning D: Society and Space*, 8: 297–321.

Eggertsson, T. (1994) The economics of institutions in transition economies, in S. Schiavo-Campo (ed.) *Institutional change and the public sector in transitional economies*, 19–50. Washington, DC: World Bank.

Elster, J. (1989) *The cement of society: A study of social order*. Cambridge: Cambridge University Press.

Fainstein, S. S. (2000) New directions in planning theory. *Urban Affairs Review*, 35: 451–478.

Fainstein, S. S. (2005) Cities and diversity should we want it? Can we plan for it? *Urban Affairs Review*, 41: 3–19.

Fischel, W. A. (1985) *The economics of zoning laws – A property rights approach to American land use controls*. Baltimore, MD: The Johns Hopkins University Press.

Friedman, M. & Friedman, R. (1979) *Free to choose – A personal statement.* New York and London: Harcourt Brace Jovanovich.

Galbraith, J. K. (1977) *The age of uncertainty.* London: BBC and Andre Deutsch.

Gilbert, A. (2004) Love in the time of enhanced capital flow: reflections on the links between liberalization and informality. In A. Roy & N. AlSayyad (eds.) *Urban informality – Transnational perspectives from the Middle East, Latin America, and South Asia,* 33–65. Oxford: Lexington Books.

Gregory, P. R. & Stuart, R. C. (1992) *Comparative economic systems,* 4th edition. Boston, MA: Houghton Mifflin.

Hall, P. & Pfeiffer, U. (2000) *Urban future 21: A global agenda for 21st century cities.* London: E & FN Spon.

Hardin, G. (1968) The tragedy of the commons. *Science,* 162: 1243–8.

Hayek, F. A. (1973) *Law, legislation and liberty.* Volume 1: Rules and Order. Chicago, IL: University of Chicago Press.

Healey, P. (1997) *Collaborative planning: Shaping places in fragmented societies.* Vancouver: UBC Press.

Heertje, A. (1989) Introduction, in A. Heertje (ed.) *The economic role of the state.* Oxford: Blackwell.

Heiner, R. A. (1983) The origin of predictable behaviour. *American Economic Review,* 73: 560–595.

Heller, M. A. (1998) The tragedy of the anticommons: Property in the transition from Marx to markets. *Harvard Law Review,* 111: 621–688.

Huang, Y. (1996) *Inflation and investment controls in China.* Cambridge: Cambridge University Press.

Innes, J. (1995) Planning theory's emerging paradigm: Communicative action and interactive practice. *Journal of Planning Education and Research,* 14: 183–189.

Jacobs, J. (1961) *The death and life of great American cities.* New York: Random House.

Jacobs, J. (1966) Where city planners come down to earth. *Business Week,* 20 August, 101–104.

Janoschka, M. & Norsdorf, A. (2006) Condominios Fechados and Barrios Privados – the rise of private residential neighborhoods in Latin America, in G. Glasze, C. Webster & K. Frantz (eds.) *Private cities – Global and local perspectives,* 92–108. New York: Routledge.

Jud, G. D. (1980) The effects of zoning on single family residential property values. *Land Economics,* 56: 142–154.

Judd, D. (1995) The rise and new walled cities, in H. Ligget & D. C. Perry (eds.), *Spatial practices,* 144–165. Thousand Oaks, CA: Sage.

Knight, J. (1992) *Institutions and social conflict.* Cambridge: Cambridge University Press.

Krueger, A. O. (1974) The political economy of the rent-seeking society. *American Economic Review,* 43(3): 291–303.

Lai, L. W. C. (1999) Hayek and town planning: A note on Hayek's views towards town planning. *The Constitution of Liberty. Environment and Planning A,* 31: 1567–1582.

Lal, D. (1983) *The property of 'development economics'.* London: Institute of Economic Affairs.

Leaf, M. (1993) Land rights for residential development in Jakarta, Indonesia: the colonial roots of contemporary urban dualism. *International Journal of Urban and Regional Research,* 17: 477–491.

Li, B. (1993) Danwei culture as urban culture in modern China: the case of Beijing from 1949 to 1979, in G. Guldin & A. Southall (eds.) *Urban anthropology in China,* 345–352. Leiden: E. J. Brill.

Matthews, R. C. O. (1986) The economics of institutions and the sources of growth. *The Economic Journal*, 96: 903–918.
National Bureau of Statistics of China (NBSC) (2017) *China Statistical Yearbook 2016*. Beijing: China Statistical Publishing House. (in Chinese)
Nee, V. (1991) Socialist inequalities in reforming state socialism: between redistribution and markets in China. *American Sociological Review*, 56: 267–282.
Nelson, R. H. (1977) *Zoning and property rights: An analysis of the American system of land-use regulation*. Cambridge, MA: MIT Press.
Nettl, J. P. (1968) The state as a conceptual variable. *World Politics*, 20: 559–92.
North, D. C. (1990) *Institutions, institutional change and economic performance*. Cambridge: Cambridge University Press.
North, D. C. (1991) Institutions. *Journal of Economic Perspectives*, 5(4): 97–112.
North, D. C. (1998) The institutional foundations of east Asian development: a summary evaluation, in Y. Hayami & M. Aoki (eds.) *The institutional foundations of East Asian economic development: Proceedings of the IEA Conference held in Tokyo, Japan*, 552–560. London: Macmillan.
Oi, J. C. (1996) The role of the local state in China's transitional economy, in A. G. Walder (ed.) *China's transitional economy*, 170–187. Oxford: Oxford University Press.
Olson, M. (1965) *The logic of collective action: Public goods and the theory of groups*. Cambridge, MA.: Harvard University Press.
Olson, M. (1982) *The rise and decline of nations*. New Haven, CT: Yale University Press.
Ostrom, E. (1990) *Governing the commons: The evolution of institutions for collective action*. Cambridge: Cambridge University Press.
Ostrom, E. (2000) Collective action and the evolution of social norms. *Journal of Economic Perspectives*, 14(3): 137–158.
Paul, E. F., Miller, Jr. F. D. & Paul, J. (1994) *Property rights*. Cambridge: Cambridge University Press.
Perlman, J. E. (2004) Marginality: from myth to reality in the Favelas of Rio de Janeiro, 1969–2002, in A. Roy & N. AlSayyad (eds.) *Urban informality – Transnational perspectives from the Middle East, Latin America, and South Asia*, 105–146. Oxford: Lexington Books.
Pigou, A. C. (1932) *The economics of welfare*, 4th edition. London: Macmillan.
Pejovich, S. (1990) *The economics of property rights: Towards a theory of comparative systems*. Dordrecht, the Netherlands: Kluwer Academic Publishers.
Popkin, S. L. (1988) Public choice and peasant organizations, in R. H. Bates (ed.) *Toward a political economy of development: a rational choice perspective*. Berkeley: University of California Press.
Posner, R. A. (1973) *Economic analysis of law*. Boston, MA: Little Brown.
Ricardo, D. (1821) 1951. *On the principles of political economy and taxation*. Cambridge: Cambridge University Press.
Roy, A. & AlSayyad, N. (2004) *Urban informality – Transnational perspectives from the Middle East, Latin America, and South Asia*. Lanham, MD: Lexington.
Sachs, J. D. & Woo, W. T. (1994) Structural factors in the economic reform of China, Eastern Europe and the former Soviet Union. *Economic Policy*, 18: 103–145.
Schotter, A. (1981) *The economic theory of social institutions*. Cambridge: Cambridge University Press.
Shackle, G. L. S. (1961) *Decision order and time in human affairs*. Cambridge: Cambridge University Press.

Shirk, S. (1993) *The political logic of economic reform in China*. Berkeley: University of California Press.
Smith, N. (1979) Toward a theory of gentrification: A back to the city movement by capital not people. *Journal of the American Planning Association*, 45: 538–548.
Struyk, R. J., Hoffman, M. L. & Katsura, H. M. (1990) *The market for shelter in Indonesian sities*. Washington, DC: The Urban Institute Press.
Turner, J. F. C. & Fichter, R. (eds.) (1972) *Freedom to build: Dweller control of the housing process*. New York: Macmillan.
Turner, J. F. C. (1976) *Housing by people: Towards autonomy in building environments*. London: Marion Boyars.
United Nations Centre for Human Settlements (1987) *Global report on human settlements 1986*. Oxford: Oxford University Press.
URA (Urban Redevelopment Authority), Singapore (1995) *Chinatown Historic District*, Singapore: URA.
Von Thünen, J. H. (1826) 1966. *The isolated state*, an English edition of Der isolierte staat. Translated by C. M. Wartenberg. Oxford: Pergamon Press.
Walder, A. G. (1992) Property rights and stratification in socialist redistributive economies. *American Sociological Review*, 57: 524–539.
Wallace, J., Parlindungan, A. P. & Hutagalung, A. S. (2000) *Indonesian land law and tenures: Issues in land rights*. Jakarta: National Development Planning Agency (BAPPENAS) and National Land Agency (BPN).
Wang, S. (1995) The rise of the regions: Fiscal reform and the decline of central state capacity in China, in A. G. Walder (ed.) *The waning of the communist state: Economic origins of political decline in China and Hungary*, 87–113. Berkeley: University of California Press.
Webster, C. (2002) Property rights and the public realm: Gates, green belts, and Gemeinschaft. *Environment and Planning B: Planning and Design*, 29: 397–412.
Webster, C. & Lai, L. W. C. (2003) *Property rights, planning and markets: Managing spontaneous cities*. Cheltenham: Edward Elgar.
Weimer, D. L. (1997) The political economy of property rights, in D. L. Weimer (ed.) *The political economy of property rights: Institutional change and credibility in the reform of centrally planned economies*, 1–20. Cambridge: Cambridge University Press.
Williamson, O. E. (1985) *The economic institutions of capitalism: Firms, markets, relational contracting*. New York: The Free Press.
Winayanti, L. & Lang, H.C. (2004) Provision of urban services in an informal settlement: A case study of Kampung Penas Tanggul, Jakarta. *Habitat International*, 28(1): 41–65.
Wolf, C. Jr. (1993) *Markets or governments: Choosing between imperfect alternatives*. Cambridge, MA: MIT Press.
World Bank (1992) *Government and development*. Washington, DC: World Bank.
World Bank (2002) *Building institutions for markets: World development report 2002*. New York: Oxford University Press.
Zhu, J. M., Sim, L. L. & Liu, X. (2007) Place-remaking under property rights regimes – A case study of *Niucheshui*, Singapore. *Environment & Planning A*, 39: 2346–2365.
Zhu, J. M. & Guo, Y. (2014) Fragmented peri-urbanization led by autonomous village development under informal institution in high-density regions: The case of Nanhai, China. *Urban Studies*, 51(6): 1120–1145.
Zhu, J. M. & Simarmata, H. A. (2015) Formal land rights versus informal land rights: Governance for sustainable urbanization in the Jakarta metropolitan region, Indonesia. *Land Use Policy*, 43: 63–73.

2 Land as a means of production

Urban and rural changes without market mechanisms prior to 1978

The founding of the People's Republic ushered in a new era of central planning that rejected market mechanisms. Industrialization was pursued fervently in order to strengthen the country in the interest of national development, whereas urbanization, a concurrent phenomenon with industrialization, was suppressed by the planning ideology that portrayed cities as bourgeois. Industrialization was implemented with an emphasis on addressing spatial inequality. Under the new political system, urban land was nationalized and designated as a means of production, instead of an economic asset. Centrally controlled urbanization was carried out without mechanisms of the land market, which subsequently gave rise to 'socialist' urban structures, where 'productive sectors' were prioritized over 'nonproductive sectors'. Socialist cities with ostensible equality were built as a result. Agrarian land reforms of 'land to the tillers' were implemented in the countryside, and rural land was finally converted to collective ownership.

Urbanization under the central planning and state landownership: spatial equality for proletarian producer cities

When the Chinese Communist Party (CCP) defeated the Nationalist Party (*Guomindang*) and commenced its governance over the country (except Taiwan, Hong Kong, and Macao) in 1949, the paramount task on top of the new government's agenda was to develop a new socialist China. A planned and centrally controlled economy was adopted following the influential Soviet model because of the common ideology of communism. The rise of the planned economy is a historic phenomenon aiming at redressing failures of the laissez-faire free market (Lipson, 1946). Moreover, the Soviet-styled socialist centrally controlled economy is founded based on the Marxist economic theories, which believe that "commodity-money relationships would disappear together with the private ownership of means of production, and that they would no longer exist in a new socialist society" (Sik, 1967: 15–16). The state ownership of means of production became a cornerstone of the newly founded People's Republic. The top-down control mechanisms for resource allocation were immediately installed, assisted by the nationalization of land, properties, and other means of production. Given the Cold War confrontation and the US-led embargo, it seemed that communist China had few alternatives but to develop an autarky. Zwass (1987: 157) echoes this view and claimed that "a centrally administered economy fits the needs of a developing country".

Since the Opium War in the 1840s, a defeated China had fallen into chaos and disintegration. It was forced to open up some cities in the coastal region and along the Yangtze River for international trading. Foreign powers were granted rights to build concessions in those cities, which changed China to a semi-colonial and semi-feudal state. The country was deeply humiliated by losing sovereignty over those cities to the industrialized foreign powers. Industrialization had, therefore, become an urgent national goal once the country was on its feet. But its pursuit was interrupted by the collapse of Qing dynasty, two world wars, Japanese invasion, and consequent civil war between the CCP and *Guomindang*. Only in the 1950s was the country able to carry out national industrialization. It was soon realized that heavy industries needed to be built so as to stand up to foreign hostile threats in the wake of Korean War. Learning from the Soviet model, the CCP decided to prioritize heavy industries, thereby to build a national industrial backbone. No sooner did the CCP come to power than the industrialization was actively and enthusiastically pursued, evident in the prompt drafting of the First Five-Year Plan (1952–1957). Before its execution, the central government categorized all existing cities into four groups with degree of priorities according to the heavy-industry components and the number of industrial projects to be constructed (see Table 2.1 and Figure 2.1). The cities in the first and second categories were to be built as main industrial bases of the new China. It was clear that important industrial cities would be in the central and northeast regions, while most coastal commercial cities were not chosen for the task. But two years later, cities were re-categorized in 1954 according to the revised national development strategies (see Table 2.2 and Figure 2.2). The designated most important industrial cities remained in the central region, while some of those old semi-colonial metropolises in the coastal region, such as Shanghai, Tianjin, Dalian, Qingdao, and Guangzhou (five coastal cities), were upgraded into Category II.

The cities in Category I, namely Taiyuan, Baotou, Lanzhou, Xi'an, Datong, Wuhan, Luoyang, and Chengdu, were designated as Eight Key Industrial Cities (EKICs) (*bada zhongdian chengshi*), which purported to be the epitome of new socialist cities. The new developments were apparently led by the placement of 156 Soviet-assisted manufacturing projects in the key interior cities (see Figure 2.3), and 694 large plants were then assigned to and planned for the 39 cities in Categories I, II, and III. The average size in terms of urban population in 1949 was 325,700 for the EKICs, while it was 1,849,600 for the five coastal cities, 5.7 times of the former. The growth rate of the EKICs in terms of urban population was 5.6 percent annually during the period 1949–1978, while that of the five coastal cities stood at 1.8 percent (see Table 2.3). The strategy of state-led spatial dispersion was clearly at work, as the smaller and less established EKICs were prioritized over larger and more established coastal cities, ditching the market-driven spatial agglomeration.

Table 2.1 Categorization of cities to be industrialized, 1952

Category I (to be developed as heavy-industrial bases)	Category II (to be developed as major industrial cities)	Category III (to be developed as industrial cities)	Category IV (to remain as what they were)
Beijing	Jilin	Tianjin	all other cities
Baotou	Anshan	Tangshan	
Xi'an	Fushun	Dalian	
Datong	Benxi	Changchun	
Qiqihar	Shenyang	Jiamusi	
Daye	Harbin	Shanghai	
Lanzhou	Taiyuan	Qingdao	
Chengdu	Wuhan	Nanjing	
	Shijiazhuang	Hangzhou	
	Handan	Jinan	
	Zhengzhou	Chongqing	
	Luoyang	Kunming	
	Zhanjiang	Neijiang	
	Wulumuqi	Guiyang	
		Guangzhou	
		Xiangtan	
		Xiangfan	

Source: Cao & Chu, 1990: 37

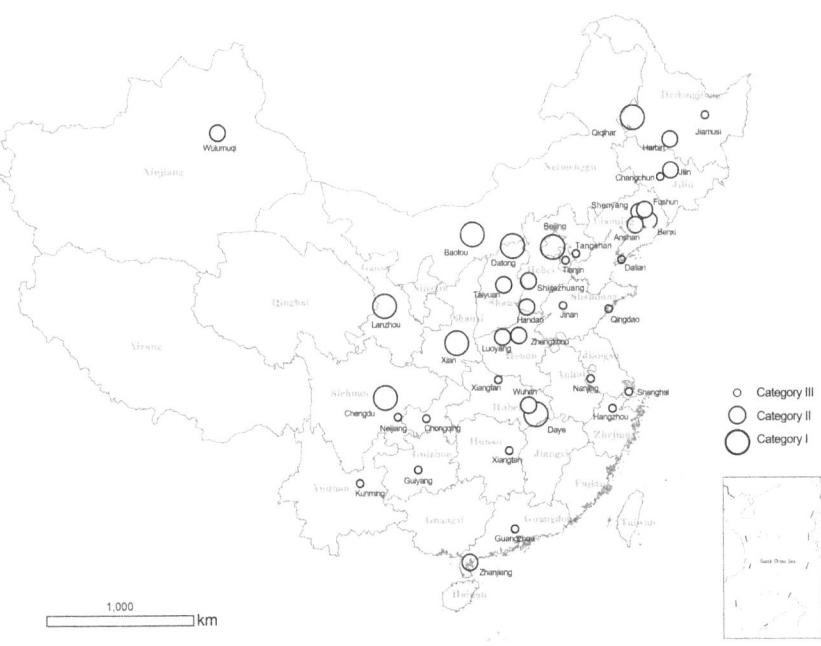

Figure 2.1 Three categories of cities to be industrialized, 1952.

Table 2.2 Categorization of cities to be industrialized, 1954

Category I (to be developed as heavy industrial bases)	Category II (to be developed as major industrial cities)	Category III (to be developed as industrial cities)	Category IV (to remain as what they were)
Taiyuan	Jilin	Tangshan	all other cities (small and medium sized)
Baotou	Anshan	Nanjing	
Lanzhou	Fushun	Hangzhou	
Xi'an	Benxi	Jinan	
Datong	Shenyang	Kunming	
Wuhan	Harbin	Guiyang	
Luoyang	Tianjin	Baoji	
Chengdu	Dalian	Changsha	
	Changchun	Nanchang	
	Jiamusi	Nanning	
	Shanghai	Huhehaote	
	Qingdao	Zhangjiakou	
	Chongqing	Xining	
	Guangzhou	Yingchuan	
	Shijiazhuang		
	Handan		
	Zhengzhou		
	Fularji		
	Zhuzhou		
	Hegang		
	Zhanjiang		

Source: Cao and Chu, 1990: 43–44

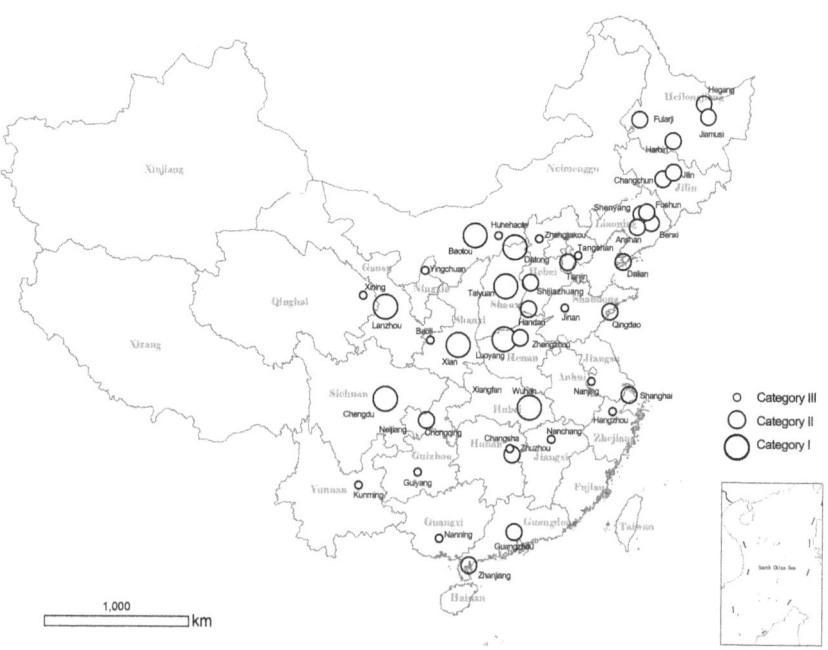

Figure 2.2 Three categories of cities to be industrialized, 1954.

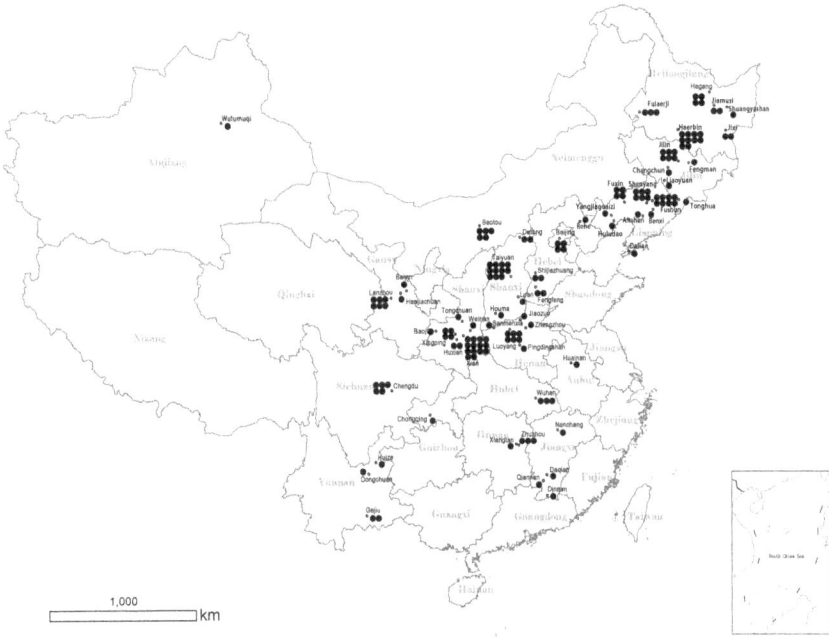

Figure 2.3 Locations of 156 Soviet-assisted manufacturing projects.

Table 2.3 Numbers of urban population in the EKICs and five coastal cities (thousands)

EKICs

	Xi'an	Taiyuan	Lanzhou	Baotou	Luoyang	Chengdu	Wuhan	Datong
1949	398	215	195	90	70	609	940	89
1978	2,102	1,456	1,285	1,005	889	2,288	2,848	799

Five coastal cities

	Shanghai	Qingdao	Tianjin	Dalian	Guangzhou
1949	4,189	640	2,432	559	1,428
1978	5,574	1,047	4,714	1,264	2,831

Sources: Li (2016: 17) for data of the EKICs in 1949. Chen (2017) for other data

After three decades' efforts, regional economic disparities were mitigated and interior regions had a strong increase in the share of industrial production (World Bank, 1985). Between 1949 and 1978, the number of medium-sized cities (population of 0.2–1.0 million) grew from 25 to 87, and the share of urban population in those cities increased from 38.6 percent to 48.4 percent of the total urban population in the country. The share of urban population residing in large cities (> 1.0 million residents) grew marginally from 36.0 percent to 37.5

28 *Land as a means of production*

percent as a result of the policy that strictly controlled the development of large cities (Lin, 2002). In 1955, 56.2 percent of urban population lived in the coastal region, and it declined to 47.9 percent in 1980. Gini coefficient that measures urban population concentration decreased from 0.591 (1953) to 0.523 (1982), suggesting a degree of regional dispersion (Ebanks and Cheng, 1990: 37, 44). The state-led central planning played a key role in achieving spatial equality instead of spatial efficiency.

The single-minded emphasis on full-scaled national industrialization was unambiguously demonstrated by the creation of the dichotomy between 'producer cities' and 'consumer cities'. Cities with dominant manufacturing production were deemed proletarian producers, while cities specialized in commercial, retail, financial and other nonmanufacturing activities were categorized as bourgeois consumers. The commended 'producer cities' and derogated 'consumer cities' revealed the tenet of urbanization policies of the new government and hinted at the priority of planned investment. The categorization of 'consumer' and 'producer' cities unveiled the central planners' obsession with the narrowly defined production. The 'consumer cities' were often referred as parasitic and unproductive. Thereby, it was logical that priority should be granted to the productive enterprises in order to fulfill the goal of rapid industrialization, whereas services were not considered as productive undertakings. Moreover, in the editorial of *People's Daily* in March 17, 1949, was it declared that socialist China needed to "transform consumer cities to producer cities" (*ba xiaofei chengshi biancheng shengchan chengshi*) (Li, 2016).

Incidentally, many of those so-called consumer cities were the trading ports built as a legacy of Opium Wars in the nineteenth century. The Treaty of Nanking (1842) after the first Opium War (1840–1842) designated five treaty ports, namely, Guangzhou, Xiamen, Fuzhou, Ningbo and Shanghai. The Second Opium War (1858–1860) led to another batch of cities opened up for international trading, namely Shantou, Haikou, Beihai, Tianjin, Hankou, Jiujiang, Nanjing, and Zhenjiang (see Figure 2.4). These semi-colonial and commercial cities actually ushered in modern urban planning and city building in China with provision of urban infrastructure and municipal services that were mostly lacking in traditional Chinese towns. Parks as public space firstly appeared in the foreign concessions, in contrast to exquisite private gardens built and owned by rich urban merchants in indigenous towns. Even Beijing as the imperial capital did not have piped water and proper sewage, and the well-known court-yard houses (*siheyuan*) did not even have flushing toilets! Despite that, these modern consumer cities needed to be transformed into industrial producer cities. The ancient imperial capital Beijing was even designated as one of the EKICs by the 1952 city categorization (see Table 2.1).

Being an industrial base at the time of the 1949 liberation, Shanghai was composed of mostly foreign and local private manufacturing. Factories controlled by foreigners and *Guomindang* were confiscated and put under the ownership of the socialist government. After forced conversion of ownership, industrial production was still dominated by the private sector. In spite of Shanghai producing

Figure 2.4 Treaty port consumer cities.

a sixth of the country's GDP with only 1 percent of total national population (1952) (NBSC, 2000; SMBS, 2001), the CCP was deeply suspicious about the role that the private sector could play in building the new socialist China. Shanghai was condemned as "the concentrated, typical expression of the colonial or semi-colonial nature of old China's economy. ...... Such colonial or semi-colonial economic status must be discarded before Shanghai can become a truly prosperous new people's city" (cited by Murphey, 1953: 27). The first Shanghai mayor of the new government, General Chen Yi, made it clear that the new government was to "change industrial policy from that of dependence on imperialism to that of serving the Chinese people" (cited by Murphey, 1953: 27).

Thereafter, the urban private sector, which still contributed more than 63 percent to Shanghai's output in 1953, was not given a free hand (Howe, 1981). Before the private sector was to be nationalized, the old industrial cities' role was restricted to maintaining the status quo. Established coastal cities such as Shanghai were requested to support the development of new industrial cities in the interior regions. Some important plants, as well as engineers and managers, were requested to move to those new industrial cities under construction. Between 1950 and 1957, 425,000 personnel, including professionals and ordinary workers, relocated from Shanghai to key cities (*zhongdian chengshi*) with given industrial significance and planned as important producer cities, to help expand capacity of industrial production (Shi and Gao et al., 1989).

Because of continuous upheavals caused by the Second World War and the following civil war, the percentage of urban population in the total population declined from 27.2 in 1943 to 10.6 in 1949, when the war ended (Sit, 1985: 6). The ensued rehabilitation (during 1949–1952) saw the country rebuild upon the rubble and debris. Urban population increased steadily to 15.4 percent in 1957. Nevertheless, the CCP leadership did not equate industrialization to urbanization. Free rural-urban migration was curbed by the introduction of the household registration system (*hukou*) in 1954, which effectively fixed residents in localities where they had resided, as all sorts of civil rights and entitlements were associated with the *hukou*. Spontaneous migration from rural areas to cities was virtually nonexistent after 1958.

Migration was restricted because the CCP wanted to promote production, either manufacturing or farming, and to curb consumption, as rural-urban migrants were usually keen on moving to large commercial cities. Between 1910 and 1949, Shanghai's population increased from 1.3 million to 5.5 million, and a quarter of them were actually living in slums, without proper jobs (Zou, 1980). Yet, these dwellers survived on doing informal and irregular work by providing simple services. Though informal economies provided meager income, which was still considered better off than farming back in their villages. Unplanned informal economies were disallowed, and services were frowned upon as parasitic by the communist ideology. As urban employment was inadequate to absorb new graduates, urban youths were sent to the countryside by the movement of 'up to mountains and down to villages' (*shangshan xiaxiang*) that ostensibly advocated the necessity of re-education of urban high school graduates by peasants according to Mao's revolutionary tenets of closing the rural-urban gap (*chengxiang chabie*). Between 1962 and 1979, 17.8 million urban youths either voluntarily or obligatorily migrated to the countryside. One-third of them, or 5.8 million, were sent during the high heat of the Cultural Revolution (1967–1970). Farming was perceived as production and therefore was encouraged. Most of the urban youths came from large cities such as Shanghai, where 1.25 million young residents had to abandon their much-liked urban life (Gu, 1997). Food shortages and famines ensued from the Great Leap Forward also forced city governments to re-rusticate urban residents. Urban population decreased to 12.2 percent in 1965. It further dropped to 11.2 percent in 1970 and then to 12.1 percent in 1978. Cities in the coastal region experienced negative population growth of 0.79 percent in the period 1965–1970 (Urban Social and Economic Survey Organization, 1990).

Following the binary logic of producer cities and consumer ones, urban components were similarly categorized into productive sectors and nonproductive ones, so that investments into the former would be given a priority (see Table 2.4). Projects such as building manufacturing plants and industrial zones were considered productive, while housing, shops, and urban services were regarded as nonproductive. In order to direct more investments into productive sectors, quality standards of nonproductive sectors were even downgraded. These urbanization policies, formulated in the historic context, had a profound

Table 2.4 State investment in capital construction (%)

Period	Productive sectors	Nonproductive sectors
1953–1957	67.0	33.0
1958–1962	85.4	14.6
1963–1965	79.4	20.6
1966–1970	83.8	16.2
1971–1975	82.5	17.5
1976–1980	73.9	26.1

Source: NBSC, 1994

impact on China's urban development thereafter and sowed the seeds, which later blossomed into serious urban problems.

State ownership of land as a means of production

Before the 1949 Revolution, private land ownership was the norm in China. In the countryside, most of agricultural land was owned by landlords, and they either hired peasants to do farming or leased it to tenant farmers. Urban land, like rural land, was owned by private individuals as well as the then government. The conversion of rural land ownership from landlords to peasants commenced soon after 1949 through the land reform that confiscated private landholdings of the landlords and redistributed them to landless peasants as a free gift of revolutionary fruits. Meanwhile, urban land ownership remained largely unchanged, except for the lands that were owned by foreigners, and *Kuomintang* government was confiscated and converted to the state ownership. The rural cooperative movement abolished the private ownership of farming land and replaced it with collective ownership in 1956, though peasants were granted land plots only a short while ago. Change of urban land ownership started with the socialist reform of private industries in 1956. Private properties and land were gradually converted to state-owned properties, and by 1958, the conversion had been almost completed in all cities. After people's commune movement in the countryside and ownership transformation in cities, private land ownership virtually ceased to exist, though the nationalization of urban land was not officially finalized until the 1982 Constitution (IFTE/CASS and IPA, 1994).

Universally recognized as one of the most important production factors, land had been excluded from economic transactions by the socialist principle of state land ownership that considered any kind of land transaction unconstitutional and unlawful. Clause 4, Article 10 of the 1982 Constitution stipulates that

> [u]rban land belongs to the state. Land in the countryside and in suburban areas belongs to collective ownership unless the law stipulates that the land is state-owned. Residential land and family plots also belong to the collective ownership. No organization or individual may appropriate, buy, sell, or lease land, or unlawfully transfer it in any way.

Due to the nature of overall state economies and the centrally controlled economic system, the government did not see it necessary to subject land users, most of them being state-owned-enterprises or institutions, to a system of land use fee and rental. It was reckoned that the planning system was supposedly more efficient than the market system, and thus planned land allocation would meet users' needs without implications of affordability and market bias. In 1954, a government decree removed the nominal use fees and rentals for using urban land by state-owned enterprises, government offices, and civic institutions (Fung, 1981a). According to the central planning, urban land was allocated to users through administration channels without payment of any fee or charge, but land users had no rights to transfer the land they occupied. From 1954 to 1984, urban land in China was virtually free goods and was not regarded as economic assets. Land was assigned according to land users' investment plans, and site selection was negotiated and determined between users and urban planners based on the land use master plan.

Urban construction was a result of top-down plans, instead of an outcome of bottom-up initiatives and interactions between private and public interests. Marxist doctrines consider that land should not have economic value, though it is a necessary factor for production, so-called a means of production. Income from any property, therefore, should be abolished. Landowners as a class were eliminated with the nationalization of land. There was no profession of real estate developers because all premises were constructed by state-owned construction companies at the command of governments, and thereby there were no property markets. Under the predominant state ownership and administrative-command system, individual initiatives were largely suppressed and market demand ignored. The absolute state ownership of urban land under the centrally controlled socialist system led to a dramatically different structure of socialist cities (French and Hamilton, 1979).

Marxism believes that land should not be a commodity, and it should be owned by the state and allocated to users according to their needs instead of their economic purchasing power. The institution of land not as an economic asset appears economically irrational and thus tends to be problematic. Nevertheless, it is an integral part of the overall economic strategy for the purpose of state-led expeditious industrialization. Given the hostile international embargo, it seemed that China had few options but to be self-reliant. This military-styled development demanded all necessary resources under the state control. Urban land being one of the indispensable resources for the industrialization, its nationalization was an essential thrust to make urban landownership compatible with the economic system and the policy of rapid industrialization. All evidences suggested that in order to speed up industrialization to catch up with capitalist countries, the government had to mobilize all resources. Prices of agricultural produce were held artificially low in order to subsidize urban workers. Prices of natural resources were controlled by plans to ensure low costs for production.

Developing socialist producer cities without a land market

The building of socialist cities was entirely a matter of the state, as the state owned all the means of production. Government provided premises, without transactions in monetary terms, to state-owned urban enterprises, which were the mainstream of the urban economy. The government, as the trustee of public resources, acted as an omnipotent financier, landowner, developer, and investor in the development of the urban built environment. Buildings were considered only as shelters for production and consumption. Governments and their subsidiary enterprises were also responsible for the provision of public housing to urban residents. Haussermann (1996: 216) suggests that "the term 'urban development' is basically not applicable to the socialist city, since it normally implies a process in which the actions of different (semi-) autonomous performers and/or systems can only partly be guided". Socialist cities are built simply to facilitate the overriding goal of industrialization as well as to provide its workers with social services. The principle of building socialist cities is to configure a functional layout to support urban productive units (Miliutin, 1974). As a result, Chinese cities suffered a syndrome of underinvestment in the urban built environment, due to the ill-prepared plans that gravely ignored the relationship between urban performance and quality of the built environment.

The CCP government regarded itself the pioneer to lead China into a brand-new era. New socialist cities should best serve as a manifesto of socialism in built-forms. The drafted plan for Beijing city firmly held that the capital of socialist China should be not only the political and cultural center but a great industrial city. It went to the extreme by declaring Beijing to be restructured into a heavy-industrial city from a traditional cultural and administrative center. Ten grand 'socialist' buildings were planned for the new capital immediately after the new government came into power and the construction of the buildings was completed by 1959, the tenth anniversary of the founding of People's Republic of China. For the party leaders, Beijing was no longer the imperial capital for emperors and scholar-official elites but the new center for its proletarian and Communist Party cadres. The imperial north-south axis was soon shifted to a socialist east-west axis in Beijing's urban structure. The ancient city-walls and buildings were relentlessly torn down to make way for new thoroughfares. *Pojiu lixin* (eradicating the old, building the new) is a revealing idiom that explains succinctly what has happened since 1949 in the Chinese cities. Horse and dog racecourses built by the Westerners in Shanghai were converted to People's Square, People's Park, and Cultural Park (Qian, 2018). "As much as one-fifth of the existing buildings and dwellings in Taiyuan and Lanchow were taken down to make way for new construction, although these buildings were still in good condition" (Fung, 1981a: 275). It was estimated that the total area of demolished buildings in 175 cities in 1956 amounted to 2.48 million square meters (Fung, 1981a). *Pojiu lixin* did not cease and continued with a vengeance in the

34 Land as a means of production

1960s–1970s 'Cultural Revolution' (*wenhua da geming*) when thousands of historical relics and artifacts were destroyed.

The socialist ideology deemed urban problems such as shortages of decent housing for low-income residents, social segregation, traffic congestion, and environmental pollution as evils related to the unplanned capitalist cities. There were 1.2 million people, about a quarter of urban residents, living in shacks and slums, and the area of very poor housing accounted for one-sixth of the municipal built-up areas of Shanghai in the late 1940s (Luo, 2007; see Figure 2.5). As the revolution subverted the old social structure where workers and peasants were in the bottom, emancipated workers and peasants became the masters in the new socialist society, so-called 'turning over to become the masters' (*fanshen zuo zhuren*). Urban workers in the socialist countries as working class were accorded a social status of leading class on top of all strata of society according to the Marxist doctrines, and thus their housing conditions had to be improved.

Public housing estates in the form of Workers' New Villages (WNVs) were built as communities located near industrial zones in order to create production-dominated working-living complexes. The term 'New Village' insinuated a new way of life and rusticated urban living, so as to symbolically narrow down the rural-urban divide. The WNVs were well planned according to modern urban planning principles, and Caoyang WNV, one of the first WNVs built in Shanghai, served as an exemplar in this regard (see Figure 2.6). In contrast to urban *lilong* housing quarters that were built mostly in the 1920s–1930s within the foreign concessions, WNVs were spacious with amenities and public facilities

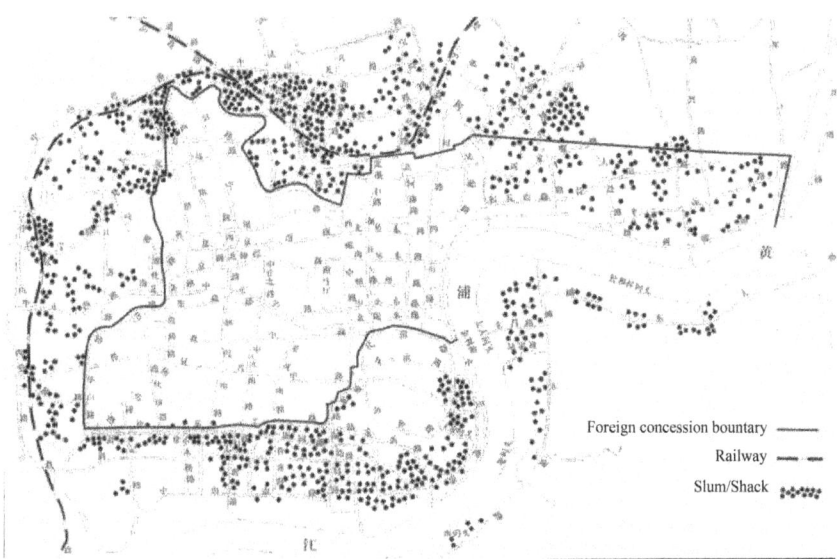

Figure 2.5 Slums and shacks in Shanghai, 1949.
Source: ERI/SASS, 1962: 7

Land as a means of production 35

Figure 2.6 Layout of Caoyang Workers' New Village.

like community centers and bathhouses. *Lilong* housing quarters demonstrated the effect of land markets on housing segregation between those of the working class and of high-income residents (see Figure 2.7). The former were often cramped with hardly any public space and greenery, while the latter had low density with ample gardens. Low-income, middle-income, and high-income *lilong* housing accounted for 52.7 percent, 19.9 percent, and 9.5 percent of the total housing floor areas, respectively, in 1949 (SMBS, 2001). Without being constrained by the land market that worked in shaping the old urban spatial structure reflective of economic affordability and social classes, WNVs provided decent living neighborhoods to the low-income working class. "By the end of 1959 a total number of 34 workers' villages had been completed" (Fung, 1981b:40). Under the scheme of workers' new villages, housing to workers had changed the structure of Shanghai housing stock. There was none in 1949, and in 1979 it accounted for more than a quarter (see Table 2.5). A socialist producer city was clearly in the making.

36 *Land as a means of production*

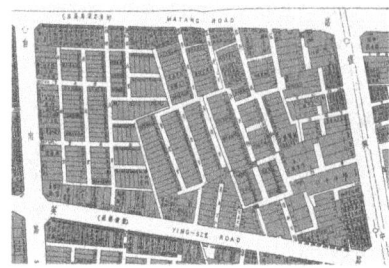

Figure 2.7 A typical *lilong* residential quarter for the working class (L) and that for the high-income class (R), Shanghai.

Table 2.5 WNV housing in Shanghai, 1949–1979

	1949		1979	
	million m^2	%	million m^2	%
Total housing stock	23.6	100.0	41.2	100.0
In which: WNV housing	0.0	0.0	11.4	27.7
Lilong housing	19.4	82.2	23.6	57.3

Source: SMBS, 2001

Socialist cities have to be producers rather than consumers that are deemed capitalist. 'Producing first, living second' (*xianshengchan, houshenghuo*) summarizes succinctly the emphasis placed on investment in the productive sectors. Building plants is paramount, while construction of housing, urban services, and infrastructure were secondary. In order to ensure that the plants obtain sufficient land sites, price mechanisms in the land allocation system were deliberately ruled out, so that market forces would not undermine the industrial policies. The determination of land allocation by the ability to pay would jeopardize the urgent need of industrialization and will only facilitate cities with 'unproductive' services of consumption. As a result, the proportion of industrial land use in Chinese cities was much higher than that in capitalist cities, where land was allocated by the market (see Table 2.6).

It was realized that initial large-scale industrial development without coordination of supporting facilities gave rise to poor performance of production, and thus unproductive use of scarce resources. In his speech 'On the Ten Great Relationships' to the Central Committee of the CCP in 1956, Mao Zedong raised the issue of relationship between 'bone' (plants) and 'flesh' (infrastructure and services), as a disproportionate amount of investment was made in plants, while little was made in residential and service sectors. However, economic rationality did not triumph over political fanaticism. In contrast to the First Five-Year Plan period (1953–1957), when industrialization was mainly driven by the top-down,

Table 2.6 Structure of urban land uses: comparison between market cities (Japanese and Paris) and planned cities (Chinese and Moscow) (% of total built-up areas)

	Japan (average)	Paris	Moscow	Nanjing	Ningbo	Shanghai	Jinan
Industrial	13.5	5.0	31.5	34.2	30.5	24.4	37.5
Residential	77.0	–	–	29.1	28.3	32.5	28.4
Others	9.5	–	–	26.7	41.2	43.1	34.1

Note: Japan's data were of 1985, and Chinese cities' were of the 1980s on average.
Source: China's Academy of Social Sciences, 1992; Bertaud and Renaud, 1994 (for Paris and Moscow data of unknown year)

state-sponsored, and Soviet-assisted industrial projects, the Second Five-Year Plan period (1958–1962) was characterized by the politically motivated mass industrialization movement at grassroots levels. The developmental focus shifted from the key cities to almost every urban and rural locality, and from the dependency on the Soviet Union's technologies and assistance to the reliance on the indigenous efforts and passion. In 1960, 100,000 plants were under construction nationwide in order to increase the contribution of industrial products to GDP so that the share of manufacturing would surpass that of agriculture in the national economy (Cao and Chu, 1990:72). This movement, termed as the Great Leap Forward, started in 1958 and ended in 1960 as a disaster.

Excessive land provision taking place in the 'new industrial cities' contrasted sharply with the extremely parsimonious land allocation to the 'old consumer cities', which were mostly in the coastal region (Zhu, 1996). The policies favored the former by directing almost all resources to new industrial bases, and thus the latter were neglected and suffered from underinvestment in urban infrastructure. A very high population density in the old cities resulted from insufficient spatial expansion and inadequate urban facilities. While the generous land development in the new industrial cities gave rise to a too-low population density to sustain urban public services (see Table 2.7). One neighborhood in Shanghai had a residential population density standing at 293.5 thousand per square kilometer – probably one of the highest in the world (Zhu, 1986a).

Because of socialism and pervasive state ownership, urban housing was considered as socialist welfare distributed to workers free of charge. The low rental for housing was consequently determined by the then-low-wage income. On the one hand, the low rental remained unchanged until the early 1980s, which by then had become a nominal charge. On the other hand, due to a misconception of housing as a consumption good rather than a basic need of urban living, only a disproportionate amount of funds was channeled into urban housing construction, whereas a lion's share of capital investment was put into industrial projects. Housing development was consistently kept very low in proportion to the total capital investment. National housing investment as a proportion of GDP averaged only 1.5 percent in the period 1949–1978. Shanghai's investment into housing only accounted for 0.49 percent of municipal GDP during the period

38 *Land as a means of production*

Table 2.7 Population density in selected Chinese cities (1,000 per sq km, 1983)

	Shanghai	Guangzhou	Beijing	Xi'an	Hefei	Lanzhou
Urban population density	40.6	32.0	11.6	10.9	8.9	5.6

Source: Zhu, 1986b: 15

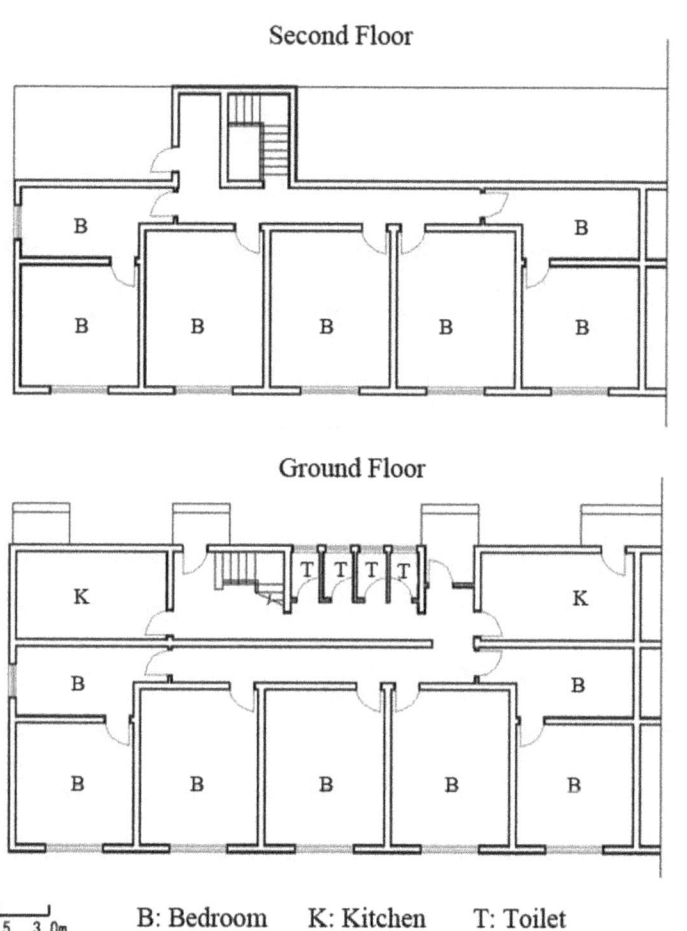

B: Bedroom   K: Kitchen   T: Toilet

Figure 2.8 The floor plans of Workers' New Village housing.

1950–1980. Housing improvement in terms of living space increased merely from 3.9 to 4.4 square meters per capita over the 30 years (SMBS, 2001).

The hallmark of 'producing first, living second' was reflected from the primitive quality of workers' housing. Toilets and kitchens were shared between ten households, and each household had living floor areas between 15 and 20 square meters for workers' housing (see Figure 2.8; Luo, 2007). Though the housing quality was kept low in the beginning, the central government even issued a directive in 1954 requiring that the cost of public housing should be cut down further so as to channel more investment into manufacturing plants. The construction cost of public housing built in 1957 was reduced to 65 percent of those built in 1952, while land for housing was free of charge (Cao and Chu, 1990; Yang, 2011). The scene of slums and shacks remained almost unchanged, as slum clearance was not deemed a high priority. Its quantity in terms of floor areas even went up sharply during 1957–1961, when the mass industrialization in the Great Leap Forward brought in many migrant workers, and in 1972, when the rusticated urban youths returned home (see Figure 2.9).

Inadequate financing for housing development inevitably resulted in housing shortages. Housing floor area per capita, a widely used indicator in China to measure the situations of housing provision, declined to a very low level in the 1970s. Acute housing shortages were basically, on the one hand, caused by underinvestment in housing for a long time. The fact that the state was the sole supplier of urban housing explained that housing provision was at the mercy of state plans and housing conditions would not be improved as long as housing investment remained low on the government's agenda. On the other hand, absence of housing markets and thus prices led to inequalities in distribution because housing welfarism delinked housing demand from affordability and excluded pecuniary contribution from tenants. Urban housing problems were exacerbated by the continuous negligence and became a crisis in cities where underinvestment led to a severe housing shortage. Insufficient rental income resulted in poor maintenance of the existing housing stock, which caused urban degradation. Inadequate housing investment coupled with rapid growth of the urban population in the late 1970s because of the return of rusticated urban

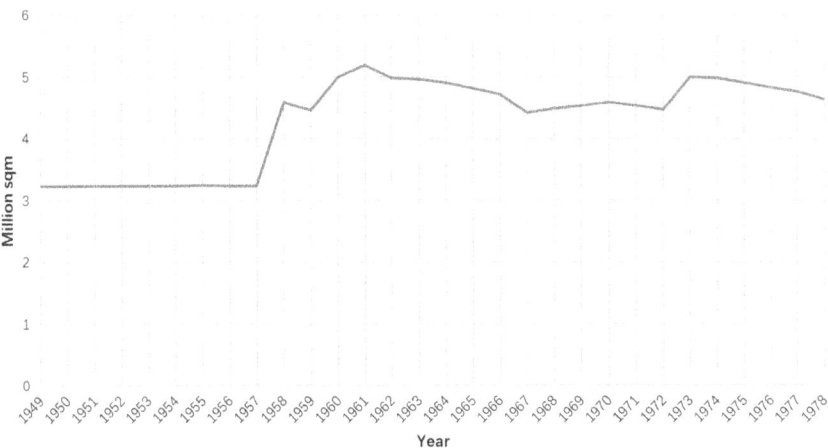

Figure 2.9 Stock of shacks in Shanghai, 1949–1978.

40 *Land as a means of production*

youths after the Cultural Revolution gave rise to a widespread deterioration of housing conditions in many Chinese cities; 192 cities witnessed a reduction in housing space per capita from 4.5 square meters in 1952 to 3.6 square meters in 1978. One-third of urban households were officially categorized as in overcrowded conditions in Shanghai (Wu, 1988).

Shanghai became a victim of the central planning as it ignored adequate investment in urban physical and social infrastructure for quality urban growth (Zhu, 1996). Over 30 years, housing stock in Shanghai, the largest city in China, only increased by 58 percent, despite city GDP expanding by 6.7 times and urban population growing from 4.2 million to 5.8 million (SMBS, 1981). According to a population census conducted in 1982, 47.6 percent of urban households in Shanghai had housing problems to various degrees: poor housing qualities such as dilapidated structures and lack of amenities, overcrowding, and homelessness. Average housing space per capita was merely 4.7 square meters, and 25.1 percent of households were virtually homeless as they temporally lived with their parents or relatives while waiting for government assignment. About half of the total housing space were of substandard quality without necessary facilities (Shanghai Housing Situations Research Team, 1983). A very high population density evolved because of insufficient development of new housing estates and related urban facilities. As a result, urban slums reappeared as unfortunate urban residents who were not properly accommodated by public housing built temporary and informal shelters to cope with their basic housing needs.

'Producing first, living second' did not make new industrial cities productive, and it degraded old consumer cities substantially. In the period 1950–1980, 8.8 percent of Shanghai GDP was invested in fixed assets (that were a proxy for the built environment), 1.8 percent in infrastructure, and 0.5 percent in utilities (SMBS, 1981), in sharp contrast with those in cities of similar size under the market economy (see Table 2.8). During 1949–1978, only the provision of industrial plants outstripped the population growth, while the increased rates of housing supply and road construction were far less than that of population. There was no additional office space built, and shops were even closed by 30.3 percent in the same period (see Table 2.9). Without mediation of land and property markets, top-down plans tended to misallocate resources in urban construction. Underinvestment strained urban functions to the limit, whereas overinvestment unnecessarily wasted valuable resources.

Inefficiency and rigidity imbedded in the urban spatial structure without land market mechanisms

An urban economy was thus structured without participation of land markets. Bertaud and Renaud (1994) discover that the internal efficiency and productivity of the former Soviet cities have been profoundly impaired by the absence of land markets. The absence of a formal land market to coordinate land allocation among competing users also resulted in an inefficient structure of land use and inequality among land users in Chinese cities (IFTE/CASS, 1994). Without

Table 2.8 Urban investment as percentage of GDP

	Shanghai (1950–1980)	Japan (1960–1980)	USA (1975–1983)	Germany (1976–1980)	UN-recommended standard
Investment in fixed assets as percent of GDP	8.8	32.4	18.1	22.1	33.0
Investment in infrastructure as percent of GDP	1.8	NA	NA	NA	NA
Investment in utilities as percent of GDP	0.5	3.1	1.5	1.8	4.0
Investment in housing as percent of GDP	0.5	NA	NA	NA	NA

Note: Fixed assets can be used as a proxy for urban built environment.
Sources: SMBS, 1990; *Chengshi Jingji Yanjiu*, 1993, 1: 15

Table 2.9 Population growth and construction of the built environment, Shanghai, 1949–1979

	1949 (a)	1978 (b)	Increase during 1949–1979 [(b−a)/a, %]
Population (million)	5.0	11.0	120.0
Industrial plants (million m^2)	10.3	25.4	146.6
Housing (million m^2)	23.6	41.2	74.6
Office (million m^2)	2.3	2.3	0.0
Shop (million m^2)	3.3	2.3	−30.3
Paved roads (km)	711	905	27.3

Source: SMBS, 2001

market signals, the plan-guided investment in the built environment often led to mismatches between what were demanded in the marketplaces and what were supplied by plans. Underinvestment and overinvestment occurred to the Chinese cities in the process of urbanization. The regime of central planning propped up government administrate centers and squares for mass assembly, while central business districts were disappearing as offices and retails were suppressed (see Table 2.9). Free resources encourage users to over-consume, let alone to consider affordability. Waste and over-claims arose as land applicants often demanded more than needed by their investment schemes. Land squandering was prevalent (Fung, 1981a). It became evident by rapid expansion of some industrial cities (see Table 2.10). Many cities uneconomically adopted great squares in their city plans. "[T]he area of the municipal central squares in the urban plans of Lanchow, Loyang and Harbin exceeded the 9-hectare Tiananmen Square in Beijing" (Fung, 1982: 275).

Table 2.10 Change in the size of built-up area of selected Chinese cities (1949–1957, square kilometer)

	1949	1957	% Growth
Beijing	109	221	103
Xi'an	13	65	400
Zhengzhou	5	52	940
Hefei	5	57	1,040
Jinan	23	37	61
Tianjin	61	97	59

Source: World Bank, 1993, p.43

The magnitude of urban problems was reckoned directly proportional to the size of the city. Thereby, socialist cities should adopt a new urban structure so as to escape from urban predicaments. The solution was logically adopted by the national urbanization policy to give preference for small- and medium-sized cities and to suggest containment of large cities, in spite of the fact that larger cities were actually associated with greater efficiency of their industrial enterprises because of economies of scale and benefits of agglomeration (Pannell, 1992). Self-contained industrial towns were planned and built around metropolises, aiming at containing further expansion of cities that were already considered too big to manage. Eight industrial towns were built in Beijing, six in Nanjing, and five in Tianjin. Some factories and their workers in metropolises had to be relocated from the central city to the suburban industrial towns.

In order to contain the expansion of Shanghai central city that already had a population of about 6 million in 1957, ten agricultural counties were severed from the neighboring Jiangsu province and annexed by Shanghai so that the area of municipality expanded from 654 to 5910 square kilometers in 1958 (SMBS, 2001). It allowed Shanghai government to comply with the policy of building small- and medium-sized cities by shifting strategies from developing the ten industrial zones (Taopu, Pengpu, Caohejin, Gaoqiao, Qingningsi, Wujiaochang, Beixinjing, Zhoujiadu, Changqiao, and Wusong) in the urban peripheries to pursuing self-contained satellite industrial towns in the far suburbs (see Figure 2.10; Qian, 2018). Seven industrial towns in the suburbs of Shanghai had been built since 1958. Wujing, Minhang, Jiading, Anting, and Songjiang had commenced their developments since the late 1950s, while those of Baoshan (with the construction of Baoshan steel mill) and Jinshanwei (with the establishment of Jinshan petrochemical plant) started since the 1970s (see Table 2.11). Each of these towns specialized on certain sectors of manufacturing. In 1982, the population of those towns accounted for about 7 percent of the total municipal urban population, producing industrial products representing 13 percent of the municipal total in value (Zheng, Zong, and Song, 1984).

The strategy of industrial satellite towns might have overlooked the merits of metropolises that were probably overshadowed by urban problems. Not intrinsically belonging to large cities, urban problems arose from inadequate investment

Land as a means of production 43

Figure 2.10 Location of ten industrial zones in the urban peripheries and seven industrial towns in the suburbs of Shanghai.

in urban infrastructure and incompetent management by the inexperienced city governments. Planned decentralization did not appeal to the factories and workers who were requested to move to the new towns. Given choices, industrial enterprises and their workers would rather remain in the central city. Only 11.9 percent of the total number of enterprises operational in seven industrial towns migrated from the central city. While workers, whose *danweis* had moved to industrial towns, voted with their feet: only 28.1 percent of them actually settled in where they worked, and the rest commuted wastefully between their workplaces and residence in the central city (Zheng, Zong, and Song, 1984).

Table 2.11 Industrial towns of Shanghai

Industrial town	Distance from central city's center (km)	Number of residents (existing, 1,000)	Number of resident (planned, 1,000)	Size (ha)	Main industry	Total number of enterprises	Number of enterprises migrated from central city
Baoshan	18	165	500	2,400	metallurgic	114	0
Wujing	25	13	500	376	chemical	21	2
Minhang	31	67		794	machinery and electrical	59	15
Jiading	33	56	250	693	instruments and researches	65	7
Anting	33	10	150	230	automobile and machinery	26	10
Songjiang	40	69	250	632	machinery and light industry	74	10
Jinshanwei	72	45	450	1,000	petrochemical	12	0

Source: Zheng, Zong and Song, 1984, p.15

Because of the industrialization policy, it was not uncommon to see factories located in the once central business districts. Quite a number of manufacturing factories occupied central locations in the downtown Shanghai even up to the 1980s. In 1985, it was estimated that 56.7 percent of the total industrial space of factories in Shanghai municipality were still in its central city where it was estimated that 30 percent of the land area was occupied by factories and warehouses (Fung, Yan, and Ning, 1992). Manufacturing premises in four central districts (Huangpu, Jing'an, Luwan, and Nanshi) still accounted for 18.9 percent of the municipal total in 1985 (SMBS, 1986). Up to 1991, there were still 1.74 million square meters of factory space in the downtown districts, which at the same time had only 0.39 million square meters of office space (SMBS, 1992). Land use changes were extremely difficult as sitting occupiers were protected by de facto property rights over their premises. It exerted an effective obstacle for potentially more efficient land users to access the land occupied, if not impossible to acquire land in the right location and at the right time. Any necessary land use change and redevelopment did not occur in the built-up central cities as land markets did not exist and land plots could not be transacted.

At the beginning of the 1980s, besides a great shortage of office space, there were not any commercial office spaces[1] for sale or for rent in the emerging market. Since 1981, the Shanghai municipal government had been searching for a location to build a new office center for the incoming international businesses, while redevelopment of old CBD was blocked by sitting tenants who did not have incentive to vacate the sites. The first commercial office premise was not available until 1983 when the Jingjiang Club, a refurbished old colonial building, was made available for leasing to tenants at market rates. By the end of 1988, there were only four office buildings (Jingjiang Club, Union Building, Ruijing

Building, Gaoyang Building), amounting to a total floor area of 58,500 square meters in the nascent office market, while Shanghai was reclaiming its status of international city in Asia (SMBS, 1989). These developments were ad hoc and haphazard responses to the emerging market demand until 1984 when Shanghai was designated as one of the 14 open coastal cities,[2] where special policies and incentives were offered to attract foreign investment.

Agrarian land reforms: land to the tillers in the backdrop of farmland scarcity

According to a well-known anthropological fieldwork of a village named *Kaihsienkung* in the 1930s by Fei (1939), farmland holdings were absolutely unequal among villagers, exacerbated by serious farmland scarcity. *Kaihsienkung* was located in the Yangtze River Delta region, one of the prosperous agrarian economies in China. There were 1,458 villagers and 274 households, and 2,758 *mu* farmland[3] in 1935. It worked out 10.1 *mu* per household and 1.9 *mu* per capita on average. Those families with farmland less than 10 *mu*, revealed by Fei, found it hard to make ends meet based on grains yielded from the meager landholding. Yet, those barely surviving farming households stood for as high as 93.8 percent of the village total (see Table 2.12). Because of scarce endowment of farmland, subsistence farming had been a principal mode of agricultural production, which gave rise to prevalent and persistent rural poverty in China. Techniques of intensive farming increased land productivity, but the growth rate of productivity could not match with that of the population. Agricultural output per land unit increased while output per capita remained the same or even dropped, and thus the production mode was of agricultural involution rather than of evolutional change (Geertz, 1963).[4]

Duo to farmland resources made increasingly scarcer by the continuous population growth, the widening gap between the haves and the have-nots in terms of farmland holding had created a large number of landless peasants. The nature of landlords basically as a rentier class gave rise to a highly unproductive agricultural economy that made peasants worse off over time, though intensive farming developed in the context of small landholdings helped mitigate the abject poverty slightly. Poverty weakened the traditional social cohesion in the

Table 2.12 Farmland holdings in *Kaihsienkung* Village, 1935

Farmland holding, mu	Household, %
50–70	0.6
30–49	0.7
15–29	0.9
10–14	4.0
5–9	18.0
0–4	75.8

Source: Fei, 1939

villages. A natural disaster such as flood and drought often became the last straw on the camel's back, and peasant uprisings brought down the old dynasties and brought in the new ones. The cycle of agricultural involution leading to peasant revolution, instead of evolution toward a more productive regime, repeated itself in China's history and prevented the country from advancement. By the promise of redistributing farmland fairly, the CCP led peasants to defeat the *Guomindang*. Agrarian land reform was carried out soon after the 1949 liberation under the banner 'land to the tillers'.[5]

According to national land statistics in 1950, farmland holding had been highly uneven between the rural social strata before the agrarian land reform, when about 90 percent of the population were living in the villages and engaged in farming (Bi and Zheng, 2000; NBSC, 2017). Farmers with little arable land and tenant peasants without any represented 52.4 percent of the rural population, but their farmland holding only accounted for 14.3 percent of the total. Landholding by the landlords, whose number stood at 4.8 percent of the total, went as high as 38.3 percent of the total farmland stock (see Table 2.13). Addressing this injustice, the state confiscated land from the landlords and rich farmers and redistributed it to the poor farmers and tenant peasants as free gifts so that farmland holdings became even (see Table 2.14). Poor peasants were

Table 2.13 Distribution of landholdings between the rural social strata prior to the land reform

	Population as rural household heads, %	Farmland holding, %	Farmland holding per household, mu
Poor farmer & tenant peasants	52.4	14.3	0.9
Middle-level farmers	33.1	30.9	3.1
Rich farmers	4.7	13.7	9.6
Landlords	4.8	38.3	26.3
Others	5.0	2.9	1.8
Total	100.0	100.0	3.3

Note: 1 *mu* is equal to 667 square meters
Source: Zou, 1998

Table 2.14 Distribution of landholdings between the rural social strata after land reforms

	Population, %	Farmland holding, %	Farmland holding per capita, mu (estimated)
Poor farmer & tenant peasants	52.2	47.1	3.0
Middle-level farmers	39.9	44.3	3.7
Rich farmers	5.3	6.4	4.0
Landlords	2.6	2.2	2.8
Total	100.0	100.0	3.3

Source: Zou, 1998

really poor as they had 0.9 *mu* per capita on average, but the landlord class, though the richest, only controlled 26.3 *mu* per capita on average, which was not considered outrageous in a normal country. It seemed a national tragedy that inequality aggravated by land scarcity induced violent revolution, and the actual differences between the haves and have-nots were not so great. The 'land to the tillers' revolution dissolved the highly concentrated landholdings to a few landlords, and landless peasants received their fair shares, though still very small.

Toward collective land ownership

Nevertheless, the private ownership of farmland created by the 'land to the tillers' revolution was not in accordance with socialist principles of the new government that promulgated state ownership of land resources. The rich might consolidate land from the poor as what had happened prior to 1949, and thus individual household farming might lead to a new divide between the rich and the poor. This potential inequality had to be pre-empted. Moreover, household farming gives rise to fragmentation in landholding that can lead to inadequate provision of farming infrastructure, such as irrigation, which needs collective action. Fragmented landholdings prevent farming of scale as well.

The cooperative movement initiated in 1953 persuaded peasants to join in with their newly obtained land and farming tools to conduct collective farming with consolidated farmland stock, while the Constitution 1954 still recognized the private ownership of farmland. However, the third plenum of the first National People's Congress declared in June 30, 1956, that members' means of production, including land in the cooperative, should be considered as owned by the members collectively, rather than individually. Thereby, the private ownership of farmland had been abolished and replaced with invented collective ownership formally (https://baike.baidu.com/item/%E5%9C%9F%E5%9C%B0%E9%9B%86%E4%BD%93%E6%89%80%E6%9C%89%E5%88%B6, accessed August 16, 2018). Fragmented private landholdings were consolidated again, albeit in the name of collective ownership.

China's agrarian collective farming with collective land ownership was finalized under the banner of People's Commune, which was established on the farming collectives in 1958. The entity of the collective was further clarified in 1962 as composed of three hierarchical bodies of the commune, the brigade, and the production team, and the collective land ownership rested with the production team mainly (*sanji suoyou, dui wei jichu*) (Tang, 2009). Collective farming, though egalitarian, did not give strong incentive to its members for wealth creation. Unfortunately, the People's Commune was mired in its inception in the absurd political campaign of Great Leap Forward (1958–1960), which proved to be disastrous to the collective farming, let alone the tumultuous Cultural Revolution (1966–1976), which was even more disastrous to almost all spheres of the nation. China was on the brink of economic collapse and social breakdown by the late 1970s.

The timely economic reforms, started from the rural domain, unleashed the Household Production Responsibility scheme, which contracted the use rights

48 *Land as a means of production*

of farmland to individual village households over a period of 30 years. The collective farming was effectively terminated in the early 1980s, so was the People's Commune. Farming households became production units, making decisions on what to grow and to sell at market prices after fulfilling the required planned output quotas. The rural economy and communities have been managed by a three-tiered governance system, which is the cornerstone for the collective land-ownership as well, with townships (*xiang/zhen*), administrative villages (*xingzhengcun*), and natural villages (*zirancun*) replacing the commune, the brigade, and the production team, respectively (Smil, 1999; Ho, 2001).

Notes

1 Commercial office space means the office space developed speculatively by development firms. Under the central planning system, offices were built by users' requests only.
2 The 14 open coastal cities are Beihai, Dalian, Fuzhou, Guangzhou, Lianyungang, Nantong, Ningbo, Qingdao, Qinghuangdao, Shanghai, Tianjin, Wenzhou, Yantai, and Zhanjiang.
3 *Mu* is a traditional measure of farmland in China. One *mu* is equal to 667 square meters, or 15 *mu* to one hectare.
4 The population of *Kaihsienkung* village increased to 1,899 in 1966, and further to 2,308 by 1980, while village farmland resources remained unchanged, reducing land-holding per capita to 1.1 *mu* (Annals of *Kaixiangong* Village Compiling Committee, 2015:134).
5 'Land to the tillers' movement started as early as 1927 in the areas controlled by the CCP, which was one of conflicts breaking up the coalition against warlords between the CCP and *Guomindang* (Zou, 1998). The nationwide movement was initiated since the liberation when Land Reform Act was passed on June 30, 1950.

References

Annals of *Kaixiangong* Village Compiling Committee (2015) *Annals of Kaixiangong Village*. Nanjing: Jiangsu People's Press. (in Chinese).
Bertaud, A. & Renaud, B. (1994) *Cities without land markets: Location and land use in the socialist city*. Policy Research Working Paper 1477. Washington, DC: World Bank.
Bi, Y. Y. & Zheng, Z. Y. (2000) Analysis of farmland change since the founding of People's Republic of China. *Resource Science*, 2: 8–12. (in Chinese).
Cao, H. T. & Chu, Z. H. (eds.) (1990) *Urban construction of contemporary China*. Beijing: China Social Science Press. (in Chinese).
Chen, X. L. (2017) *Annual statistics of China's cities, 2017*. Beijing: China Statistics Press. (in Chinese).
China's Academy of Social Sciences (1992) China's urban land management system and its reforms,. *China's Social Sciences*, 2: 63–81. (in Chinese).
Ebanks, G. E. & Cheng, C. Z. (1990) China: a unique urbanization model. *Asia-Pacific Population Journal*, 5(3): 29–50.
Economic Research Institute, Shanghai Academy of Social Sciences (ERI/SASS) (1962) *Transition of Shanghai shacks*. Shanghai: Shanghai People's Press. (in Chinese).
Fei, H. T. (1939) *Peasant life in China; a field study of country life in the Yangtze valley*. London: G. Routledge and Sons.

French, R. A. & Hamilton, F. E. I. (1979) Is there a socialist city? in R. A. French & F. E. I. Hamilton (eds.) *The socialist city – Spatial structure and urban policy*, 1–21. Chichester: John Wiley & Sons.
Fung, K. I. (1981a) Urban sprawl in China: Some causative factors, in L. J. C. Ma & E. W. Hanten (eds.) *Urban development in modern China*, 194–221. Boulder, CO: Westview Press.
Fung, K. I. (1981b) Satellite town development in the Shanghai city region. *Town Planning Review*, 52(1): 26–46.
Fung, K. I. (1982) The spatial development of Shanghai, in C. Howe (ed.) *Shanghai: Revolution and development in an Asian metropolis*, 269–300. New York: Cambridge University Press.
Fung, K. I., Yan, Z. M. & Ning, Y. M. (1992) Shanghai: China's world city, in Y. M. Yeung & X. W. Hu (eds.) *China's coastal cities: Catalysts for modernization*, 124–152. Honolulu: University of Hawaii Press.
Geertz, C. (1963) *Agricultural involution: The processes of ecological change in Indonesia*. Berkeley: University of California Press.
Gu, H. Z. (1997) *History of Chinese urban youths' rustication*. Beijing: China Jiancha Publishing. (in Chinese).
Haussermann, H. (1996) From the socialist to the capitalist city: Experiences from Germany, in G. Andrusz, M. Harloe & I. Szelenyi (eds.) *Cities after socialism: Urban and regional change and conflict in post-socialist societies*, 214–231. Oxford: Blackwell.
Ho, P. (2001) Who owns China's land? Property rights and deliberate institutional ambiguity. *The China Quarterly*, 166: 394–421.
Howe, C. (1981) Industrialization under conditions of long-run population stability: Shanghai's achievement and prospect, in C. Howe (ed.) *Shanghai – Revolution and development in an Asian metropolis*, 153–187. Cambridge: Cambridge University Press.
Institute of Finance and Trade Economics, Chinese Academy of Social Sciences (IFTE/CASS) and Institute of Public Administration (IPA) (1994) *Urban land use and management in China*. Beijing: Economic Science Publishing. (in Chinese).
Li, H. (2016) *The planning of the eight key new industrial cities – Urban planning history of PR China in the 1950s*. Beijing: China Press of Construction Industry. (in Chinese).
Lin, G. C. S. (2002) The growth and structural change of Chinese cities: A contextual and geographic analysis. *Cities*, 19: 299–316.
Lipson, E. (1946) *A planned economy or free enterprise – The lessons of history*. London: Adam & Charles Black.
Luo, G. (2007) Production of space and transition of space: Workers' New Villages and socialist urban experience in Shanghai. *Journal of East China Normal University (Philosophy and Social Sciences)*, 39(6): 91–96. (in Chinese).
Miliutin, N. A. (1974) *Sotsgorod: The problem of building socialist cities*. Cambridge, MA: MIT Press.
Murphey, R. (1953) *Shanghai - Key to modern China*. Cambridge, MA: Harvard University Press.
National Bureau of Statistics, China (NBSC). (1994, 2000, 2017) *China statistical yearbook*. Beijing: China Statistics Press. (in Chinese).
Pannell, C. (1992) The role of great cities in China, in G. E. Guldin (ed.) *Urbanizing China*, 11–39. Westport: Greenwood.
Qian, Z. (2018) Shanghai's socialist suburbanization 1953–1962. *Journal of Planning History*, 17(3): 226–247.

Sik, O. (1967) *Plan and market under socialism*. White Plains and Prague: IASP and Academia Publishing House of the Czechoslovak Academy of Sciences.

Shanghai Housing Situations Research Team (1983) *Report on solving housing problems in Shanghai in eight years (1983–1990)*. unpublished report. (in Chinese).

Shanghai Municipal Bureau of Statistics (SMBS) (1981, 1986, 1990, 2001) *Shanghai statistical yearbook*. Shanghai: Shanghai People's Press. (in Chinese).

Shanghai Municipal Bureau of Statistics (SMBS) (1989, 1992) *Shanghai real estate market*. Beijing: China Statistical Publishing. (in Chinese).

Shi, S. Z. & Gao, Q. S. (eds.) (1989) *Shanghai encyclopaedia*. Shanghai: Xuelin Publishing. (in Chinese).

Sit, V. F. S. (ed.) (1985) *Chinese cities – The growth of the metropolis since 1949*. Hong Kong: Oxford University Press.

Smil, V. (1999) China's agricultural land. *The China Quarterly*, 158: 414–429.

Tang, J. J. (2009) Collective ownership belonging to three entities [the commune, the brigade, and the team], and with the team being the basic holder. *Archives World*, 4: 17–21. (In Chinese).

Urban Social and Economic Survey Organization (1990) *Forty years of urban development*. Beijing: Urban Social and Economic Survey Organization. (in Chinese).

World Bank (1985) *China – Long-term development issues and options*. Washington, DC: The World Bank.

World Bank (1993) *China - Urban land management in an emerging market economy*. Washington, DC: The World Bank.

Wu, W. Q. (1988) Chinese housing problems and policies. *City Planning Review*, 1: 13–17. (in Chinese).

Yang, C. (2011) Spatial practice of socialist city – Worker's new village in Shanghai (1949–1978). *Human Geography*, 26(3): 35–40, 64. (in Chinese).

Zheng, Z., Zong, L. & Song, X. D. (1984) Comments on the policy of satellite town development in Shanghai. *Urban Planning Forum*, 3: 15–23. (in Chinese).

Zhu, J. M. (1986a) Development of urban resident density and hypothesis of logistic curve. *Urban Planning Forum*, 6: 2–16. (in Chinese).

Zhu, J. M. (1986b) A basic research on urban population distribution and re-distribution. *Urban Planning Forum*, 5: 10–19. (in Chinese).

Zhu, J. M. (1996) Denationalization of urban physical development – The experiment in the Shenzhen Special Economic Zone, China. *Cities*, 13: 187–194.

Zou, Y. R. (1980) *The study of demographic change of old Shanghai*, Shanghai: Shanghai People's Press. (in Chinese).

Zou, Y. C. (1998) *Contemporary China's land management*. Beijing: Contemporary China Press. (in Chinese).

Zwass, A. (1987) *Market, plan, & state – The strengths and weaknesses of the two world economic systems*. Armonk and London: M.E. Sharpe.

3 Restoration of land as assets
Genesis of a market of land leasehold

The economic reforms since 1978 have introduced marketization to the management of the economy, which has changed the modes of China's urbanization profoundly. Shenzhen Special Economic Zone acts in the vanguard, pioneering the market-driven land development with institutional change that phases out free land utilization initially. Dynamic market demand for premises has facilitated the growing-up of a new generation of state-owned developers who benefit substantially from land rent created by a dual land market. Shenzhen becomes the 'instant city', built with emerging land markets that formally bring up the newly invented land leasehold, though arbitrage opportunities are created by a dual land market. Transformation of housing provision is successfully achieved from public welfare housing to private commercial housing.

Shenzhen as a pioneer for market-driven land development

In 1978 a grand and unprecedented economic reform was launched in China, a bold political decision to initiate the transformation toward a decentralized economy with a mixture of market mechanisms and planning controls. The new initiative calls for a change from self-reliance and self-sufficiency to joining the global economy, so as to improve economic performance. Few people believe that a planned economy, after being in place for 30 years, would ever lead the country to prosperity, and the state has given up its doctrine of class struggle and proletariat dictatorship. Public opinions maintain that political legitimacy of the government should be established by its successful management of economic development, because economic growth is the sole goal capable of uniting China's citizens after decades of perennial political upheavals. The transformation from the centrally controlled system to a socialist market economy and from the closed socialist autarchy to an open economy with market orientation inevitably entails restructuring of the economy and formation of new social relations. However, a free market system, with its cornerstone of private ownership, is not expected to replace the existing regime at a stroke. Public ownership and the roles of the state in production are rigorously maintained.

Officially inaugurated in 1980, the Shenzhen Special Economic Zone (SSEZ) was earmarked to experiment with the integration of home enterprises into the international economy. It was used primarily as a laboratory in a confined locality to test an innovative regime by using foreign capital, modern technologies, and advanced management to stimulate the domestic economy. Therefore, the SSEZ is meant to be an exemplar for other cities to follow its development that can live up to reformists' expectations. Land and building development had not been considered as independent economic activities since socialist China was established, because of an all-inclusive public economy and dominant state ownership. Governments acted omnipotently as financier, land owner, builder, and investor in all urban land and building development projects. Governments provided public housing to urban residents and supplied offices and factories to urban enterprises where the state-owned accounted for the absolute majority. The SSEZ has an area of 327.5 square kilometers as its territory. The whole zone in its inception was of greenfield in agricultural farming, except for a small town center named Luohu, functioning as a marketplace for the county. Infrastructure construction to equip land for urban use was the first compelling task for the new government, which was handicapped by inadequate fiscal capacity. Having seen the inflow of external investment from both overseas and inland provinces to take advantage of low production costs, tax relief, and proximity to Hong Kong – a gateway to the world market – the SSEZ government contrived new measures to promote urban physical development by various modes. It rejected the mode of sole government sponsorship, which was still the norm elsewhere in China. It became imperative to introduce market mechanisms and participation of multiple actors into land and building development, so as to speed up the growth of SSEZ.

Institutional change to urban land rights: phasing out free land utilization

The old land regime was challenged for the first time in Shenzhen. No sooner had Shenzhen been designated as a special economic zone than its government found itself in a handicapped situation for want of finance, except for the autonomy granted to try experimental policies for the building of a pro-market economy. Firstly, grants from the central government for construction of urban infrastructure were far from adequate to take on large-scale land development. Secondly, a practical problem arose when overseas investors came to commit themselves to Shenzhen: they were not entitled to free land use as domestic firms that were mostly state-owned socialist units still under the centrally controlled state economy. The purpose of setting up the SSEZ was to build a city with characteristics of a socialist market economy by luring as much overseas and private investments as possible. Shenzhen was thus expected to deal with privately owned enterprises, and it had been successful in this regard. By the end of 1996, the total contractual inward investment in SSEZ reached US$23.1 billion, of which US$11.9 billion had been materialized (Shenzhen Bureau of Statistics,

1997). Therefore, a commercial relationship between the government as the landowner and private land users as tenants had to be established and legalized.

The issue was how to reinstall the notion of land as economic assets and to strengthen the status of the state as the landowner. For a joint-venture firm, the property rights over the land parcel contributed to the venture should be claimed formally by its owner. Pragmatically, the value of land contributed by Shenzhen partners as a share to joint ventures had to be worked out. In this connection, the first benchmark of a land use fee of HK$5,000 per square meter was established in December 1980, when a plot at a size of 4,000 square meters was rented to a Hong Kong developer for an apartment/office project. The lease was to be valid for 30 years, and the developer paid the rental in a lump sum. There were up to 10 cases of such land renting by December 1981. Prior to that, a Shenzhen catering firm together with a Hong Kong investor initiated a joint development named Bamboos Garden Hotel in 1979 (Shenzhen Bureau of Construction, 1989). It was the first case of land commercialization. The Shenzhen partner provided the land plot allocated by the government, and the Hong Kong investor covered development costs, including expenses for land requisition from a village. Upon completion of the construction and the hotel coming into operation, both parties shared profits based on their terms of agreement. The Donghu Liyuan project, a residential development of 460 units, was implemented under a similar contract. Profits were divided between Shenzhen–Hong Kong parties at 85–15 percent split after sales. A form of joint venture between foreign development capital and local land resources was conceived. SSEZ Development Corporation (SDC) (*Shenzhen Tequ Fazhan Gongsi*), a state-owned company, was appointed in charge of comprehensive physical development. By the end of 1983, the number of cases of joint property development had risen to 36, with a pledged capital inflow of HK$5.88 billion and a total land area of 86 hectares (Zhang, 1993).

However, this bold experiment did not accord with the existing regime that considered land as a means of production. Only on January 1, 1982, did the belated *SSEZ Land Management Regulation* legalize the practice and declare the end of the era of free land use. In order to strengthen the status of the state as the landowner, all land users were required to pay a land use fee. Rates of land use fee for various categories were made known to the public. As such, Shenzhen acted in the vanguard of terminating the old land regime, which was ostensibly concerned with social equity but, in fact, was gravely inefficient in the economic sense and seriously undermined effective management of land resources. The land use fee announced on January 1, 1982, was nevertheless received as a heavy financial burden to local land users. The strong resistance from the local land users was caused by the lagging state-owned enterprise (SOE) reforms, which only allowed SOEs certain degree of autonomy in managing their businesses.

Heavy lobbying from SOE land users pressured the government to reduce the rates on July 1, 1984, after having been in place for two and a half years. However, the land use fee did not constitute a barrier to overseas investors. In facing still more complaints of claimed overcharges on land use from the local land users, the Shenzhen government in 1985 succumbed to the pressure to further reduce the rates to the level of only one-tenth of the 1982 rates. Despite the imposition of land use fee and compromises made, many land users were still exempted from the payment over land occupation. By 1987, out of 82 square kilometers of land that had been allocated, only 17 square kilometers were levied a land use fee. The income from the land use fee was far behind government expenditure on land development. Land development had so far cost ¥1.7 billion, while only ¥52.5 million land use fees were collected (Zhang, 1993). SOEs enjoying a substantial discount or even to the degree of zero on land use expenses constituted land rent captured by land users, which reflected the nature of incremental and gradualist economic reforms. It sowed the seeds of rent-seeking in the later transition from the old land regime to the new system of land marketization. Cashing out land rent became the startup capital for a new generation of public developers.

A new generation of market-oriented developers brought up by land rent

The urban built environment under a capitalist market system is shaped by many individual players and is primarily determined by developers and the state. The government is generally responsible for the provision of urban infrastructure and public facilities, such as social housing and civic structures, whereas the property development industry decides within a statutory framework what building should be developed at what location. The real estate industry is 'the main progenitor' of changes in the urban physical form (Reckinger et al., 1991; Fainstein, 1994).

While many Chinese city governments faced a daunting task of renovating dilapidated old urban structures, Shenzhen, as a new town, needed to develop a vast amount of greenfield to fill it with urban infrastructure and buildings in order to accommodate forthcoming social and economic activities. Handicapped by the financial constraint of inadequate funds granted from the central treasury, the Shenzhen government itself was not financially capable of carrying out the mission on a full scale. Various forms of participation had to be tried instead of sole government sponsorship. A local property industry had to be nurtured so as to conduct urban construction and development under a new set of market conditions.

The implementation from 1978 of grand economic reforms had moved the system of central planning toward market orientation. Market-oriented enterprises, albeit many still being state owned, were to a certain extent given autonomy in decision-making. The emergence of private industries, foreign-local joint ventures, and non-state-owned enterprises had created a quasi-market, and their business decisions were largely market driven. A property user market was thus emerging. Overseas investment, the reforming autonomous SOEs, and private enterprises constituted a considerable amount of commercial demand for land and buildings. Premises were needed in great magnitude to accommodate production and consumption because of dynamic economic growth as well as insufficient investment in urban physical structure in the past. Establishment of property markets was in the pipeline, driven by the demand from users, tenants, and investors, who had to acquire premises at market prices and rentals. Potential value of land and buildings was widely perceived and anticipated to appreciate in time in the background of long-time pent-up demand for premises. This perception was reinforced by an envisaged tendency of urban land stock toward great scarcity due to looming rural-urban migration in great magnitude.

Demand for premises from SOEs was emerging as well, stimulated by the SOE reforms that would put SOEs under hard budget constraints by instilling economic responsibility and financial accountability in them. In 1983, profit remittance was partially replaced by profit taxation. SOEs were to remit 50 percent of profits to governments and pay 55 percent income tax on the other 50 percent (Lim, Cai, and Li, 1996). Meanwhile, government grants had been replaced by repayable bank loans with interest, and SOEs were required to purchase or rent their premises according to their needs and affordability. With a new profit-sharing formula between governments and SOEs, SOEs were stimulated to operate in the market by responding to market demand. After a proportion of after-tax profits was submitted to the state as dividends paid to the owner, the rest could be retained and invested at the discretion of the enterprise. It provided SOEs with a means to invest in fixed assets, which was strictly controlled by the erstwhile central planning (Bei, 1990). Enterprise profits accumulated by SOEs under the control of the Shenzhen Investment Management Corporation stood at only ¥51 million in 1980 but increased to ¥5.1 billion in 1995 (Shenzhen Enterprise Reforms Committee, 1997).

After 30 years of building up the socialist economy, state-owned construction firms were seen as the only plausible candidates to be nurtured as property developers operated in an emerging property market. Land, a state asset within the reach of local government, was used as start-up capital offered to the developers-to-be. The recipients did not pay for the land transfer initially. Although the Shenzhen government, a *de jure* landowner, reserved the right to collect land rental as soon as developers could make profits from their commercial undertakings, there were no legal constraints guaranteeing the obligation.

In 1984, the State Economic Commission and Ministry of Urban and Rural Construction and Environmental Protection, in the document *Temporary Measures for Urban Construction and Comprehensive Development Companies*, gave the green light for state-owned development companies to become independent business entities. Thereafter, real estate developers formally registered, initially dominated by SOEs, and began to participate in urban spatial development and redevelopment. According to IFTE/CASS and IPA (1994), the rise of property developers had contributed significantly to the profound changes in the landscape of Chinese cities, notably, those cities in the coast region. The Shenzhen municipal government in 1983 granted full status of developer to eight SOEs for land development that was to undertake 'leveling and six connections' (*liutong yiping*) (connections of electricity, water, sewers, drains, access roads, and telecommunication to the site, as well as site leveling). The Shenzhen government only charged nominal rentals for the raw land leasing in the form of revenue remittance by the developers as SOEs. The rest of the development profits were retained by the developers as financial assets for further development.

China Merchant's Steam Navigation (CMSN) (*Zhaoshang Ju*), a large Chinese SOE established by the Qing dynasty (1872) and operating in Hong Kong since 1949 (Hou, 1965), went to Shenzhen in 1979 to develop the *Shekou Industrial Zone*. One of its divisions specializing in land development undertook land leveling of ten square kilometers with an alleged outlay of US$100 million invested in infrastructure, raised from international capital markets (Oborne, 1986: 125). Land was transferred free of charge in the first instance. When land development was completed by CMSN, in addition to its own use, some surplus land was subleased to other users at market rates. As the first lessee, CMSN paid only nominal land use fee to the municipal government. It benefited substantially from subsequent property booms because of a large land bank given only at the cost of equipping land with basic infrastructure. Having a large land bank, CMSN could diversify into property development. By March 1984, CMSN had signed 11 contracts with partners for joint-venture property development (Oborne, 1986: 123). The success of CMSN in developing a benchmark of *Shekou* industrial new town could not be isolated from its benefits derived from the preferential land provision.

CMSN was not an exception. Another large urban development project with government blessing in the preferential land policy was *Huaqiaocheng*, which was a mini new town of 4.8 square kilometers developed by Huaqiaocheng Development Corporation (HDC) – an SOE set up by China Travel Service (HK), another SOE registered in Hong Kong – since 1985. The site was appropriated by the city government and transferred to HDC free of charge in the first place, though internal agreements on settlement of land rentals between the two parties at later stages might exist. The built-up area of 2.6 square kilometers had been completed with a residential population of 30,000 by 1997. From 1986 to 1995, *Huaqiaocheng* submitted ¥950 million taxes, standing for 2.9 percent of the total fiscal income to the municipal government during the period (Shenzhen Enterprise Reforms Committee, 1997). Development profits derived from the free land factor obviously helped CMSN and HDC expand their businesses. *Huaqiaocheng* has subsequently become a well-known trademark for the development of private housing estates in China. Other similar projects include Nanshan Chiwan Petroleum Logistic Base of 38 square kilometers (1983), Wenjindu Industrial Zone of 6 square kilometers (1983), and Chegongmiao Industrial Zone (1987).

SSEZ Development Corporation (SDC) (*Shenzhen Tequ Fazhan Gongsi*) had been transformed from a company with only six employees and an asset of four bicycles to a transnational corporation with 6,500 staff and ¥4.2 billion assets in 1994 (ECSREY, 1994). On September 4, 1980, an agreement was reached to develop two office towers of 20 stories. SDC joined the agreement with a provision of 1.2 hectares of land, while Hong Kong partners provided a development fund of HK$60.2 million. Upon completion, SDC retained the retail space on the ground and first floors, as well as 58 percent of proceeds from sales of office space, and the rest, 42 percent, went to the Hong Kong partners. By the end of 1983, this type of joint development for housing, shops, offices, and hotels had aggregated to 36 contracts with a pledged capital inflow of HK$5.88 billion and a total land area of 86 hectares (Zhang, 1993). As a result, Shenzhen experienced the first property boom in its history.

Shenzhen's property development set a precedent in the history of Chinese socialist urbanization that urban development can be done based on the commercial principle of profitability. The number of developers mushroomed: 8 in 1983 and then 107 in 1989. In 1991 there were 109 developers, of which 79 were SOEs, representing 72.5 percent of the total. In 1994, the number of developers increased to 337, of which 207 were SOEs, accounting for 61.4 percent of the total. Foreign capital played an essential role in the first stage of Shenzhen development toward the establishment of a good showcase of a socialist market system. Those early adventures served as exemplars of how projects should be handled. Market forces started to demonstrate influence on the course of urbanization. However, the impact of foreign capital on the local property market declined from its prime time, 1979–1983, when funds from overseas accounted for 31 percent of the total capital investment, to the period of 1992–1996, when foreign capital took only 16 percent (Shenzhen Bureau of Statistics, 1997).

The pace of urban construction and the role of the new property development industry in shaping new urban structures demonstrated that interactions between market demand and supply were instrumental in the process of property development. Public developers were learning to be market players. Shenzhen developers accomplished several milestone-projects of significance to the city landscape. Development expertise, which had been built up gradually over years, was so crucial that it determined the fate of project in a market where customer preferences began to dominate. The ITC Mansion (*Shenzhen Guoji Maoyi Zhongxin Dasha*) was such a case to demonstrate how a nascent property industry was learning to develop a project to maximize output. Many provincial and municipal governments in China wanted to have offices in Shenzhen to handle outward investment from their provinces to Shenzhen and to attract inward investment to their inland cities. Having perceived the demand for offices, the state-owned developer SSEZ Real Estate & Properties (*Shenzhen Wuye Fazhan Jituan*) initiated development of an office building named ITC Mansion in October 1982. Despite 38 prospective tenants turning up with down payments for the intended office space, the developer was still two-thirds short of development expenses. Development finance constituted a major obstacle, on the one hand. On the other hand, after a visit to Hong Kong to learn the design of similar buildings, the developer realized that the original building design did not have a proper combination of tenants to maximize the value of building and to make best use of the location. Its architectural design was subsequently revised to reflect new ideas by adding a shopping mall at the ground floor and a rotating restaurant on the top. The height of the building increased to 53 floors from its original 38 floors for the purpose of enhancement of prestige. The revision turned an otherwise purely office tower into a visual and functional focus in the central business district where it was located. The alterations, however, exacerbated the problem of shortage in development finance. Having seen the booming housing market at that time, the developer conceived a remarkable strategy of developing housing using the down payments with an intention to multiply the capital, in the faith that housing could be quickly built and sold at great profit margins. It succeeded. Profits made from the housing development were used to finance the ITC Mansion project, and it was completed successfully. The ITC Mansion has become the 1980s' landmark of Shenzhen, where Deng Xiaoping made his famous 1992 South-Tour Speech to stimulate and deepen China's economic reforms after the 1989 political crisis (http://shenzhen.sina.com.cn/news/n/2015-06-27/detail-ifxenncn6741762.shtml, accessed November 4, 2018).

Shenzhen: the 'instant city' built with land markets

Under the centrally planned system, urbanization was artificially suppressed and thus proceeded slowly. In 1949, 10.6 percent of the population lived in cities; the ratio increased to 17.9 percent in 1978. The number of urban population grew from 57.7 million in 1949 to 172.5 million in 1978, at an annual increment of 4.0 million. With the initiated economic reforms in 1978, people were set free from rigid economic controls and abundant initiatives were released from ideological cages. A variety of economic entities was emerging to break the dominance of the state economy. Rapid urbanization took place. By 1988, urban population reached the level of 25.8 percent of the total national population, with a net increment of urban population at 114.1 million (NBSC, 1989). This accelerated development is largely attributed to the participation of new nonstate actors that created nonagricultural jobs in cities. Economic liberalization also opened up the cities where the service sector permitted free entry of self-employed individuals such as tailors, barbers, peddlers, salespersons, real estate agents, and so on.

Property development as an economic activity usually contributes substantially to the general national product and employment in the countries experiencing rapid urbanization. After many years under the doctrines of Marxism-Leninism, which emphasize narrowing down the gaps between the countryside and cities by suppressing urbanization, the economic change has brought in the user demand for buildings, which provides a strong stimulus to the newly founded property industry. The released pent-up demand for buildings, suppressed by the former planning regime, added to the pressure on the market. The process of property development, from initiation to transaction, has to follow commercial principles and equilibrium between demand and supply. Forecasting market demand and identifying buyers and tenants become part and parcel of essential feasibility studies for property development, in contrast with the previous practice, where construction was commissioned by government and built for users who did not need to pay for the premises.

As a forerunner in the national urban reforms, Shenzhen has tried market mechanisms in its urban construction in the very beginning of its new town development. Its supply of physical structures is responsive to market demand, and development of buildings is presumably directed by market prices, which suggests equilibrium between demand and supply. Shenzhen property stocks have multiplied, along with vibrant economic growth (see Tables 3.1 and 3.2). It has been the first time since China adopted socialism in 1949 that property market mechanisms replace central plans in guiding the production of the urban built environment. Market forces appear more effective than plans in allocating resources to urban construction. It constitutes a sharp contrast to urban construction under the previous central planning, where investment in the urban built environment was entirely manipulated by government whims. With no mechanisms to receive market feedback, the plan-guided investments in the urban built environment often led to mismatches between what are demanded by marketplaces and what are supplied by plans. Owing to its low priority on the government agenda, investment in the urban built environment is generally neglected.

Real estate as assets with investment value appears under the reins of market forces as well, which seemingly regulate property prices along with changing market circumstances. Property prices and price changes begin to serve as a barometer to decode interactions between demand and supply. It is remarkable for a country where market prices were absent for 30 years to see economic democracy making inroads into a totalitarian entity. Strong economic growth pushes up property prices, reflecting relative scarcity at a time when supply lags behind demand. Property oversupply drives down real estate prices, which subsequently discourage launches of new projects. In a period of ten years, Shenzhen properties experienced a substantial appreciation in value, and price changes ranged

Table 3.1 Shenzhen GDP and population, 1979–2016

Year	GDP (¥billion)	Population (million)
1979	0.2	0.3
1985	3.9	0.9
1995	84.2	4.5
2005	495.1	8.3
2016	1,949.3	11.9

Source: Shenzhen Bureau of Statistics, 2017

Table 3.2 Shenzhen property stocks, 1985–1999 (million square meters)

Year	Housing / Index	Offices / Index	Factories / Index	Shops / Index
1985	2.4 / 100	0.3 / 100	0.6 / 100	0.5 / 100
1988	5.5 / 230	1.1 / 323	1.4 / 243	0.8 / 148
1994	13.8 / 579	1.6 / 462	3.4 / 618	1.8 / 328
1999	29.1 / 1220	3.2 / 916	–	3.9 / 719

Source: ECSREY, 2000

from 4 to 18 times for varied sectors (see Table 3.3). The considerable growth in property value and sufficient supply of premises are mainly due to robust economic growth, high inflation, and speculative investment behavior. Buildings as economic assets are seemingly sold and bought at prices determined by buyers and sellers. Albeit not perfectly and efficiently, property prices have been changing and adjusting according to situations in the marketplace. During the period 1988–1994, Shenzhen's housing prices had fluctuations of between +95 percent and −22 percent (see Table 3.3). Entry into the development market does not seem restricted, either.

An economic system liberalized by the reforms should be an indisputable factor attributing to Shenzhen's incredible growth at extraordinary rates. It is also due to the fact that the city is of new town development starting from a very small and humble base, with GDP only 196 million in 1979 (see Table 3.1). Inflation, a new phenomenon never seen during the era of central planning, occurred in the end of the 1980s and amplified the nominal prices. In spite of that, the Shenzhen property markets have empirically proved the premise that investment in property serves as a hedge against inflation. Speculation in property investment, which is considered related only to the capitalist free market, appears in Shenzhen. It is induced by rapid appreciation of property value. Short-term speculation plays a positive role by mobilizing finance into the property market.

When private property rights were ill defined in the early 1980s, developers could hardly sell their completed projects. Buildings had to be held and leased to users. Development capital was thus taken as a hostage, which impeded further development. High rentals because of the consequent relative undersupply of rental properties induced users into owner occupation and investors into property investment. High risks resulting from unclear property rights were compensated by high yields from investment. Examination of the primary market of

Table 3.3 Changes in property price indexes

Year	Housing / Annual change rate (%)	Offices / Annual change rate (%)	Factories / Annual change rate (%)	Shops / Annual change rate (%)
1984	100 / –	100 / –	100 / –	100 / –
1985	118 / 18.0	113 / 13.0	108 / 8.0	106 / 6.0
1986	121 / 2.5	128 / 13.3	105 / −2.8	138 / 30.2
1987	147 / 21.5	143 / 11.7	117 / 11.4	210 / 52.2
1988	179 / 21.8	183 / 28.0	143 / 22.2	306 / 45.7
1989	349 / 95.0	241 / 31.7	256 / 79.0	454 / 48.4
1990	489 / 40.1	331 / 37.3	282 / 10.2	537 / 18.3
1991	705 / 44.2	366 / 10.6	292 / 3.5	926 / 72.4
1992	1061 / 50.5	603 / 64.8	405 / 38.7	1323 / 42.9
1993	1292 / 21.8	733 / 21.6	497 / 22.7	2130 / 61.0
1994	1012 / −21.7	753 / 2.7	484 / −2.6	1996 / −6.3

Source: ECSREY, 1995

properties in Nanshan district, one of the three districts of SSEZ, reveals that holding of properties by developers became less over the period 1987–1996. The share of property sold directly to users as well as to investors as a percentage of the total development rose significantly for offices and factories (see Table 3.4). The emergence of a rental property market differentiates the market into two submarkets for use and investment, and it attracts investors who consider property a worthwhile investment option. It facilitates the economy by providing property occupiers with the option of long-term and short-term holding. The rental property market has been active and dynamic ever since. Accordingly, the secondary property markets have been active as well.

A case study disclosed that a state-owned developer, Shenzhen Development Bank Real Estate Company, attained 76.2 percent development profit from a typical project of mixed-use building with retailing, offices, and housing in 1989. The profit was calculated based on a valuation of ¥9.16 million and total development costs of ¥5.20 million, inclusive of interests paid on loans and taxes. The land lease was purchased in November 1988 at a price of ¥1,200 per square meter. Building construction commenced five months later and was completed in one year. Upon completion, part of the building was sold immediately, and the rest was retained for the developer's own use (Shenzhen Bureau of Construction, 1990). Capital appreciation occurred in all property sectors of Shenzhen to various degrees. Total investment yields seemed very high in comparison with other normal investment opportunities. An anecdotal story of successful property investment influenced profoundly on luring investment capital into the Shenzhen property market. The Shenzhen International Trade Mansion was presold of 80 percent of floor areas by its developer to a Hong Kong investor in 1988 at HK$77 million. One year later, after some refurbishment, it was sold again to another investor when its capital value appreciated to HK$106 million after deduction of the expenditures for improvement. The net annual appreciation rate

Table 3.4 Property transactions in the primary markets, Nanshan district, Shenzhen

Year	Sold (%)	Rented (%)	Vacant (%)
Housing			
1987	77.3	17.6	5.1
1996	80.3	6.7	13.0
Office			
1987	13.4	86.6	0.0
1996	40.7	49.1	10.2
Factory			
1987	35.1	57.5	7.4
1996	81.5	14.5	4.0

Source: NPLBS, 1997

was 37.7 percent. This case is one of the many sensational stories of property investment in good times.

Unlike urban construction during the central planning era, where government was the sole actor, Shenzhen's urban physical development has involved many actors: the central government, the local government, foreign capital, local developers, private individuals as tenants and investors, and banks. Local developers, foreign capital, and local government are three principal builders of the Shenzhen city. Up to 1996, local developers contributed 35.0 percent, foreign capital 18.0 percent, and local government 13.3 percent to the total investment in urban properties and facilities, indicated by the data of Capital Construction Investment[1] (see Table 3.5).

Induced by the first property boom, which was basically caused by the sensation of Shenzhen's opening up to the world, foreign capital led investment into commercial properties that were far from sufficient at the time in coping with inward investments. Foreign capital then receded to a less prominent position, replaced by local developers that were growing, until the second property boom, starting from the early 1990s, when it revived its interests in property. Local enterprises, after their investment capacity was strengthened by greater profit retention and preferential fiscal policies, have become a leader in investment in the built environment. At the outset of Shenzhen's construction, the role of the central state was already marginalized. Its financial contribution continued to decline drastically up to 1994, when it ceased to allocate any grant to the Shenzhen government. About half of the property in floor area developed during 1979–1996 was built during 1992–1996, the period of the second property boom in Shenzhen. Seventy percent of capital investment was made in the same period, which meant that much improvement in urban infrastructure was made recently when local government fiscal strength was enhanced (see Table 3.6). The construction industry has become a pillar of the municipal economy, and a substantial amount of capital has been invested in the built environment. Although there were about 400 developers in 1993, the top 30 developers produced 70.1 percent of total floor area; the top 50 ones, 85.1 percent (ECSREY, 1993). During the period 1987–1999 in Shenzhen, 3,669 hectares of land were leased to developers and the city built-up area expanded from 58.0 to 132.7 square kilo meters (Shenzhen Bureau of Statistics, 2000).

Table 3.5 Capital Construction Investment by source (%)

Period	State	Local government	Foreign capital	Bank loans	Local enterprises	Others	Total
1979–1983	8.7	9.7	31.0	29.3	18.1	3.2	100.0
1984–1988	1.4	13.9	15.5	20.4	36.7	12.1	100.0
1989–1993	0.1	11.2	18.0	23.6	34.4	12.7	100.0
1994–1996	0.0	14.4	18.2	16.1	35.6	15.7	100.0

Source: Shenzhen Bureau of Statistics, 1997

Table 3.6 Property development and Capital Construction Investment by period

	01/1979 – 06/1983	07/1983 – 12/1987	01/1988 – 06/1992	07/1992 – 12/1996	1979 – 1996
Floor areas built during each period as % of the whole period 1979–1996	3.5	20.7	30.2	45.6	100.0
Capital Construction Investment in each period as % of the whole period 1979–1996	1.1	6.3	19.2	73.4	100.0

Source: Shenzhen Bureau of Statistics, 1997

Institutional change toward land leasehold

Land use fee constrains land users to the position of tenants, who do not have full property rights over the land in question, which constitutes great uncertainties to the long-term operation of business. The debate on land marketization lasted so long that impatient Shenzhen reformers decided to let practice move ahead of ideological deliberation. A milestone in China's urban land system was set by the first land transaction in Shenzhen on September 9, 1987, when the Shenzhen municipality sold the leasehold of a land plot of 5,000 square meters to a local company (Shenzhen Industrial and Trade Center, ancillary to the China Aviation Technology Import and Export Company) at a price of ¥200 per square meter for a lease term of 50 years. Although the land price was settled by negotiation behind closed doors, this case was the first land leasehold transfer, even running the risk of violating the national Constitution, whose Clause 4, Article 10 reads categorically: "No organization or individual may appropriate, buy, sell, or lease land, or unlawfully transfer it in other ways."

With a mind to deepen reform in urban land system, on September 25, 1987, the Shenzhen government issued an invitation to bid for another piece of land with an area of 46,355 square meters meant for residential land use. Shenhua Development Company won the bid at a price of ¥368 per square meter. Purposely, a third form of land transaction was tried on December 1, 1987, when a plot of 8,600 square meters planned for housing land use was auctioned. SSEZ Real Estate & Properties Company won at a price of ¥611 per square meter. This series of land transactions set a precedent for the forthcoming reforms in the property rights over urban land and finalized the formality of leasehold transfer.

Having broken the ideological taboo, on January 3, 1988, the new legislation, the Provisional Ordinances on Land Management of Shenzhen Special Economic Zone, was promulgated by the Guangdong Provincial People's Congress. It stipulated that the rights over leased land could be transferred, assigned, bequeathed, and mortgaged at the lessee's will within a validated term. After a ten-year informal trial in the Shenzhen Special Economic Zone, privatization and marketization of urban land have formally replaced the tenet of land as 'a means of production' since 1988 when the National People's Congress approved an amendment on April 12, 1988, to the 1982 Constitution that states: "the right of land use can be transferred in accordance with the law" (Zhu, 1999). Complementing an emerging market economy, land leasing is legalized such that urban land can be leased to developers or users for a fixed period of time after a payment of rental in lump sum to the state. Land leasehold can be acquired through tender, auction, or negotiation. After 30 years' practice of free allocation as a socialist production means, urban land has been restored as an economic asset.

Land leasehold would cast a drastic impact on China's urbanization. First, it would facilitate introduction of market forces into urban development. Second, it would allow the state to quit its omnipotent position in urban construction and to re-establish its role of a regulator. Third, urban infrastructure would have a designated financial source for its development, so that the problem of underinvestment in infrastructure, dragging urban economies behind, would be alleviated somewhat by guaranteed funds from land sales. Finally, the urban land use pattern would undergo radical changes as market competition replaces administrative allocation. The marketization of urban land was to have a profound impact on China's urban landscape. Land leasehold under the drive for marketization has expedited the pace of urbanization. From 1988 to 2016, urban population increased at 18.1 million per annum on average, and 57.4 percent of the populace were urbanites in 2016. While urban population grew at 11.4 million per annum on average between 1978 and 1988, 25.5 percent of the population were urbanized in 1988 (see Table 1.1). Between 1981 and 1986, 681.5 square kilometers of land per annum were added to the urban built-up areas. The figure increased to 1,421.1 square kilometers during 1986–2016 (see Table 1.2).

An incipient dual land market and arbitrage opportunities

In hindsight, urban-centered reforms have significantly transformed China from an agrarian economy toward an urban society. Urban land privatization and marketization promulgated in 1988 are one of the most important events that have changed China's cities and urban landscape fundamentally. Land leaseholds are supposedly acquired at market prices. Transfers of land rights through auction and tender are allocated through market mechanisms, reflecting the full market value of land, while purchasing leaseholds through negotiation is a practice where land prices are determined by negotiations between two parties: the local government as a seller and developers as buyers. Sales by auction and tender are transparent to the market, whereas sales through negotiation are non-transparent deals, where land prices can vary very much. Obtaining leasehold by agreement is a market allocation with government subsidies, through which local government implements its policy of facilitating targeted industries or investments. In accordance with the common belief that inexpensive land supply would act as one of the many incentives to facilitate local economic growth, the Shenzhen government decided to supply land at subsidies to certain land tenants in the good faith that they would fully utilize the allocated land and realize their investment intentions. Nevertheless, a dual land market has thus been invented (Zhu, 1994).

Buildings were commercialized as properties whose prices were largely determined in the market. The property user markets were booming, but land, as the most important factor, was monopolized by the state in the primary market, where land was largely transferred to state-owned *danwei* as the mini-state at discounted prices to a considerable degree. It is the land rent, created by the difference between market prices of properties and nonmarket allocation of land, that has brought up new state-owned developers. By 1987, of its total 155 square kilometers of usable land stock in SSEZ, 49.5 percent or 76.8 square kilometers had been released to mostly SOE users. A large land bank controlled by the holders had been built up (ECSREY, 1991; 1996). Although land leasehold system has been in place since 1987, the new rules do not seem retroactive to the earlier allocated land. A substantial amount of land laid idle in the hands of land users. A quarter of the total land supplied, or 19.8 square kilometers, remained vacant in 1987, and overall land hoarding mounted to 37.3 square kilometers in 1989. Over-claim of subsidized land was evident in mounting land hoarding to 38.7 square kilometers by 1992, accounting for 34.1 percent of the total land provided. Industrial land had been in generous supply all the time to meet the final land users' demands, in accordance with the government determination to absorb inward industrial investment. However, industrial land hoarding was also the most substantial among the overall categories, which reached a peak of 10.6 square kilometers, accounting for 56.4 percent of the total industrial land supplied up to 1990.

Land hoarding constituted a large land reserve controlled by landholders in comparison to the primary land market managed by the government land bureau. The land reserve is ready to leak into the secondary land market. Joint development schemes are the cases of illegal land transfer in the secondary market. Lessees of subsidized land benefit, to a great extent, by capitalizing the price differences – an arbitrage of two markets. Land undersupply in the open market resulted in an upsurge in land prices and property prices. A straw poll carried out by the author revealed that 55.6 percent of manufacturing respondents indicated that, among three factors, cheap land was the least important incentives, behind labor costs and tax reduction, while the rest saw it the second least important factor. On the whole, subsidized land provision was ranked the lowest in terms of significance by the respondents. Of sampled users, 88.9 percent thought their premises not expensive at all, which implied that they could pay more for the same space. In the office sector, all users did not regard the prices paid for space occupation as too high (Zhu, 1994). A comparison between the aggregate take-up of industrial land and the aggregate built-up industrial floor areas shows that the overall industrial land use density had substantially increased. If the floor area density in 1983 was taken as 1.0, it rose to 3.5 in 1986 and 5.1 in 1990 (ECSREY, 1992). The rising industrial land use density suggests that the genuine land users might have been squeezed by speculative land hoarding. Industrial land became less readily accessible to the final tenants.

The second property boom in Shenzhen during the period 1988–1993 constituted such an irresistible pulling force to the development industries. In five years, partly as a result of speculation, the prices of housing and shops increased by 6 times, offices by 3 times, and factories by 2.5 times (ECSREY, 1995). The number of new development firms, mostly private, increased significantly. Most of those newly set-up development companies did not have a land bank at hand. They had to compete in the open land market in order to obtain land parcels for property development. In terms of the percentage of land released to the total usable land stock, it was 49.5 percent in 1987 and reached 66.7 percent in 1990. However, much of the land released was not available on the open market.

A fierce competition was clearly displayed in the 1990s' land-bidding events. It was unambiguously demonstrated by three land-bidding competitions in 1991. The first bid was held on 6 August. A total of 2.6 hectares subdivided into three plots were competed for by 26 developers. The average land price was bid up to ¥1,875 per square meter of floor area allowed by the predetermined plot ratio (Shenzhen Real Estate Express, [*Shenzhen Fangdichan Shichang Kuaibao*], August 12, 1991). One month later, a second land bid was publicly announced and held on 26 December. A total of 3.25 hectares in five plots attracted participation of 47 developers, resulting in 19 bidders at least and 31 at most hunting for each single plot. The strong competition apparently drove the land prices up, reaching ¥2,914 per square meter on average, an increase of 55 percent over the last benchmark (Shenzhen Real Estate Express [*Shenzhen Fangdichan Shichang Kuaibao*], October 2 & 12, 1991). Being afraid of an imminent overheating of the property market driven by the escalating land prices, the Shenzhen authorities put financial restrictions in place in order to cool down the heated land chasing by reducing the number of participants. The new measures increased bid deposits from ¥200,000 to ¥1 million, which were to be expropriated in case of any default, and the period by which payment for land acquisition should be cleared was reduced to 20 days from two months. The new regulations effectively made fewer developers qualified for the third bid of 2.75 hectares of four land parcels. Only 20 developers turned up, and the winners obtained their land at a price of ¥2,674 per square meter on average (Shenzhen Real Estate Express [*Shenzhen Fangdichan Shichang Kuaibao*], November 2, 1991).

The primary land market was not responsive to demand, as much land was still allocated to land users directly with explicit subsidies. The late-coming developers without a land bank had to resort to poaching on the secondary land market, which was composed of hoarded land by SOE users for their production as well as for their employees' housing building under the old *danwei* system. An active, but covert, land market had been created as a black, secondary land market. The hidden, secondary land market was much larger than the primary land market. Those capital-poor and land-rich SOEs could capitalize on land rent. Joint developments between capital-rich developers and land-rich SOEs were proposed where developers bore all development costs, and landholders contributed land parcels. Upon completion, land contributors could claim up to 70 percent of the output.

It was found that tenants were generally paying more due to the tight supply of rental premises. By and large, the benefits derived from subsidized land and gained from the property development and investment were retained in the forms of rising rentals, capital appreciation, and substantial development profits. Therefore, landholders were the prime beneficiaries. The disparity between the two modes of land provision creates a built-in pressure on subsidized land release, which leads to a vicious spiral of ever-greater pressure of demand for cheap land supply for whatever reasons. Because of a unique government structure and having a tradition of an omnipotent state and public sector economy, it has been very hard for the Shenzhen local government to resist land demand pressures from the state enterprises and various public bodies that have turned to commercial business. And in an environment where entrepreneur spirit is encouraged, illegal land trading is hardly controllable, for land transactions occur in the name of joint ventures or something else of ostensible respectability.

In a country where free land utilization had existed and the state economy had been overwhelming for more than 30 years, resistance to land use reform was enormous. The old land use system had been closely incorporated into the system of public enterprises, which still formed the majority part of the national economy. In the absence of an effective legal system, administrative control on the disciplines of land use and land transactions was hard to implement, particularly in a period of drastic transformation where innovations were specifically encouraged. Without effective management from the government, corruption in land markets was bound to occur if alternative market disciplines were not applied.

Impact of land marketization on the changing provision of urban housing

The housing reforms aim to put an end to the universal state provision of urban housing in the socialist countries. Housing commodification and privatization and decentralization of housing provision are two thrusts in parallel of this significant change, along with the ending of free land utilization. The tenets of housing commodification are to make the maintenance of existing housing stock commercially viable, on the one hand, and to commercialize housing development for the new supply, on the other hand. It is recommended that housing development and maintenance be regulated by market forces. A commercially viable housing lease market should be created to sustain a sizable housing stock for leasing. In line with the gradual economic reforms, changes in the urban housing system are gradually progressing from 'welfare' to commodity. As opposed to housing provision being solely dependent on the state prior to 1978, individual households were required to contribute more from their living expenditure to housing consumption. The policy of low housing rental remained unchanged until the early 1980s, when the housing rentals became a nominal charge in comparison with wages. Low rents not only undermined good maintenance of housing stock but also were blamed as a main culprit causing the inflation that became phenomenal in the late 1980s, given the fact that urban households spent about 1 percent of their cash income on housing and thus had a relatively high purchasing power for durable commodities (Tolley, 1991). Low expenditure on housing also induced unreasonably high demand for housing and thus led to difficulties in its fair distribution.

In 1982, pilot housing commodification was advanced with an experiment in a few cities where households paid one-third of the market price, and the rest was paid one-third each by the government and *danwei* to which the prospective buyer was affiliated (Cao and Chu, 1990). However, this experiment did not last long enough to be further refined. Although the burden on the state was lessened and households were required to contribute much more than before to housing consumption, the state was still held responsible for housing provision, and property rights over the acquired housing units were unclear. What the buyers obtained were 'partial property rights' because the buyers paid only one-third of the market price. The quasi-owners had rights to reside but did not have rights to alienate the units to the market at will. The residents were still tied up with the *danwei*, which subsidized the housing.

The 1988 State Council Plan for Housing Reform in Urban Areas formally set guidelines for the reform of housing rental and promotion of home ownership. The procedure of raising housing rentals was consequently designed to increase rentals to a degree of full maintenance cost recovery for the existing housing stock and then to raise rents to eventually cover the full economic cost of housing development as a commercial undertaking. Simultaneously, raising wages was recommended as a way of cashing out the housing in-kind remuneration to offset housing rental increases. A drive for privatization was also initiated to sell housing to those who could afford it. The so-called 'commodity housing' was to be delivered by property developers rather than by government or *danwei*. It was based on the premise that housing rentals would be increased gradually to the point that buying housing units became a more sensible decision than renting.

The voucher model emerged. The vouchers, used only for paying housing rentals or purchases, served as a way of cashing out housing in-kind remuneration. The use of vouchers was to control the money supply so as not to fuel inflation, which was menacing enough at the time to cause social unrest. The issuing of housing vouchers was connected with gradual rental increases. The fashion of gradualism determined that the raised rentals were still far from the market rate. However, inequality in the public housing distribution was redressed by the introduction of rental surcharges on households holding 'excessive' housing space as choices for housing consumption and linkage with household affordability were established.

As for sales of commodity housing, housing freely available at market prices in a newly founded market remained a privilege for a small minority who became rich during the economic reforms and could not wait long to obtain a unit from the state. For most, the incentives to purchasing commodity housing did not exist because a multitude of tenants were not yet required to pay rentals at market rates. Commodity housing only accounted for 1.7 percent of the total housing provision in Shanghai from 1981 to 1985 (SMBS, 1997). Sales of public housing to the sitting tenants were tried in some cities as another pragmatic measure to get rid of maintenance burdens and to raise funds for housing development. Public housing has been sold since 1994 in Shanghai at a discount by considering factors such as the tenant's number of years working in *danwei* and entitlement to benefits based on seniority, deemed as the cashing out of housing benefits that tenants deserve over the years of low-wage employment. Up to the end of 1996, 51 percent of salable public housing was sold to 659,000 households, representing 20 percent of total urban households (Zhang, 1998).

As land leasehold has introduced the cost factor to the land use, private housing would inevitably become the norm. In Shanghai, the proportion of private housing in the total housing supply rose from 11.3 percent (1986–1990) to 41.4 percent (1991–1996). It reached 69.8 percent in 1997. The per capita housing space increased from 4.5 square meters (1978) to 9.3 square meters (1997) as a result of increased investment spurred by privatization (SMBS, 1998). The investment in housing as a proportion of GDP stood at 3.4 percent from 1981 to 1992, a substantial increment in comparison with 0.78 percent from 1949 to 1978 (SMBS, 1993).

Note

1 Capital Construction Investment (CCI) is investment in new projects, including construction of completely new facilities or addition to existing facilities. It includes construction of plants, mines, railways, bridges, harbors, water conservation facilities, stores, residential buildings, and schools, and purchase of machinery and equipment, vehicles, ships, and planes. CCI and technical upgrading and transformation (TUT) are two major components of investment in fixed assets. TUT covers renewing, replacing, and rebuilding existing fixed assets.

References

Bei, Q. Z. (1990) *Special Economic Zones' fiscal and financial policies*. Beijing: Ocean Publishing. (in Chinese).
Cao, H. T. & Chu, Z. H. (eds.) (1990) *Urban construction of contemporary China*. Beijing: China Social Science Press. (in Chinese).
Editorial Committee of Shenzhen Real Estate Yearbook (ECSREY) (1991–1996) *Shenzhen real estate yearbook, 1990–1995*. Beijing: People China's Publishing. (in Chinese).
Editorial Committee of Shenzhen Real Estate Yearbook (ECSREY) (2000) *Shenzhen real estate yearbook, 1999*. Beijing: People China's Publishing. (in Chinese).
Fainstein, S. S. (1994) *The city builders – Property, politics & planning in London and New York*. Oxford: Blackwell.
Hou, C. M. (1965) *Foreign investment and economic development in China, 1840–1937*. Cambridge, MA: Harvard University Press.
Institute of Finance and Trade Economics, Chinese Academy of Social Sciences (IFTE/CASS) and Institute of Public Administration (IPA) (1994) *Urban land use and management in China*. Beijing: Economic Science Publishing. (in Chinese).

Lim, J. Y., Cai, F. & Li, Z. (1996) *The China miracle – Development strategy and economic reform*. Hong Kong: The Chinese University Press.

Nanshan Planning and Land Bureau, Shenzhen (NPLBS) (1997) *A survey on real estate of Nanshan, Shenzhen*. Shenzhen: NPLBS. (in Chinese).

National Bureau of Statistics, China (NBSC) (1989) *China statistical yearbook, 1988*. Beijing: China Statistics Press. (in Chinese).

Oborne, M. (1986) *China's Special Economic Zones*. Paris: OECD.

Reckinger, J. D. et al. (1991) The government's perspective on the land development process, in P. W. Nyden & W. Wiewel (eds.) *Challenging uneven development – An urban agenda for the 1990s*, 166–179. New Brunswick: Rutgers University Press.

Shanghai Municipal Bureau of Statistics (SMBS) (1993, 1998) *Shanghai statistical yearbook*. Shanghai: Shanghai People's Press. (in Chinese).

Shanghai Municipal Bureau of Statistics (SMBS) (1997) *Shanghai real estate market, 1996*. Beijing: China Statistics Press. (in Chinese).

Shenzhen Bureau of Construction (1989) *The history of Shenzhen urban construction*. Shenzhen: Shenzhen Bureau of Construction. (in Chinese).

Shenzhen Bureau of Construction (1990) *Guidelines to Shenzhen property development*. Shenzhen: Shenzhen Bureau of Construction. (in Chinese).

Shenzhen Bureau of Statistics (1997, 2000, 2017) *Shenzhen statistical yearbook*. Beijing: China Statistics Press. (in Chinese).

Shenzhen Enterprise Reforms Committee (1997) *Practice and search to establish the system of modern enterprises in Shenzhen*. Shenzhen: Haitian Publishing. (in Chinese).

Tolley, G. S. (1991) *Urban housing reform in China: An economic analysis*. Washington, DC: World Bank.

Zhang, E. Z. (1998) Development of housing financing in Shanghai. *Shanghai Investment*, 2: 4–9. (in Chinese).

Zhang, Z. C. (1993) *Shenzhen Real Estate Market*. Shanghai: Tongji University Press. (in Chinese).

Zhu, J. M. (1994) The changing land policy and its impact on local growth: The experience of the Shenzhen Special Economic Zone, China, in the 1980s. *Urban Studies*, 31(10): 1611–1623.

Zhu, J. M. (1999) Local growth coalition: The context and implications of China's gradualist urban land reforms. *International Journal of Urban and Regional Research*, 23(3): 534–548.

4 Land markets in the making
A dual land market and land rent seeking

Full land market mechanisms are not created straightforwardly under the gradualist reforms. A dual land market appears instead. Gradualism and dualism, though politically sensible, worsen the problems of emerging principal-agent relations, leading to ambiguous delineation of land rights. The two new local agents of the local developmental state and *danwei*-enterprises have developed an informal local growth coalition, and land rent derived from the dual land market is used for strengthening local government-enterprise coalitions and by the local developmental state as instrument for intervention. As a result, the state as the third party for market mediation is absent. Land rent seeking and grabbing are rampant, evidenced in the impact on the resultant built environment.

Emergence of a dual land market: growth machine

This dual land market is derived from the practice of gradual urban land reforms, that is, parallel provision of land at both market and subsidized prices under the new land leasehold. On the one hand, land can be obtained at negotiated and thus subsidized rates to an extent way much below the prevailing market prices. On the other hand, those land users who do not have access to land subsidies have to compete in a much-contested open land market. Land allocated through negotiation behind closed doors has been overwhelming and out of proportion to land released at market prices in Shenzhen, a pioneer of the urban land reform (see Table 4.1). Subsidized provision has become less substantial since the early 2000s than in the 1990s, which shows the effect of progressive marketization (see Table 4.2).

Price discounts implied in the land leasing by negotiation are 80 percent on average and, in many cases, are as much as 100 percent (Liao, 1994). The old system of free land allocation survives in the guise of land leasing by negotiation. Subsidized land provision that gives rise to the dual land market is offered for two apparent reasons: giving incentives to end users in order to encourage direct investment and thus to promote local growth, and providing land subsidies as a protective cushion to SOEs for their stable transition to fully fledged players exposed to market disciplines. The political goal of SOE transition is to avoid large-scale bankruptcy destabilizing a society where its citizens have paid heavily

Table 4.1 Subsidized land lease in Shenzhen

Year	1988	1989	1990	1991	1992	1993	1994	1995
Land leased through negotiation as % of total land supply under land leasehold	97.5	98.2	94.8	97.7	99.2	99.3	100.0	85.7

Source: ECSREY, 1991–1996

Table 4.2 Land supply by leasing modes, 1987–2016

Period	Total (ha)	By negotiation as % of the total	By bidding & auction as % of the total
Shenzhen			
1987–1994	2093.4	98.1	1.9
2004–2006	3537.5	91.2	8.8
2007–2009	2517.0	80.8	19.2
2010–2012	1014.8	77.7	22.3
2013–2016	2109.4	67.8	32.2
Shanghai			
2004–2007	23,487	64.7	35.3
2008–2011	9,441	6.1	93.9
2012–2016	6,205	5.2	94.8
National			
2003–2007	1,008,679	65.1	34.9
2008–2012	1,347,909	11.5	88.5
2013–2016	1,088,887	7.7	92.3

Sources: ECSREY, 1991–1995; Ministry of Land and Resources, China, 2004–2017

for perennial political and social changes. The implicit intentions in the hidden agenda are to retain land-related benefits in the locality and for the mayors to use underpriced land as a tool to implement what can enhance their political careers.

China has changed its strategies of economic management for market orientation, as few people believe that the central planning after 30 years in place would ever lead the country to prosperity. The state is giving up its philosophy of class struggle and proletariat dictatorship. Public opinion maintains that popular acceptance of government should be established by its successful management of economic development. From the perspective of political economy in the context of American capitalist framework, cities are interpreted as a place where landed and other place-bound interests seeking financial gains from their assets are strongly motivated to drive the urban "growth machine" in order to capture the exchange value of property and spin-offs of urban growth (Molotch, 1976, 1990; Logan and Molotch, 1987). From this view, urban growth and development are used by those in the control of city politics as "growth machines to benefit their own fortune building" (Molotch, 1990: 176). The distribution of growth benefits is clearly a key notion to explain the aspiration for local growth. The concept of 'urban regimes', used to describe local coalitions in the American urban politics, captures the process of local actors participating in and benefiting from local growth by the formulation of urban regimes for the management of common interests (Stone, 1989). Local government is deemed to play a key role in the regime where "governments must blend their capacities with those of various non-governmental actors" (Stone, 1993: 6). It is the interplay between markets and politics that forms pro-growth coalitions in the context of competitive reformation toward the postindustrial city (Mollenkopf, 1983; Swanstrom, 1988).

Ambiguous delineation of land rights: gradualism, dualism, and principal-agent problems

After a disappointing performance of the planned economy for 30 years (1949–1978), economic reforms were launched in 1978, aiming toward the grand goal of building an efficient and strong economy. The rigid, centrally controlled, planning system is under restructuring in order to give room to bottom-up initiatives. Decentralization of economic management has set off an unprecedented transformation, which is gradually replacing central directives with material incentives to the agents at local levels. Marketization, penetrating into the economic system at the margin initially, has been driving the economy from plan-controlled to market-led.

Nevertheless, institutional change brought about by the economic reform is intended in principle to improve productivity without fundamental changes to the political system (Wang, 1994). The goal of establishing a socialist market economy has initiated changes in the economic organizations, but the political organizations, which used to be crucial components of the outgoing planned economy, are still more or less in place. A noticeable trait is that pragmatism has substituted for socialist idealism. This pragmatism implanted in the reform process determines that transformation is incremental and gradual, as opposed to the drastic 'shock therapy' adopted by the former Soviet Union and Eastern European socialist countries. Gradualism is meant as an instrument to legitimize rather than undermine the existing political system. The reform has thus turned out to be a process of 'muddling through' without a blueprint to guide the unprecedented changes. 'Crossing the river by groping for stones' is a succinct adage revealing the underlying philosophy. It is not unreasonable if one knows the contemporary history of China, where the multitude have suffered tremendously from seemingly perennial political and social upheavals. The government is fully aware of the political risks associated with the economic reforms that inevitably result in disruptive economic and social restructuring. After numerous political movements prior to 1980, the party-led government has been keenly making efforts to legitimize its existence and to maintain the political status quo by being sensitive to social dissatisfaction. The ethos of the gradual reform is to avoid any social turmoil probably caused by the hardship in transition. There is "developmental coalition deriving political legitimacy from what be called the nation's collective aspirations" (Bardhan, 1990: 5).

It is exemplified by how the country has opened up to foreign capital and how non-state-owned sectors grow. Both foreign capital and the private sector were driven out after the Communist Party gained control over China in 1949. Foreign investment was sought out at first in four Special Economic Zones set up in 1979 and then in 14 'coastal open cities' in 1984. It was in 1992 that cities in other regions were granted autonomy to attract foreign investment with favorable policies (Qian, 2000). Initially, foreign partners were allowed as a minor party, and later majority ownership was permitted. Foreign capital returning to China since 1978 has been in a dual process of gradual penetration: geographical expansion and ownership domination (Morris, Hassard, and Sheehan, 2002). In the course of the reforms, non-state-owned enterprises have been growing and have become an indispensable component of the economy. State-owned and collective-owned enterprises accounted for 77.6 and 22.4 percent of the total industrial output in 1978, respectively. There were no private-owned industries then. In 1999, state-owned and collective-owned enterprises contributed 28.2 and 35.4 percent, respectively, and the remaining 36.4 percent was produced mainly by private-owned industrial firms (NBSC, 2000).

In spite of these fundamental changes, gradualism remains the key spirit of the economic reform, which has already been ongoing for 40 years.[1] In the process of phasing in market elements and phasing out planning factors, dualism appears as a result of compromise and cooperation between plan and market, as well as between old political interests and new economic rationality (Wang, 1994). It is meant to provide a mechanism that introduces market elements while retaining planning controls for the sake of social stability. It is expected to provide a path to transition by mitigating the effects of the redistribution of political powers and economic benefits entailed in the reform process. In short, it is "to implement a reform without creating losers", who are likely to hamper the reform (Lau, Qian, and Roland, 2000: 122). One of the dualist measures was dual-track pricing, implemented in the 1980s and early 1990s (Wu and Zhao, 1987). Lau, Qian, and Roland (2000: 121) explain its rationale as that "a market track is introduced under which economic agents participate in the market at free-market prices, provided that they fulfill their obligations under the preexisting plan".

It was applied to agricultural goods at first and then extended to industrial goods and labor markets (Sicular, 1988; Byrd, 1991; Lin, 1992). Markets are, therefore, expected to "grow out of the plan" (Naughton, 1995). Local governments as well as SOE agents take more responsibility for making decisions. Incentives for profit maximization mediated by the market have come to fore on the one hand. On the other hand, socialist redistribution between profit-making and loss-making SOEs, coordinated by the remnants of planning control, remains effective to a certain extent (Xiao, 1991). Both coordination mechanisms of top-down directives and bottom-up initiatives are at work. Both material and coercive incentives, which link the principal's goals to agents' performance, are in place to motivate agents (Zhu, 2000).

The gradual reforms without a blueprint led institutional change on an uncharted route. The distinctions between the governing rules of the two economic entities created by dualism are often blurred to the advantage of parties with vested interests (Wong, Heady, and Woo, 1995). The local government pushes local autonomy to the limit. Since 1978, the consistent growth of extra-budgetary funds, which are outside the central planning system, has testified to the extent of decentralization that localities have gained (Blecher, 1991; White, 1991; Wang, 1995). While decentralization is the spirit of the economic reforms, the central government does not wish to see its roles of central coordination and regional redistribution marginalized. The scope of decentralization is thus made negotiable.

In the socialist, centrally controlled system, the state holds full ownership of the means of production. SOEs and local governments, as units of the state economy, operate under central command with little autonomy; they are compliant and passive agents, obeying orders from the principal without self-interests to pursue. The state is not so much a 'fictitious' owner in this centralized public ownership system, for the economy is predominantly a state economy. Almost all revenues are remitted to the central treasury and then transferred back to local governments and SOEs according to expenditures planned by the state. The state determines the allocation and utilization of resources through directives, rather than by pricing mechanisms. With the separation of control over enterprises from ownership by the state under the economic reform, local governments and SOEs have begun to command assets under their use and are thus becoming agents in pursuit of their own interests (Aram and Wang, 1991; Su and Zhao, 1997). Principal-agent problems arise, as agents are likely to maximize utility within the limit of the existing institutional structure, which may hurt the interest of the principal (Jensen and Meckling, 1976). On the one hand, autonomous agents are induced to appropriate state land assets, abetted by ambiguous delineation of property rights. Managers of SOEs can attenuate the state's ownership of the firms, and it is observed that they are inclined to collude with local governments and workers to enhance their own interests at the expense of state revenues (Furubotn and Pejovich, 1972; Lee, 1991; World Bank, 1997). Urban land values are accentuated by the market forces, on the other hand. The ambiguous delineation of property rights over land between the principal (the central state) and agents (local governments and SOEs) is to the advantage of the agents and at the expense of the principal's land revenue income. Maximization of land rent by the local agents under the decentralization may not accord with the interests of the state as the principal.

The two local agents: the local developmental state and *danwei*-enterprises

The socialist state and SOEs are two essential actors in the outgoing centrally planned system. Acting as an omnipotent provider, the state, together with its agents – SOEs and local governments – dominated the economy and society.

Without these two actors, the centrally controlled economy could not have been sustained. The state is transforming itself from an economic producer and socialist welfare provider to an advocate of marketization. The socialist, authoritarian state is changing from its preoccupation with political campaigns to the pursuit of economic growth in order to legitimize itself by improving the livelihood of its citizens, with the progressive reforms that are gradually phasing out unsustainable socialist welfarism and letting the market take over its role of provision. In the same vein, SOEs as agents of the socialist state are shedding their obligatory social responsibilities to become independent enterprises.

After many years of preoccupation with ideological battles, the Chinese government has finally altered its path to the pursuit of economic growth. The most striking change that has occurred is that governments at various levels are much more development-oriented and committed to growth than ever before. Markets are gradually taking responsibility for the provision of goods to its citizens. As the leading paradigm for the development of East Asian capitalist economies, the developmental state places top priority on economic development, productivity, and national competitiveness (Johnson, 1982). China's developmental state emerges from its origin as a socialist state in this context (White and Wade, 1988; Woo-Cumings, 1999). The socialist, political state is clearly changing to a socialist, developmental state (Oi, 1996). The developmental state plays an active and strategic role in guiding market forces to achieve the goal of economic growth. A capitalist, developmental state is "a plan-rational economy with market-rational political institutions" (Johnson, 1995: 28). 'Embedded autonomy', or insulation from political and social pressures, allows the developmental state to be relatively free from predation and rent seeking (Evans, 1995). By this definition, China's developmental state has close links (embedded) to society, but it is not independent from the political and business interests of society (insulation) (Zhu, 1999a; 2002).

For historical reasons, economic development in China was biased toward the coastal regions prior to 1949. The vast hinterland was thus left underdeveloped. During the period 1949–1978, the new socialist government promoted the policy of equal development between regions. New industrial projects were evenly distributed throughout the country in order to diminish the existing regional disparities in economic well-being. After three decades' efforts, regional economic disparities were reduced, with coastal regions sustaining a modest decline and interior regions having a strong increase in the share of industrial production (World Bank, 1985). However, it had always been debatable whether to pursue the strategy of equal development with scarce capital evenly invested across regions without consideration of investment performance. The new policy of economic reforms has nevertheless considerably changed the strategy by shifting the focus from countrywide equality in development to economic productivity. Economic efficiency is given priority over social equity, and regional equality is replaced by regional competition. Local factors are given more weight in the decision-making process for resource mobilization than before. Market forces play the role in strengthening some localities' economic capacity due to their inherent socioeconomic and geographic advantages. Coastal regions have received more resources for manufacturing and services than the inland provinces where the economic reform policies have not entailed much market-driven investment. The foreign-investment-led developments have concentrated almost exclusively on the cities along the east coast. Thus, gaps between regions in their economic well-being are again widening (Lakshmanan and Hua, 1987). In terms of per capita GDP, the ratio of the richest (Shanghai) to the poorest (Guizhou) was 14.2 in 1978 and remained as high as 10.8 in 2000 (NBSC, 1979, 2001).

Building an effective state is being vigorously pursued in order for the state to lead development efficiently. For the party-led national government, development policies are adopted in order to legitimate and justify its existence. The same rationale applies to local governments as well. Devolution occurs in the central-local intergovernmental power structure, and localities are given more latitude in making investment decisions and managing local growth. This process is led by the fiscal decentralization initiated in 1984 to change the fiscal system from profit remittance to taxation levy. Local fiscal revenue and expenditure were controlled by central planning to a great extent in the pre-reform era, as the control of revenue resources was one of the very essential components of the centrally controlled planning system (Oksenberg and Tong, 1991; Huang, 1996). The kernel of revised fiscal contracts between the central and local governments is that the latter have become 'residual claimants' of fiscal revenue – a strong incentive for local governments to pursue local economic development (Qian, 2000). While urban society becomes increasingly diverse, NGOs and social groups interested in social, cultural, and environment issues emerge with their various agendas. Some interest groups, however, are keener on growth than others. Business elites, whether they are foreign investors or local enterprises, and local governments are motivated to pursue local growth as they have strong stakes in the locality; that is, they expect to benefit more than others from local growth. It is observed that the gradual land partial reforms have benefited those holding 'redistributive power' greatly (Nee, 1991; Walder, 1992; Shirk, 1993; Zhou and Logan, 1996). The arena of urban development is made more intriguing by the marketization of land and property since 1988, which has obviously created landed interests.

No longer being passive agents of the central government, China's provincial and municipal governments are made active actors pursuing local growth because of decentralization, which results in competition between the center and localities (Solinger, 1992; Wang, 1994; Nolan, 1995; Oi, 1995; Unger and Chan, 1995; Wong, Heady, and Woo, 1995; Huang, 1996). Advancing development strategies that can stimulate local growth and expanding fiscal capacity become two indispensable goals of local governments (Wong, 1987, 1992), resulting in the reemergence of localism in China's national politics.[2] As a result, autonomous local governments are highly motivated to maximize local revenues, and subsequent increases in the state budget deficit have compromised the central government's capacity (Breslin, 1996; Lin, 2000). China's local governments have become an economic interest-group with their own policy agenda and preferences and thus have become *the local developmental state* – a term coined to capture its unique characteristics.

It is the three-pronged decentralization that motivates a locality toward a local developmental state. First, the participation of alternative economic interests other than state-owned, though not many in quantity, provided a stimulus to the local economy. Second, the SOE reforms entitle state enterprises autonomy in decision-making and, thus, instill economic responsibility and financial accountability in their operations. Third, the fiscal reforms, which are intended to redefine central-local relations, are an attempt to provide incentives to local growth. The problematic formulation of fiscal relations, however, reflects the scope of central-local conflicts regarding the extent of decentralization (Agarwala, 1992; Wong, Heady, and Woo, 1995). Each local government is keen to generate 'extra-budgetary' revenues for its own purposes in 'entrepreneurial' ways. This leads to retention of much resources at local levels. The scope of local 'extra-budgetary funds', which are mainly used to construct local government–initiated projects, has expanded as the economic basis of local governments expands (Blecher, 1991; White, 1991). In the late 1980s and early 1990s, there is ample evidence that local governments aggressively lobbied the central state for special policies to localities in order for them to attract foreign capital by offering preferential measures (Reich, 1991; Nolan, 1995). Economic transition and inward investment have changed the position of many localities in the process of restructuring the national economy. Localism, which has deep roots in the long Chinese tradition of place-bound social alignment and even survives in the overseas Chinese communities in their host countries (Lang, 1946; Siaw, 1983), is instrumentally used as a political strategy to circumvent outmoded structures of central bureaucracies in order for localities to emerge as winners of regional competition (Goetz and Clarke, 1993).

The competition for favorable market positions among localities has pressed local governments to mobilize as much revenue as possible in order to finance local development. According to Wang (1994: 95), local officials have become highly motivated to maximize local revenues due to their own interests. Local government treats enterprises within its administrative jurisdiction as one component of the local corporate whole (Solinger, 1992; Oi, 1995) and behaves like a state "that coordinates economic enterprises in its territory as if it were a diversified business corporation" (Oi, 1992: 101). The common pro-growth interest has bound local bureaucracy, enterprises, and inward foreign capital into an informal coalition to deal with regional competition and to circumvent central pressure for revenue submission. Under tacit agreement, local states subsidize local enterprises at the expense of the central revenue income, and, in turn, enterprises pay back tributes in one way or another.

In this regard, having the same rationale of pro-growth legitimization, China's local developmental state is different from the paradigm of Asian developmental states in three aspects: its socialist origin, competition between localities, and the tenure of its local leaders being dependent on the authorities at a higher level. Dependence is twofold. On the one hand, the common interests in local growth entice a reciprocal relationship between the local developmental state and business interest-groups. Facing intense competition from other localities, the local developmental state endeavors to create a favorable business climate for businesses to prosper, which directly leads to local growth. On the other hand, political, central control over local developmental states is still retained as a main instrument. Despite the considerable experience gained by local officials in managing the locality, their political existence and advancement are still determined by the central state according to their performance and loyalty. This performance has been largely measured by economic growth rates and urban changes. Short-term quantitative growth is thus pursued at the expense of long-term quality development.

The reform of SOEs is intended to substitute market mechanisms for mandatory planning coordination. Under the central planning system, the state and state-owned economic units or *danwei* were closely related as one entity, rather than as two entities – the principal and independent agents. By separating management from the state ownership of enterprises, the SOE reform has taken several steps to change the business decision-making process and to improve production efficiency with instilled managerial responsibility and financial accountability (Aram and Wang, 1991; Fan, 1994; Perkins, 1995; Hope, 1996). After almost two decades of SOE reforms, SOEs have gained a certain, but not a complete, degree of autonomy. It is believed that government officials are still making important decisions for many large-sized SOEs based on noneconomic logic (Hu, 2000). Although there has been a remarkable achievement in the ownership change of enterprises (Xu and Wang, 1999; Zweig, 2001) and although non-state-owned firms contribute an ever-increasing share to the industrial output (Scalapino, 1999), SOEs remain important employers in the country. SOEs are still more or less a profound socialist institution in the post-reform era (Putterman and Dong, 2000). Socialist comprehensive welfare had been phased out in the course of reforms, but a social security system was yet to be fully established.

Nevertheless, rising unemployment rates, increasingly a menace to social and political stability (Weller and Li, 2000), prevent the SOE reform from further deepening (Hu, 1996; Liu, 1997; Hassard, Morris, and Sheehan, 2002). SOEs still have to shoulder some of social responsibilities on behalf of the governments to avoid a massive outbreak of social problems. Having to retain redundant workers and take on the heavy burdens of welfare obligated to retired workers, SOEs could easily justify their continuous access to the soft-budget guarantee[3] provided by the government, until the transfer of welfare provision (social safety net) from *danwei* to local governments finally took place.[4] Thus, SOEs are concerned with profits and losses but are not entirely responsible for them. The state has to help some loss-making SOEs survive for the overriding goal of political stability. Socialization of losses is often allowed as an alternative to bankruptcy, and losses are covered through income redistribution by governments (Xiao, 1991; Uvalic, 1992). An allowance is made for agents to appropriate the assets of the principal with the latter's tacit agreement, which is extended by the old socialist institution of use rights. However, the line between implicit state subsidies and illegitimate poaching of state assets is blurred by the ambiguously delineated property rights between the principal and agents, that is, between the central state and the local governments and *danwei*, when agents are actively pursuing their interests. Therefore, SOEs are transformed to take a dual role. Many SOEs are both an agent of the state (*danwei*) and an actor in the emerging market (enterprise). The notion *danwei-enterprise* is coined to suggest this dual nature, between a quasi-state and an enterprise. *Danwei*-enterprises, being a hybrid of independent enterprises and apparatuses of the local developmental state, possess characteristics of both *danwei* and autonomous firms.

Economic growth, physical change, and social stability are the fundamental objectives of the local developmental state, while *danwei*-enterprises struggle to survive and keenly pursue expansion. It is the local growth that bonds the two actors. Growth coalitions are formed between the local developmental state and *danwei*-enterprises in China's urban politics. Ambiguous delineation of property rights over land is one of the key mechanisms in the operation of growth coalitions. The local developmental state, because of its intimate involvement in the economic sphere, may still be engaged in active management of local economies (Wei and Wang, 1997; Nanto and Sinha, 2002; Wang, 2002), instead of being a disinterested state for third-party enforcement of market rules and social redistribution. As agents of the local developmental state, *danwei*-enterprises are engaged in a dual role as production units for profit and as quasi-states because of their residual role in managing social stability. A reciprocal relationship is thus found between these two actors. *Danwei*-enterprises receive assistance so as to shoulder some responsibilities on behalf of the local developmental state (Wang, 2002) and undertake unprofitable but socially significant projects (such as slum clearance and redevelopment of dilapidated high-density housing estates).[5]

Subsidized land leasing: land rent for local coalition and government intervention

The transformation from the centrally controlled system to a socialist market economy and from the closed socialist autarchy to an open economy with market orientation inevitably entails restructuring of the economy and formation of new social relations. The reforms are gradual, incremental, and experimental in nature. Public ownership and the roles of the state in production are rigorously maintained. Departure from the central planning is clearly demonstrated by fiscal decentralization, the SOE reforms, and the emergence of alternative economic sectors (Walder, 1995). The gradualist urban land reforms are intrinsically linked to the incremental economic reforms in transitional China. Decentralization has made latent localism explicit. In the process of mobilizing local resources, the land factor has been incorporated into local development strategies. Land rent derived from the gradualist urban land reforms has been used by the local developmental state as a program to nurture local government–enterprise coalition. It has been used by the local developmental state as an instrument of positive intervention in the peculiar Chinese political structure to further the interests of local leaders.

Some degrees of 'collusion' between municipal governments and enterprise managers became apparent. Underpriced, and even free, land was considered one of the aids local governments could offer at their discretion. On the one hand, enterprises received benefits in the form of tax reduction and land subsidies. On the other hand, these gains could be to a certain extent recouped by local government. Imposing ad hoc local fees on enterprises and extending governmental obligations to enterprises, such as providing public goods or urban amenities in the public domain, were common practices. According to a survey conducted in the mid-1980s, about 5 percent of enterprise profits were appropriated as fees by local authorities (Tseng et al., 1994). Developers received the benefits of subsidized land provision and were then subject to fee collection imposed by various local authorities. Eighty-five kinds of fees were reportedly collected from real estate development in Guangzhou, which accounted for 25–30 percent of the total development costs (Xu, 1996). It was reported that Guangzhou had been practicing this kind of transaction of land leasehold. The winning bidders were responsible not only for the costs of compulsory farmland requisition, relocation of and compensation to sitting peasants, infrastructure and accessory facilities but also for other facilities such as greenery, school buildings, and substations. These projects were carried out as a payback for receiving land leasehold at subsidized prices (IFTE/CASS and IPA, 1994). Thus, the land sale income, part of which was supposed to accrue to the central government, was retained in the form of local built-up environment.

As such, the local government–enterprise coalition benefited both parties by sacrificing the interest of the central government. Local enterprises grew and expanded with the facilitation from the local government, and then in due course the beneficiary firms paid back in the form of commitments to projects with high risks and low profits but great significance, such as high-tech industrial parks. Developers were sometimes persuaded to take up unprofitable social projects that were nevertheless useful for various reasons. For instance, because of its location in a prime area, a residential quarter was renovated by a Shenzhen developer so as to enhance the city's image, but without commercial profits. Profitable state-owned developers were occasionally cajoled to sponsor national social projects, such as donations to poor provinces, or sponsor projects to alleviate poverty on behalf of the government at advanced municipalities.

Under the old centrally controlled system, the economic and political interests of localities were subdued by the central government. Local governments were hardly considered as politically independent entities. Decentralization has redefined the roles of local government to the extent that an accountable local state appears to serve the locality. However, due to the existing undemocratic political structure where top officials of all levels of government below the central state are appointed and assessed by the bodies at upper levels, mayors cannot be fully responsible to municipal citizens. Not only is it a case of political reforms lagging behind economic change, but it is also a measure intended to curb ever-growing localism. The governance structure where municipal governments are only partially accountable to the constituencies will continue unless political reforms are called for.

On the one hand, the officials employed in a developmental state have to be development minded. They need to legitimize their position by their performance in office and to pave the way for the progress of their political careers. On the other hand, their accomplishments are assessed by the bodies at upper levels who are not local residents living in the local constituencies. Visible physical accomplishments apparently look more impressive to nonresidents than those invisible but really beneficial to locals. The landmark-styled projects can obviously serve as conspicuous achievements affiliated to the local leaders in charge. During Shanghai's renaissance in the 1980s, the then-mayor favored building of grand bridges over the Huangpu River instead of tunnels underneath, and this clearly explains that the former were more visible and impressive despite being more expensive than the latter. Frequent reshuffles of mayors in important municipalities have created a sense of anxiety among local chiefs and an urgency to deliver what will appeal to superiors. Reshuffles have become more frequent than earlier due to the reconfiguration of the central leadership and consequent political alliances. The first two mayors of Shenzhen, Liang Xiang (1981–1985) and Li Hao (1985–1991), each held the position for five to six years in the 1980s. In the 1990s, once Shenzhen had become a heavy weight and an important city in southern China, the tenure of mayorship was shortened. The third mayor, Zeng Liangyu (1991–1993), served two years in office. The following mayor, Li Youwei, commenced his term in 1993 and was soon replaced by Li Zhibing in 1995. A long-term agenda for urban development is not deemed affordable as mayors may have stepped down before the vision has materialized. Short-term quantitative instead of long-term qualitative urban changes are pursued as a result.

The road project of Binhai Avenue, involving the city east-west thoroughfares, was put up for development without hesitation clearly for its visual impact rather than claimed utilitarian function, as the east-west transportation was no more a problem than the north-south traffic flows. When affordable housing, for example, was a more urgent and tougher challenge for the government to tackle, it was the modernist expression of its seafront section and the speediness of its construction that prompted the city leaders to give the Binhai Avenue project priority over others. Municipal leaders were keen to maximize the impact of limited resources on the city profile by investing in visible projects in strategic locations. The newly built modernist Diwang Commercial Centre in Luohu, frequently appearing on the government brochures as a symbol for the 1990s' Shenzhen, evidently revealed the importance of image-building for the municipality.

There is no doubt that market mechanisms should play a role in the management of urban development. But the nature of developmental state determines that government plans cannot be totally discarded in favor of market actions. The growth-oriented local developmental state must find an instrument to transmute government plans to market actions. Land subsidies seem a convenient instrument in hand to lever market agents in the implementation of local government's or more precisely mayor's plans. Given the situation that many local governments in China were in a state of weak financial capability, granting subsidies or waiving taxes were the only means by which governments could create an impact. Science and technology parks and several other industrial zones, which were meant to spearhead high-tech manufacturing in Shenzhen, were developed in such a fashion. Developers were further subsidized by the permission given to develop private housing for foreigners to cover the possible losses, because the housing supply of this market was strictly controlled while the demand was strong.

Luohu was the center of now-defunct Bao'an County and still remained the city center of the new Shenzhen. Due to the expansion of Shenzhen city, Luohu's capacity was reaching its limit. It had been a dream of consecutive city mayors to build a new city center in order to project a new image of Shenzhen – which could also serve as a landmark symbolizing the achievement of Shenzhen municipal government. Futian was identified and planned as the future new downtown. As early as 1986, Hopewell China Development Corporation, a Hong Kong developer, was approached to explore the possibilities of its development. Land would be given at very low prices as an attraction. Although the scheme was dropped before it reached the final stage, the enthusiasm and determination of the city government were unambiguously demonstrated. In 1996, this grand project was again put on the city government's agenda. An international competition was held in August 1996 for the new city center design. Four architecture design firms, coming from France, Hong Kong, Singapore, and the United States, were invited to submit their designs. Following the selection of the final winner, the government declared four incentives to promote the new downtown development. All of them were land or property related. First, developers would enjoy 30 percent discount on land prices. Second, the local and foreign housing markets would be merged in the new downtown so that the price differences between the two markets would be effectively eliminated in favor of local housing developers. Third, no capital gains tax would be imposed on the first transaction of newly built properties. Fourth, special property mortgages would be arranged and offered to property purchasers by the domestic finance institutions (Chinese and Foreign Real Estate Times, 1996). Although the property markets were not buoyant and oversupply of buildings was looming, the city government remained determined to push for the new city center development. Eighty-five out of 160 hectares of developable land had been leased at negotiated prices below the market rates to six Hong Kong developers of repute. The land factor had been mobilized by the mayors to the full extent to fulfil their vision under the auspices of gradualist urban land reforms.

An absence of the state as the third party: substandard development

Commoditization and marketization of land and buildings since 1988 have initiated the process of creating market mechanisms for urban physical development. Nevertheless, no serious attempts have ever been made to lay down the

84 *Land markets in the making*

'the rule of the game' for the emerging land market. The fiscally deficient local developmental state is not in a position to provide adequate public goods and social facilities, and thus its capacity to exercise effective planning controls is questionable, while its top priority is quantitative growth. It is not able to prevent the emerging market from providing inferior and unhealthy buildings to the low-income residents. Inferior and deteriorating habitations are generated from places which, owing to the absence of government rules and market order, are virtually the commons. The commons emerge from the gap between the socialist central planning order and the market order yet to be established. Spontaneous land development without planning controls as the rules imposed by the state tends to produce a substandard built environment.

Under the centrally controlled economic system, urban planning was a tool to facilitate urban economic plans that were prepared in a top-down manner. The blueprint land use plan was instrumental in converting 'bourgeois consumer cities' to 'proletarian producer cities' and assisted socialist industrialization to a great extent by securing sites for plants (Cao and Chu, 1990). However, the old planning system has not adapted to the new situations arising from the economic reforms, because institutional reform is lagging behind the economic transformation. The traditional land use plans do not have the capacity to offer effective development controls in the face of dynamic urban growth and a new phenomenon of multiple actors participating in urban development. Planning procedures and operations are often interpreted and manipulated at the whim of the authorities (Xu and Ng, 1998), due to a deficient and underdeveloped legal framework. The local developmental state gives itself much power in the handling of development projects with ample flexibility, and thus development controls are highly discretionary without sufficient transparency. While inward investments are keenly pursued by the financially strained local developmental state, cajoling developers into committing their investments to the city usually results in governments yielding to individual developers' interests. Planning controls are used as a mechanism by which the local developmental state negotiates with developers for mutual benefits (Zhu, 1999a; 1999b).[6] Most of the negotiations bargain for the construction of more floor areas and higher buildings. Consequently, externalities imposed by those projects are not internalized. A capricious planning system with little accountability to the public does not foster stabilities in the land market, while land use planning is supposed to provide certainty with respect to the future characteristics of the neighborhood.

Urbanizing villages, or *chengzhongcuns*, having proliferated mostly in the booming southern coastal cities, are urbanizing enclaves of rural settlement amid urban built-up areas, as rapid urban development has encroached on the agricultural hinterland on an unprecedented scale and speed since the 1980s. Because of the historical dichotomy of rural and urban entities, urban land is owned by the state, whereas agricultural and village land comes under collective ownership. When almost all farmlands of the villages in the suburbs are acquired by the city government for urban expansion, villagers are allowed to retain 10–15 percent of acquired farmland to conduct nonagricultural economic activities.[7] Peasants have to live in their village housing as well because it is hard for city governments to compensate urban housing to peasants for the loss of village housing because of constrained fiscal capacity. *Chengzhongcuns* emerge when villages are encircled by the surrounding areas developed as urban districts. The transformation from rural villages to *chengzhongcuns* suggests an intriguing issue of land rights at play. Urbanizing villages are the products of rapid urbanization without effective governance over drastic market-driven change, in the context of the ambiguity and incompleteness of village land rights accentuated by the enhanced land rent.

Land in villages, according to the Land Management Law, 1998, should be managed by the village committee. The village committee is an autonomous administrative organ empowered by the Village Committee Law, formed to manage collective matters. Enhanced by the progressive urbanization. which radiated rapidly from the urban core, the land value of the villages became explicit and multiplied within a short span of time. An irresistible urge to capitalize on land value arose as a challenging issue to the village committees. Since the dissolution of People's Communes, the peasant household has been restored as an independent unit of rural economic activities. Kinship and some traditional institutions are still in place, functioning as effectively as they used to in managing the life of the village. Located in the suburbs of Shantou, Guangdong, Jingsha Village was mainly composed of members of the Li clan. By the 1990s, when it was surrounded by the urban districts and became a *chengzhongcun*, the Taoist *Shanshan Guowang* Temple remained a center for the villagers to socialize and worship in. Some traditional values are still held by the villagers, evident in the conversion of the long-standing Li's Ancestral Hall to an elderly home in 1986. However, in the face of dramatic changes, traditional and informal institutions (*xianghui mingyue*) that used to govern the village have become inadequate to cope with the pressure of urbanization.

Although kinship remains a social relation in village life and members of the village committee are often related to villagers by kinship ties, the era when social order was maintained by kinship hierarchies has gone owing to the dual force of collectivization and urbanization. Elements of the traditional rural lifestyle have blended with individualism, which is usually characteristic of urban society. In the early 1990s, when development pressure was mounting, Jingsha Village Committee set up a taskforce to work out a plan for redeveloping the village collectively. With the engagement of a professional planning consultant, a redevelopment plan was produced, recommending a building density 50 percent higher than the existing one. Expecting much more housing space, the majority of villagers did not see the benefit of this collective action. As a result, collective agreement brokered by the Village Committee could not be reached and the redevelopment plan was abandoned. This illustrates that the Village Committee no longer has the authority that the village elders enjoyed in earlier times. Yet, on the other hand, the diminishing authority of the Village Committee has not been replaced by the third-party rules of modern urban planning, for the villages are deemed rural jurisdictions. An institutional vacuum has appeared when the old order has gone and a new order has not been established owing to the ambiguous status of *chengzhongcuns*.

Having seen a rising demand for affordable housing from migrants in search of jobs in the cities of Pearl River Delta, villagers in *chengzhongcuns* realized that the housing land they were sitting on could be utilized to build apartments. Spontaneously, the villagers started to construct apartment buildings that were much bigger than their families actually needed on their own land parcels for family living, or *zhajidi*, with an expectation of leasing extra housing space on the market. As landowners or landholders naturally want to enhance the quality of living as well as land values, zoning as a community right is beneficial to both individuals and neighborhood as a whole (Fischel, 1985). No formal land use control mechanism (zoning) renders village land rights incomplete. *Zhajidi* parcels are usually small at about 150 square meters in size and good for housing of two to three floors high in a compact settlement, thanks to the prevailing land scarcity in the Pearl River Delta. When individual village households spontaneously start redeveloping their houses to a higher density in order to capitalize on the enhanced land rent, negative externalities, such as reduction of fresh-air ventilation and of exposure to nature light to the neighboring sites, occurs, but it is at little cost to the imposer who owns extra space that enhances use value of *zhajidi*. Having seen the benefits recouped by the imposers, neighbors follow suit. The similar externalities generated consequently diminish the use value of housing space built earlier. When everyone else follows suit in the village, negative externalities are aggregated and exacerbated, and the value of built-up housing space drops on aggregate. The damage of negative externalities to neighboring sites is costless to the imposer initially, which then provides an incentive to all landholders to do the same. Because the land development market follows the logic of the commons, failure to internalize externalities produces suboptimal use of scarce land resources and substandard habitats. Infrastructure and amenities are provided at a minimum level.

Illegal constructions encroach upon open spaces, minimizing the space between buildings. On some occasions, the distance between buildings is as short as one meter, so that residents could literally shake hands across the gap between two adjacent buildings. Thus, a notorious term 'shaking-hands buildings' has been coined. Chaos arises and hazards are ubiquitous (Jin, 1999). Shipai *chengzhongcun* in Guangzhou is a case in illustration (see Figure 4.1). Shipai has an area of 26.5 hectare, with a plot ratio at 3.98 and site coverage at 83.9 percent. The height of housing buildings averages at 4.8 floors. Fire safety, open spaces, fresh-air ventilation, and exposure to nature light are seriously compromised so that untidy, unsafe, and unhealthy *chengzhongcuns* have become a synonym of urban slums. In Luohu, a district of Shenzhen, residential density reached on average 1,000 residents per hectare for its 24 *chengzongcuns*, but the highest density peaked at 4,110 residents per hectare in Hubei that was in a good location (Du, 1999). According to a survey carried out in 1999, 91.2 percent of 553,747 residents who were living in *chengzhongcuns* of Shenzhen were temporary migrant tenants (SIUPD, 2001). In Futian district of Shenzhen, *chengzhongcuns* provided rental housing space accounting for 68.4 percent of its whole housing rental market (Zhou, 1999). Social

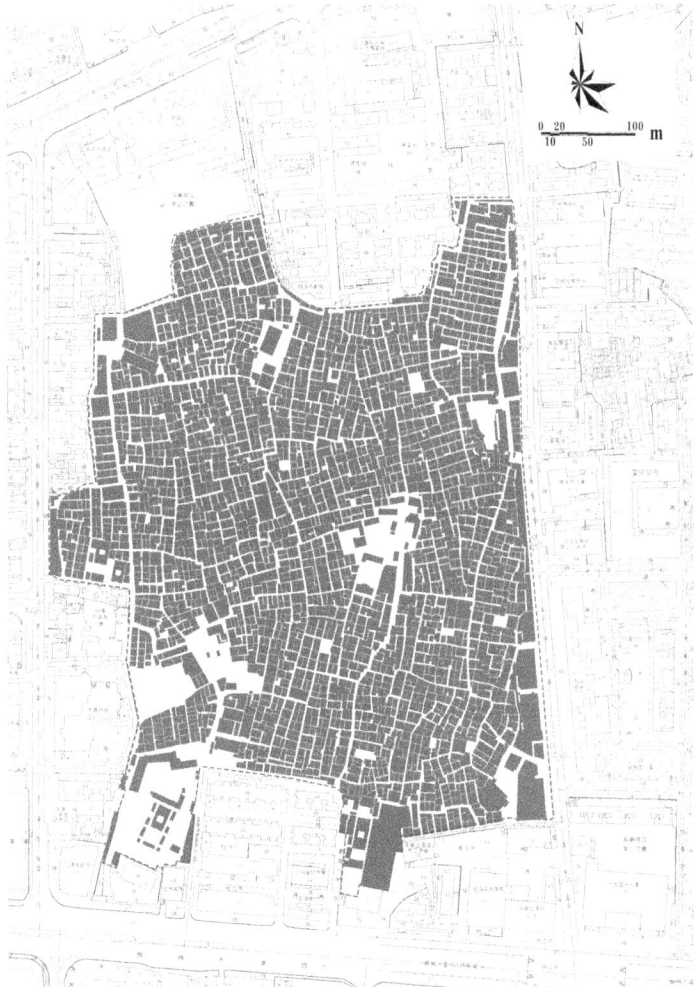

Figure 4.1 Spatial layout of *zhajidi* housing in Shipai *chengzhongcun*, 2015.

disorganization occurs to Jingsha, attracting a concentration of criminal activities on a disproportionate scale to the community. In the year 1996 alone, 226 arrests were made of prostitutes, gangsters, and drug dealers.

Luohu was the center of defunct Bao'an county and stands as a main retail district of new Shenzhen. Although there is plenty of greenfield sites available for new developments along with the rapid expansion of Shenzhen city, the old, crowded Luohu remains commercially attractive because of its location close to the Luohu Customs, through which thousands of travelers between Shenzhen and Hong Kong pass every day. Redevelopment of Luohu was initiated as early as 1982, when the Shenzhen Special Economic Zone had just been established.

88 *Land markets in the making*

A joint venture between Hong Kong's capital (HK$1.1 billion, reportedly) and Shenzhen's land (about 20 hectares) was soon set up with a 30-year long-term plan. Dilapidated buildings were torn down, some refurbished, and affected residents relocated. MacDonald's, a symbol of American capitalism, gained its foothold in the center of Luohu in the late 1980s, when the area was in the midst of redevelopment. The density of Luohu before renewal was indicated by a plot ratio below 2.0, and most were single-story buildings (see Figure 4.2). The 1989 master plan stipulated that plot ratios should not exceed 3.0 for the redevelopment. However, the subsequent redevelopment had substantially intensified land use to the extent where density now stood at two to three times what the plan regulated (see Figure 4.3).

Figure 4.2 Spatial layout of Luohu before redevelopment, 1988.

Environmental quality soon declined because of a lack of open spaces and amenities. Traffic jams and congestion, which existed before redevelopment, were not alleviated and the same chaos still prevailed. Redevelopment of Luohu did not achieve its objective of upgrading spatial quality. Before too long, rapid deterioration of the shopping ambience caused by overcrowding resulted in customer complaints and declining retail performance. A second round of urban renewal had to be called for in 1998.

Land rent grabbing

The incomplete land reforms do not assist the construction of land market mechanisms so as to utilize land resources efficiently. Instead, the dual land market corrupts the integrity of land marketization. Favoritism in the land market

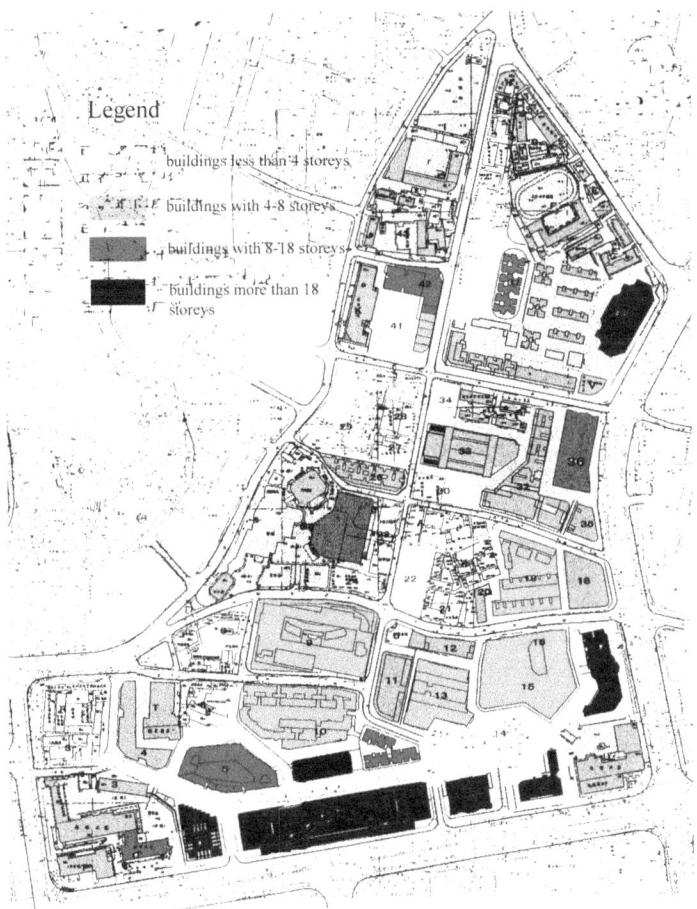

Figure 4.3 Spatial layout of Luohu after redevelopment, 1998.

discourages improvement of economic efficiency in property development. Protection to SOEs does not necessarily warrant the expected results. More often than not, it renders inefficient utilization of discounted resources by the recipients. Price disparities between the two land markets (land leasing by auction/tender and land leasing through negotiation) generate land rent.[8] It has been estimated that, during the period 1987–2000, 300,000 hectares of land were leased out nationwide, of which only 5 percent was through auction and tender (see http://www.people.com.cn/GB/14857/15304/21521/2081658.html, accessed September 10, 2003). Rent dissipation reportedly occurred at a rate of about ¥10 billion every year at the cost of the state landowner's revenue income (see http://www.peopledaily.com.cn/GB/14857/22238/28463/28464/2015058.html, accessed September 10, 2003). It is the two-tier incentive structure that has constructed the dynamics of building construction booms. On the one hand, the commoditization and marketization of buildings make property development a viable business driven by profit-pursuing. On the other hand, the capitalization of land rent generated between the two land markets is another driving force behind rapid land (re)development. Since property development projects on publicly leased land make up an insignificant fraction of the total supply of commodity space, the unprecedented urban physical change in the 1990s is mainly accounted for by the developments in another land market, which was driven by property demand as well as by the capitalization of land rent.[9]

Uncertainty induces hasty capitalization of land rent, because rent generated from the dual land market cannot be safely stored for long during an uncertain transition period. Gradualism implies unpredictable changes and dualism will not be perpetual. The ambiguous property rights, based upon gradualism and dualism, are thus insecure. When uncertainty occurs, it prevents actors from making rational and most appropriate decisions because of not knowing the causality, which deprives actors of a long-term perspective. Land-leasing projects can wait for the best timing to be initiated because of secure property rights. Furthermore, risk is part and parcel of real estate businesses. Underpriced land causes a weak sense of risk-bearing, which makes developers less cautious in initiating projects than they should be if land is acquired at market prices. Capitalization of land rent has to be materialized only through undertaking land development. The opportunity of rent capitalization could be otherwise lost. Between 1997 and 2002, 1,466 hectares, out of a total of 8,550 hectares of sites that were not promptly developed, were taken back from landholders by the Guangzhou municipal government (Li, 2002).

Notes

1 Twenty-eighteen was the 40th anniversary of the economic reforms and opening-up to the world.
2 On March 2, 2003, a report on the competitiveness of Chinese cities was published by the China Academy of Social Sciences, which ranked cities according to their achievements in sciences and technologies, economic growth rates, etc. Hong Kong

was ranked the first, followed by Shanghai and Shenzhen (http://finance.sina.com. cn/g/20030303/0751316063.shtml; accessed July 16, 2003). Seeing Guangzhou ranked sixth, behind Shenzhen in the same province, the mayor of Guangzhou complained and doubted if the ranking was fairly done (http://news. sina.com.cn /c/2003-03-09/1402939281.shtml; accessed July 16, 2003). After Beijing had won the 2008 Olympic Games, and Shanghai 2010 Expo, Guangzhou felt left behind these competitors and decided to bid for the 2010 Asian Games. It won the bidding.

3 The concept 'soft budget constraints' is coined by Kornai (1986) to explain the behavioral differences between a capitalist firm and a production unit in a centrally planned economy. A capitalist firm that fails to cover its costs out of current revenue (or, in the case of borrowing from outside sources, out of expected future income) is ultimately forced to exit the market. In a centrally planned economy, such an exit threat is non-existent. As long as a firm has access to implicit or explicit subsidies from government, there are no incentives to cover the costs of production or behave as a cost minimizer. The forms of soft budget constraints include following cases. First, the two-tier pricing system is an example of a soft budget that offers large profit margins to those SOEs able to obtain most of their inputs at below-market prices and sell part of their output at free market prices. Second, explicit subsidies come from government budgetary funds. Third, firms may enter into political negotiations about the level of effective taxation, lobbying for tax exemptions and reductions in tax rates. The contract responsibility system offers ample opportunities for selective tax waivers and discretionary taxation. Fourth, as the banking system takes on a larger role in the financing of investment, soft loans become a way of keeping loss-making SOEs afloat.

4 SOEs had heavy 'social burdens', providing an array of social services (housing, medical insurance, pensions). A quick look at the issue of retirees revealed the enormous social obligation borne by SOEs. Retirees accounted for 25 percent of the total number of urban workers in 1997; about 20 percent of SOEs' capital assets were buried in social projects; housing for employees cost SOEs an extra 35–40 percent of total wages; and, the cost for medical care accounted for 12 percent of total wages (Liu, 1997).

5 Shanghai's housing development and provision in the 1980s and 1990s are an example in illustration. Commoditization or privatization leads to an increasing share of private housing in the market over the years, and private housing has become the norm for housing supply since the late 1990s. There was no private housing as late as in 1982. However, provision of private housing accounted for 95.2 percent of total housing space supplied in 2000 (SMBS, 2001a, 2001b). Private housing sold to households had to be subsidized by the state in the 1980s. While the percentage of households buying housing at market prices has been increasing since the late 1980s, *danwei*-enterprises have taken over the role of the state by assigning their employees subsidized housing, which is purchased directly from the market. During 1982–1984, *danwei* acquired 31.0 percent of total housing units at market prices. In the period 1991–1993, *danwei* purchased 78.5 percent of total housing units in the market (SMBS, 1994).

6 For the sake of local development, the local development state often colludes with and yields to developers. Having sampled the cases of development controls dealt with by the Shanghai Municipal Planning Bureau during the 1980s, a survey disclosed that 46.8 percent of the cases were in discordance with the land use plan (Sun and Deng, 1997).

7 *Chengzhongcun* is the product of market-driven urbanization. In the pre-reform era of socialist central planning (1949–1979) was urbanization led by the state and state-owned-enterprises. Acquisition of agricultural land for urban uses was undertaken by the local governments that offer the affected peasant families urban apartments and urban jobs as compensation, so that whole villages are urbanized, land as well as peasants. The economic reforms since 1979 have changed the economy significantly. Enterprises, whether public or private, have become autonomous.

Governments are no longer able to offer urban jobs on behalf of enterprises to the displaced peasants. Therefore, villagers need to find urban jobs in the market. As a transitional measure, villages are given certain land parcels to conduct nonagricultural economies in order to generate incomes for the collective welfares.
8 According to Krueger (1974) and Tullock (1993), rent-seeking normally arises in the context of artificial interference with markets by the state, whose restrictions give rise to rent in a variety of forms. It is a societally costly pursuit of transfers, when individual efforts to maximize value generate social waste rather than social surplus (Buchanan, 1980: 4), so-called the welfare-reducing effects of political competition over redistribution (Olson, 1982).
9 Several in-depth case studies can be found in Wang and Hung (1997), Zhao, Bao and Hou (1998), Wu and Zhang (2000), and Zhu (2002: 50–51).

References

Agarwala, R. (1992) *China: Reforming intergovernmental fiscal relations*. Washington, DC: World Bank.
Aram, J. D. & Wang, X. (1991) Lessons from Chinese state economic reform. *China Economic Review*, 2(1): 29–46.
Bardhan, P. (1990) Symposium on the state and economic development. *Journal of Economic Perspectives*, 4(3): 3–7.
Blecher, M. (1991) Development state, entrepreneurial state: The political economy of socialist economy in Xinju Municipality and Guanghan County, in G. Write (ed.) *The Chinese state in the era of economic reform – The road to crisis*, 265–291. Armonk: M. E. Sharpe.
Breslin, S. G. (1996) China: Developmental state or dysfunctional development? *Third World Quarterly*, 17(4): 689–706.
Byrd, W. A. (1991) *The market mechanism and economic reforms in China*. Armond, NY: Sharpe.
Cao, H. T. & Chu, Z. H. (eds.) (1990) *Urban construction of contemporary China*. Beijing: China Social Science Press. (in Chinese).
Chinese and Foreign Real Estate Times (1996) 17: 14. (in Chinese).
Du, J. (1999) The choices faced by urban villages in the new millennium. *City Planning Review*, 23(9): 15–17. (in Chinese).
Editorial Committee of Shenzhen Real Estate Yearbook (ECSREY) (1991–1996) *Shenzhen real estate yearbook, 1990–1995*. Beijing: People China's Publishing. (in Chinese).
Evans, P. B. (1995) *Embedded autonomy: States and industrial transformation*. Princeton, NJ: Princeton University Press.
Fan, Q. (1994) State-owned enterprise reform in China: Incentives and environment, in Q. Fan and P. Nolan (eds.) *China's economic reforms – The costs and benefits of incrementalism*, 137–156. London: Macmillan.
Fischel, W. A. (1985) *The economics of zoning laws – A property rights approach to American land use controls*. Baltimore, MD: The Johns Hopkins University Press.
Furubotn, E. G. & Pejovich, S. (1972) Property rights and economic theory: A survey of recent literature. *Journal of Economic Literature*, 10(4): 1137–62.
Goetz, E. G. & Clarke, S. E. (1993) *The new localism – Comparative urban politics in a global era*. Newbury Park, CA: Sage.
Hassard, J., Morris, J. & Sheehan, J. (2002) The elusive market: Privatization, politics and state-enterprise reform in China. *British Journal of Management*, 13(3): 221–231.

Hope, N. C. (1996) Opening remarks, in H. G. Broadman (ed.) *Policy options for reform of Chinese state-owned enterprises*, 13–16. Washington, DC: World Bank.

Hu, X. (1996) Reducing state-owned enterprises' social burdens and establishing a social insurance system, in H. G. Broadman (ed.), *Policy options for reform of Chinese state-owned enterprises*, 125–148. Washington, DC: World Bank.

Hu, X. (2000) The state, enterprises, and society in post-Deng China – Impact of the new round of SOE reform. *Asian Survey*, 40(4): 641–657.

Huang, Y. S. (1996) *Inflation and investment controls in China*. Cambridge: Cambridge University Press.

Institute of Finance and Trade Economics, Chinese Academy of Social Sciences (IFTE/CASS) and Institute of Public Administration (IPA) (1994) *Urban land use and management in China*. Beijing: Economic Science Publishing. (in Chinese).

Jensen, M. C. & Meckling, W. H. (1976) Theory of the firm: Managerial behavior, agency costs and ownership structure. *Journal of Financial Economics*, 3(4): 305–60.

Jin, D. (1999) A survey on urban villages. *City Planning Review*, 23(9): 8–14. (in Chinese).

Johnson, C. (1982) *MITI and the Japanese miracle: The growth of industrial policy: 1925–1975*. Stanford, CA: Stanford University Press.

Johnson, C. (1995) *Japan: Who governs? The rise of the developmental state*. New York: Norton.

Kornai, J. (1986) The soft budget constraint. *Kyklos*, 39(1): 3–30.

Krueger, A. O. (1974) The political economy of the rent-seeking society. *American Economic Review*, 64: 291–303.

Lakshmanan, T. R. & Hua, C. (1987) Regional disparities in China. *International Regional Science Review*, 11(1): 97–104.

Lang, O. (1946) *Chinese family and society*. New Haven, CT: Yale University Press.

Lau, L. J., Qian, Y. Y. & Roland, G. (2000) Reform without losers: An interpretation of China's dual-track approach to transition. *Journal of Political Economy*, 108: 120–143.

Lee, K. (1991) *Chinese firms and the state in transition – Property rights and agency problems in the reform era*. Armonk, NY: M. E. Sharpe.

Li, H. W. (2002) *Urban land use and management – A case study of Guangzhou*. Guangzhou: Guangdong People's Press. (in Chinese).

Liao, K. Y. (1994) China's urban land market, in Institute of Finance and Trade Economics, Chinese Academy of Social Sciences (IFTE/CASS) and Institute of Public Administration (IPA) (eds.) *Urban land use and management in China*, 109–153. Beijing: Economic Science Publishing. (in Chinese).

Lin, J. Y. F. (1992) Rural reforms and agricultural growth in China. *American Economic Review*, 82: 34–51.

Lin, S. (2000) *Too many fees and too many charges: China streamlines its fiscal system*. Background Brief No. 66, East Asian Institute, National University of Singapore.

Liu, W. (1997) On the process of China's SOE reforms. *Special Economic Zones' Economy*, 1: 13–15. (in Chinese).

Logan, J. R. & Molotch, H. L. (1987) *Urban fortunes: The political economy of place*. Berkeley: University of California Press.

Ministry of Land and Resources, China (2004–2017) *China land and resources statistical yearbook, 2004–2017*. Beijing: Geological Publishing House. (in Chinese).

Mollenkopf, J. H. (1983) *The contested city*. Princeton, NJ: Princeton University Press.

Molotch, H. L. (1976) The city as a growth machine: Toward a political economy of place. *American Journal of Sociology*, 82(2): 309–332.

Molotch, H. L. (1990) Urban deals in comparative perspective, in J. R. Logan and T. Swanstrom (eds.) *Beyond the city limits*, 175–198. Philadelphia: Temple University Press.

Morris, J., Hassard, J. & Sheehan, J. (2002) Privatization, Chinese-style: Economic reform and the state-owned enterprises. *Public Administration*, 80(2): 359–373.

Nanto, D. K. & Sinha, R. (2002) *China's banking reform, post-communist economies*, 14(4): 469–493.

National Bureau of Statistics, China (NBSC) (1979) *China statistical yearbook, 1978*. Beijing: China Statistics Press. (in Chinese).

National Bureau of Statistics, China (NBSC) (2000–2001) *China statistical yearbook, 1999–2000*. Beijing: China Statistics Press. (in Chinese).

Naughton, B. (1995) *Growing out of the plan: Chinese economic reform, 1978–1993*. Cambridge: Cambridge University Press.

Nee, V. (1991) Socialist inequalities in reforming state socialism: Between redistribution and markets in China. *American Sociological Review*, 56, 267–282.

Nolan, P. (1995) Politics, planning, and the transition from Stalinism: The case of China, in H. J. Chang & R. Rowthorn (eds.) *The role of the state in economic change*, 237–261. Oxford: Clarendon.

Oi, J. C. (1992) Fiscal reform and the economic foundations of local state corporatism in China. *World Politics*, 45(1): 99–126.

Oi, J. C. (1995) The role of the local state in China's transitional economy. *The China Quarterly*, 144: 1132–1149.

Oi, J. C. (1996) The role of the local state in China's transitional economy, in A. G. Walder (ed.) *China's transitional economy*, 170–187. Oxford: Oxford University Press.

Oksenberg, M. & Tong, J. (1991) The evolution of central-provincial fiscal relations in China, 1971–1984: The formal system. *The China Quarterly*, 125: 1–32.

Olson, M. (1982) *The rise and decline of nations*. New Haven, CT: Yale University Press.

Perkins, F. (1995) *Productivity, performance and priorities for the reform of China's state-owned enterprises*. Economics Division Working Papers 95/1, Research School of Pacific and Asian Studies, Canberra.

Putterman, L. & Dong, X. Y. (2000) China's state-owned enterprises – Their role, job creation, and efficiency in long-term perspective. *Modern China*, 26(4): 403–447.

Qian, Y. Y. (2000) The process of China's market transition (1978–1998): The evolutionary, historical, and comparative perspectives. *Journal of Institutional and Theoretical Economics*, 156(1): 151–171.

Reich, R. B. (1991) *The work of nations – Preparing ourselves for 21st-Century capitalism*. New York: Alfred A. Knopf.

Scalapino, R. A. (1999) The People's Republic of China at fifty. *National Bureau of Asian Research Analysis*, 10(4): 1–30.

Shanghai Municipal Bureau of Statistics (SMBS) (1994) *Shanghai real estate market, 1993*. Beijing: China Statistics Press. (in Chinese).

Shanghai Municipal Bureau of Statistics (SMBS) (2001a) *Shanghai statistical yearbook, 2000*. Beijing: China Statistics Press. (in Chinese).

Shanghai Municipal Bureau of Statistics (SMBS) (2001b) *Shanghai real estate market, 2000*. Beijing: China Statistics Press. (in Chinese).

Shenzhen Institute of Urban Planning and Design (SIUPD) (2001) *Policies on redevelopment of urban villages in Shenzhen*. (unpublished report, in Chinese).

Shenzhen Planning Bureau (2000) *A report on Luohu redevelopment*. Shenzhen: Shenzhen Planning Bureau. (in Chinese).

Shirk, S. (1993) *The political logic of economic reform in China*. Berkeley: University of California Press.

Siaw, L. K. L. (1983) *Chinese society in rural Malaysia: A local history of the Chinese in Titi, Jelebu*. Kuala Lumpur: Oxford University Press.

Sicular, T. (1988) Plan and market in China's agricultural commerce. *Journal of Political Economy*, 96: 283–307.

Solinger, D. J. (1992) Urban entrepreneurs and the state: The merger of state and society, in A. L. Rosenbaum (ed.) *State & society in China – The consequences of reform*, 121–141. Boulder and Oxford: Westview.

Stone, C. (1989) *Regional politics: Governing Atlanta 1946–1988*. Lawrence: University of Kansas Press.

Stone, C. (1993) Urban regimes and the capacity to govern: A political economy approach. *Journal of Urban Affairs*, 15(1): 1–28.

Su, Y. & Zhao, X. B. (1997) The process of Chinese state-owned-enterprise reforms. *SEZs' Economy*, 1: 13–15. (in Chinese).

Sun, S. W. and Deng, Y. C. (1997) A Study of the role of urban planning in Shanghai. *Urban Planning Forum*, 2: 31–39. (in Chinese).

Swanstrom, T. (1988) Semisovereign cities: The politics of urban development. *Polity*, 21(1): 83–110.

Tseng, W. et al. (1994) *Economic reform in China – A new phase*. IMF Occasional Paper 114, Washington, DC: International Monetary Fund.

Tullock, G. (1993) *Rent seeking*. Hants: Edward Elgar.

Unger, J. and Chan, A. (1995) China, corporatism, and the East Asian model. *The Australian Journal of Chinese Affairs*, 33: 29–53.

Uvalic, M. (1992) *Investment and property rights in Yugoslavia*. Cambridge: Cambridge University Press.

Walder, A. G. (1992) Property rights and stratification in socialist redistributive economies. *American Sociological Review*, 57: 524–539.

Walder, A. G. (1995) The quiet revolution from within: Economic reform as a source of political decline, in A. G. Walder (ed.) *The waning of the communist state – Economic origins of political decline in China and Hungary*, 1–24. Berkeley: University of California Press.

Wang, S. (1994) Central-local fiscal politics in China, in H. Jia & Z. Lin (eds.) *Changing central-local relations in China – Reform and state capacity*, 91–112. Boulder, CO: Westview.

Wang, S. (1995) The rise of the regions: Fiscal reform and the decline of central state capacity in China, in A. G. Walder (ed.) *The waning of the communist state – Economic origins of political decline in China and Hungary*, 87–113. Berkeley: University of California Press.

Wang, H. K. & Hung, C. T. (1997) *Shanghai's industrial relocation under land marketization: A case study on Shanghai electrical instrument works*, paper presented at International Symposium on Marketization of Land and Housing in Socialist China, Organized by Hong Kong Baptist University, 31 October – 1 November. (in Chinese).

Wang, X. (2002) State-owned enterprise reform in China: Has it been effective? in R. Garnaut & L. Song (eds.) *China 2002 – WTO entry and world recession*, 29–44. Canberra: Asia Pacific Press at the Australian National University.

Wei, S. J. & Wang, T. (1997) The Siamese twins: Do state-owned banks favor state-owned enterprises in China? *China Economic Review*, 8(1): 19–29.

Weller, R. P. and Li, J. (2000) From state-owned enterprise to joint venture: A case study of the crisis in urban social services. *The China Journal*, 43: 83–99.

White, G. & Wade, R. (eds.) (1988) *Developmental state in East Asia*. New York: St. Martin's.

White, G. (1991) Basic-level government and economic reform in urban China, in G. White (ed.) *The Chinese state in the era of economic reform – The road to crisis*, 215–242. Armonk: M. E. Sharpe.
Wong, C. P. W. (1987) Between plan and market: The role of the local sector in post-Mao China. *Journal of Comparative Economics*, 11: 385–398.
Wong, C. P. W. (1992) Fiscal reform and local industrialization: The problematic sequencing of reform in post-Mao China. *Modern China*, 18 (2): 197–227.
Wong, C. P. W., Heady, C. & Woo, W. T. (1995) *Fiscal management and economic reform in the People's Republic of China*. Hong Kong: Oxford University Press.
Woo-Cumings, M. (ed.) (1999) *The developmental state*. Ithaca, NY and London: Cornell University Press.
World Bank (1985) *China – Long-term development issues and options*. Washington, DC: World Bank.
World Bank (1997) *China's management of enterprise assets: The state as shareholder*. Washington, DC: World Bank.
Wu, J. & Zhang, G. H. (2000) Large scale urban redevelopment in the 1990s – Empirical survey of Jing'an District. *Urban Planning Forum*, 4: 47–54. (in Chinese).
Wu, J. L. & Zhao, R.W. (1987) The dual pricing system in China's industry. *Journal of Comparative Economics*, 11: 309–328.
Xiao, G. (1991) State enterprises in China: Dealing with loss-makers. *Transition* (World Bank), 2(11): 1–3.
Xu, J. and Ng, M. K. (1998) Socialist urban planning in transition – The case of Guangzhou, China. *Third World Planning Review*, 20(1): 35–51.
Xu, S. Q. (1996) Guangzhou developers appealing for 'slimming', *Chinese and Foreign Real Estate Times*, 21: 6–13. (in Chinese).
Xu, X. & Wang, Y. (1999) Ownership structure and corporate governance in Chinese stock companies. *China Economic Review*, 10(1): 75–98.
Zhao, M., Bao, G. L. & Hou, L. (1998) *Reforms of land use system and development of cities and the country*. Shanghai: Tongji University Press. (in Chinese).
Zhou, J. S. (1999) *A survey of rental housing in urban villages, Futian*. (unpublished report, in Chinese).
Zhou, M. & Logan, J. R. (1996) Market transition and the commodification of housing in urban China, *International Journal of Urban and Regional Research*, 20 (3): 400–421.
Zhu, J. M. (1999a) *The transition of China's urban development – From plan-controlled to market-led*. Westport, CT and London: Praeger.
Zhu J, M. (1999b) Local growth coalition: The context and implications of China's gradualist urban land reforms. *International Journal of Urban and Regional Research*, 23(3): 534–548.
Zhu, J. M. (2000) Urban physical development in transition to market. *Urban Affairs Review*, 36(2): 178–196.
Zhu, J. M. (2002) Urban development under ambiguous property rights. *International Journal of Urban and Regional Research*, 26(1): 41–57.
Zweig, D. (2001) China's stalled 'fifth wave' – Zhu Rongji's reform package of 1998–2000. *Asian Survey*, 41(2): 231–247.

5 Urban restructuring along with a transitional institution of land development right

Although urban land was designated as free goods given to state-owned land users and workers, the socialist land use right became a unique institution incorporated in the building of socialist cities. Lacking a market of transactions, it hampered spatial restructuring of the built-up areas. The market called for institutional change to 'buy out' the socialist land use right, and the land development right was designed as transitional institution to phase out the former. Drastic urban restructuring ensued, as well as land rent seeking and dissipating. Zoning as a land right was compromised, while land markets began to work, though structured by local growth coalitions. Rapid urban redevelopment ensued and gave rise to a new pattern of central business districts where two prestigious commercial centers of Huaihai Road East and Nanjing Road West were not designated by the strategic plan beforehand but were built anyway in Shanghai. Path-dependent institutional change went on with organizational changes, along with regional disparities.

Land as a means of production: the rigid socialist land use right

Under the socialist people's ownership, land was allocated to users (agents of the state) through administration channels that did not charge users for land utilization, and land users had no rights to transfer their land parcels either. Urban land was virtually free goods. Tenants' entitlement to land use rights became a unique socialist institution, which was incorporated in the formation of socialist cities. The drastically different structures of socialist cities from those of capitalist counterparts attest to the effect of this institution (French and Hamilton, 1979; Bertaud and Renaud, 1994). Under the socialist, centrally controlled economic system, natural resources and the means of production were nationalized. Urban land has been entrusted to and controlled by the state, which is held accountable to the people. The ownership is officially termed socialist people's ownership (*shehui zhuyi quanmin suoyouzhi*). As the trustee for 'all the people' (*quanmin*), the state has full ownership, enabling it to handle resources and assets in the interest of the general public. Following the dogma of Marxism and the socialist principle of public landownership, land was excluded from economic transactions in China.

Although land leasing has evolved as a new institution since 1988, initially it only led primarily to a land market of greenfield sites, which was a process of urbanization – conversion of land from agricultural to urban uses. Potential redevelopment of the built-up land stock remained hampered. Once SOEs and 'the people' have been allocated land for their uses, it was very difficult in practice for the state to retrieve land from the users, because SOEs were the basic units of the socialist state economy and 'the people' were the 'masters' of the socialist society. The land use right became a distinctive socialist institution, namely, the socialist land use right. Rigidity in land resource mobilization constituted an immediate obstacle to the operation of urban land markets.

The tenacious socialist land use right was also found in other former socialist Eastern European countries. Marcuse (1996: 135) observed: "[i]n capitalist systems, *the right of use is derived from, and subordinated to, the rights of ownership; in socialist systems, the right to use …was accorded a higher position than the rights of ownership*" (original emphasis). It was strengthened by the practice of land being excluded from market transactions, according to the Constitution of 1982. There were no market mechanisms with which land users could exchange land use rights for other benefits in case of relocation. There were no incentives to relinquish occupied land, as there was no compensation for doing so. Land users held on to their land parcels firmly; even the users did not use them productively.

Although officially there were no land markets in China's cities prior to 1988, there was an active informal market where residents exchanged their state-owned housing. There seemed to be an explicit value for the housing use right, when a unit in a good location could be traded for a larger one in a not-so-good location. The housing value in the most unfavorable location was only 59.2 percent of that in the most favorable location in the 1980s when open housing markets did not exist (Tang, 1986). When there were occasional land use changes in the exiting built-up area, government had to offer land at other locations as a replacement to displaced tenants. This was equivalent to the transfer of a tenant's land use right to the new sites. A survey of six residential land redevelopment projects in Shanghai in the 1980s indicated that the cost of new housing, to which the affected residents' use rights over the demolished apartments were transferred, was between 30 and 70 percent of the total redevelopment costs (World Bank, 1993).

The institution of socialist land use right was firmly rooted in residents' minds. Even before urban housing was formally privatized, residents could openly trade their public housing (with use rights only) in the market under the auspices of housing commoditization (see Table 5.1; http://www.peopledaily.com.cn/GB/jinji/32/177/20010816/536670.html, accessed August 17, 2001). Buyers' willingness to pay clearly showed their confidence in the security of housing with only use right attached, while the government's tacit approval of transactions verified this faith (Beijing Youth, April 28, 2001, cited by http://www.realestate.cei.gov.cn, accessed October 14, 2002). According to the statistics of the Shanghai real estate market, it seemed that the price differences between

Table 5.1 Housing transactions in the secondary market, Shanghai

year	Total (in floor area, square meters)	Housing with full property rights (in floor area, square meters)	Housing with use rights only (in floor area, square meters)	Housing transactions with use rights only as % of total
1998	2,141,906	1,975,561	166,345	7.8
1999	3,796,961	3,366,940	430,021	11.3
2000	7,164,430	6,482,277	682,153	9.5

Source: SMBS, 1999a–2001a

housing with full property rights and with use right only were insignificant (SMBS, 1999a–2001a).

During 1988–2000, 10,224 hectares of land were leased and 26.3 million square meters of buildings were constructed in Pudong, Shanghai (SMBS, 2001b). It is noted, however, that between 1988 and 1992, land leasing to developers/users was mainly of greenfield sites (1,725 hectares) (Research Institute of Communist Party's History, 2018). Together with several small industrial zones, there were two sizable development projects in Shanghai – the Hongqiao Development Zone (since 1988) and the Pudong Development Zone (since 1990). All were greenfield sites where the leasing of agricultural land was coordinated by the municipal government (SMBS, 1992a). There was hardly any leasing of built-up sites for redevelopment in Shanghai before 1992. Redevelopment of the old central city was prevented by the sitting land users. Once China recovered from the Tiananmen crisis in 1989, the economic reforms were forcefully pushed forward by Deng Xiaoping in his historic tour of southern China in 1992. Inward foreign investment inundated coastal cities, looking for low-cost production sites and expecting to penetrate into a potentially huge market. Demands for offices and housing were shown strongly and clearly in Shanghai (see Table 5.2). The potential value of existing built-up areas was pushed up by the emerging market forces, which favored locations in the central city over those in the outskirts. The widening gap between the potential capital value of 'the highest and best land use' and the present capital value[1] of the existing land use constituted a powerful incentive for land redevelopment in the central area, where many existing physical structures had been built before 1949. However, capitalization of the land capital value gap had a supply-side constraint: the tenants' land use rights had become de facto ownership rights.

As a legacy of socialist industrialization in the pre-reform era when urban land was a free means of production and industrialists' demand overtook that of others in land allocation (Fung, 1981), it was not unusual to find factories located in the central business district. Between 1985 and 1990, only 103 plants were relocated from the central city, where there were 5,600 factories occupying an area of 430 hectares (World Bank, 1993:19). Up to 1991, there were still 1.74 million square meters of factory space in downtown Huangpu district, which at the same time only had 1.39 million square meters of office space (SMBS, 1992b).

Table 5.2 Private housing price and office rental indexes, Shanghai

Year	1985	1990	1992	1995
High-rise housing	100	235	774	1015
Multistory housing	100	291	742	1029
Office rental	100	148	264	497

Source: SMBS, 1996a

Institutional change: the land development right

The foremost task of the urban reform[2] is to transform cities that have been molded by central planning into cities that are market orientated. The commodification of buildings is advocated as a point of departure from the command resource allocation and of entry into the marketization of urban development. Marketization has opened up Shanghai to the international economy, and transnational corporations are drawn to establish or re-establish their presence in the city. Shanghai's indispensable role in the country, reflected in its economic strengths and its pivotal position for international trades and commences, has been rediscovered. The city has been transforming itself rapidly from a manufacturing city to a service hub with an international orientation since the 1980s, and it has reinvented its image as an international open city.[3]

The new land leasehold, ushered in at 1988, has accentuated land values. The notions of land being a means of production and land as an economic asset give rise to the coexistence of two land markets, the other dual land market: those parcels acquired previously through administrative allocation under the old system and held thereafter by users, and those plots acquired through newly invented land leasehold. The former are now in the urban built-up area, whereas the latter consist mainly of former agricultural land on the fringes of the city that have been converted into urban uses. A survey showed that 96 percent of development in terms of land area occurred on the outskirts and in the suburbs between 1980 and 1990 in Shanghai (Sun and Deng, 1997). The redevelopment of the built-up central area was blocked by the socialist land use right.

Driven by a formidable market demand for premises in the central locations, institutional change is called for to remove supply-side constraints by offering incentives to the actors participating in land redevelopment. The Shanghai Municipal Ordinances on Urban Land Management promulgated in 1992 paves the way for land redevelopment in the built-up areas through land leasing by making a clear distribution of revenues from land sales among the parties with vested interests. According to the ordinances, 70 percent of the revenues should be used for compensation to displaced sitting tenants, demolition, and redevelopment of infrastructure on site. The remaining 30 percent is split among de jure owners of the central (5 percent), municipal (12.5 percent), and district (12.5 percent) governments. Compensation for relinquishing land use rights has been formalized since then, although it is not clear how much compensation land users should be entitled to. It was not finally made explicit until October 2001 when the Management of Housing Demolition and Tenant Relocation ordinance was issued by Shanghai Municipal Government; it stated that, for residential quarters, evicted tenants should receive compensation at 80 percent of the prevalent market value of the demolished housing, while the 'owner' or 'provider' (an organization or a *danwei*) receives the remaining 20 percent (http://www.shanghai.gov.cn, accessed November 1, 2002). Residents with only socialist land use rights to their state-owned housing claiming at least 80 percent of its prevalent market value reflects an informal process of housing privatization, which gives sitting tenants benefits in-kind as compensation for their many years of working in state-owned enterprises with low salaries. However, for those land parcels controlled by the *danwei* land users, compensation for demolished premises only is not considered an incentive strong enough for them to give up their de facto ownership rights.

Nevertheless, the degree of control over land conferred by de facto property rights varied among users, depending on their positions. Those with high position in the party-state bureaucracy had more control than those in the lower strata. Ordinary urban residents, in the lowest rungs of the social structure, could only claim the least control over the land they occupied for living, though they were not powerless. De facto property rights based on use rights were therefore hierarchical. Informal entitlements attached to the land use right are varied among different users, although legally these users are only tenants who have not paid for landholding. Private residents are entitled to a proper compensation for their lost accommodation when requested to leave, but the *danwei* land users are entitled to more than compensation. The higher in the hierarchy a *danwei* is, the more secure is the amount that the *danwei* could claim from its land use right (see Table 5.3).[4] In short, private residents do not have bargaining power, whereas *danwei* land users do. The higher level a *danwei* land user is, the more bargaining power it has. A *danwei* is controlled by a supervising authority of the same level, but it is beyond the control of the authorities of lower levels. Since 1992, the enacted Shanghai Municipal Ordinances on Urban Land Management have decentralized the administration of land development from the municipal authority to district governments. Thereafter, district governments are able to

Table 5.3 Hierarchy of socialist land users

Category of land users	Supervising authority	Level in hierarchy
Danwei land users	Central government – ministries	1 (highest)
	Municipal government – bureaus	2
	District government – offices	3
	Jiedao office*	4
Individual residents	District government	5 (lowest)

Note:
* A *jiedao* office is a representative or an agency of district government. It provides basic social services to those unemployed (Wu, 2002).

control the land users of Level 3 downward. These land users at Levels 1 and 2 are not managed by the district government, and their land use rights virtually cannot be taken away by the district authorities that are managing redevelopment of the most central area.

Before the initiation of land redevelopment to capture the land rent gap, a *danwei*'s property rights over the present land capital value have to be defined and clarified, and the property rights of the local government (one of the de jure landowners) over the potential land capital value have to be manifested. A new institution, the land development right (LDR), for the *danwei* land users is invented in this context. The institution is intended to unlock the land supply for redevelopment while accommodating the existing institution of the *danwei*'s land use right. The land development right is what a sitting *danwei* can claim, based on its land use right, to redevelop the site occupied by itself and, if necessary, neighboring sites occupied by other *danwei* land users or residents.

Jing'an district, with an area of 8 square kilometers in Shanghai central city, was chosen for an investigation to probe how urban redevelopment unfolds within the new institutional structure of a dual land development mode (land leasing and LDR). The survey was also intended to find out how LDR is acquired and defined. During 1992–2000, only 36 sites, amounting to 30.7 hectares, where previous land users were in the categories of Levels 3, 4, and 5, were offered through land leasing for land redevelopment, while 260 sites were acquired under LDR where land was occupied by land users affiliated to the central and municipal governments (Levels 1 and 2) as well as other users of Levels 3, 4, and 5. A total of 6.4 million square meters of building floor area, or 77.6 percent of the total, were developed by either *danwei* land users or developers under LDR, while 1.8 million square meters, or 22.4 percent of the total, were developed on the sites through land leasing (see Table 5.4). A dual land rights regime has therefore been formulated in such a fashion for the redevelopment of built-up central area in Shanghai.

Acquisition of LDR depends on the hierarchical order and financial capacity of *danwei* land users who intend to conduct redevelopment, as well as the blessing of local government. In an old, high-density district, redevelopment often

Table 5.4 Dual land acquisition in Jing'an district, Shanghai (1992–2000)

Mode of land acquisition	Developer	Number of projects	Amount of building floor area built (sqm)	Building floor area as % of total
Land leasing	Foreign developers	36	1,849,043	22.4
Land acquired under LDR	Local developers and *danwei* land users	260	6,415,399	77.6
Total		296	8,264,442	100.0

Source: author's survey

involves multiple land users and thus gives rise to land assembly. Acquisition of LDR thereby entails competition among land users whose sites are involved. To win LDR depends very much on the bidder's financial strength and whether they can compensate sitting land users for giving up their land use rights. Usually, either those *danweis* in higher hierarchical positions or those *danweis* with better financial capacities win the bid, as they could 'buy out' other land users who are often residents and small *danwei* tenants. As an informal institution, LDR is not formally tradeable in the market, though it is valuable. While holders of LDR do not possess full property rights, land assets are not secured and ownership remains ambiguous. However, once land plots are redeveloped, developed buildings with titles are tradeable at market prices and thus development profits materialize, subject to a prior fee payable to the municipal government to certify the land transfer. The value of LDR can be realized only by pushing the redevelopment project through until the building is ready for sale or rent and then the land rent gap captured. If in funding difficulties, those holders of LDR need to seek development capital to join in proposed partnerships.

Shanghai Dianbiaochuang (SD), a state-owned manufacturer of electrical apparatus since 1954, occupied a site of 6.1 hectares for its production. The potential value of the factory site had been enhanced significantly by the surrounding development of residential and commercial activities in the area over the years. Once LDR was granted, SD has been in active pursuit of redevelopment opportunities, with the blessing of the district government, which allowed change in the land use from industrial to commercial and residential. Establishment of a joint venture to carry out private housing and office real estate development was planned, and it was expected that, with SD's land and the investor's capital, SD could diversify into the real estate business. Since 1993, SD had conducted a few marketing seminars overseas, aiming to persuade foreign capital to invest in this proposed project. At one time, a deal was nearly closed with a Hong Kong developer who was about to join the partnership when he received another offer at a better location and decided to pull out (Wang and Hung, 1997).

While SD was still on the lookout for a buyer of the redevelopment option, in the same area of Anshan Road, there were 15 redevelopment projects under construction in 1996 with a total floor area of 720,000 square meters of private housing, offices, and shops. Six of those projects were initiated by the sitting *danwei* landholders (Zhao, Bao, and Hou, 1998). Statistics show that Jing'an district approved redevelopment projects with a total floor area of 8.2 million square meters between 1993 and 1998, of which 4.0 million square meters were proposed by *danwei* landholders (Hu and Zhang, 2000). The Shanghai Real Estate Fair, held in Singapore, Sydney, and Melbourne in 1997, keenly promoted 38 land sites in the tiny Huangpu district to potential foreign investors for redevelopment on behalf of *danwei* landholders (Huangpu Investment & Development Company, 1997). Enticed by lucrative prospects in real estate development, many *danwei* landholders participated in the real estate business by setting up joint ventures or sole-proprietary development firms. There were 95 developers registered in 1988. The number of developers rocketed to a staggering 2,099

104 *Urban restructuring*

in 1994 and further escalated to 4,012 by June 1998 (SMBS, 1989a; 1995a; Jiefang Daily, October 22, 1998).

A common form of partnership between LDR and development capital has been that one party contributes land with LDR and another party is responsible for financing the building construction. Out of the 23 samples investigated, 14 cases involve collaboration of this type: 4 overseas, 7 SOEs, and 3 private partners. The completed projects are split in ownership between the two partners. The share (30–50 percent of the total) to the land party reflects the value of LDR to the project. This partnership also provides a channel through which private capital participates in urban construction. This provides an opportunity for developers in the private sector to grow.

Implications of the land development right for urban spatial changes

Large-scale redevelopments have taken place since the early 1990s for the first time after 1949 Liberation in Shanghai central city, where old industrial structures have been demolished and new office buildings are erected. Many industrial tenants and residents have been relocated to the suburbs. Restructuring of urban land uses has occurred. Sensational media coverage of the city reported that Shanghai was the world's biggest construction site in the 1990s (Straits Times, January 15, 1998). Between 1993 and 2000 in Jing'an district, 4.81 million square meters of building floor area were constructed, while 2.49 million square meters of old structures were demolished (SMBS, 1994b–2001b). The total building stock by 1990 was 9.08 million square meters (SMBS, 1991b). This suggests that a quarter of the stock was demolished and 53 percent more was added during the period. Similarly, during the same period, building construction and demolition in the whole city of Shanghai were undertaken at an unprecedented scale: 131.2 million square meters constructed and 30.5 million square meters demolished (SMBS, 1994b–2001b). In all, 17.7 percent of the total building stock of 172.6 million square meters that had existed in Shanghai municipality in 1990 was demolished during the 1993–2000 period. Given that development under LDR accounted for 77.6 percent of the total (see Table 5.4), rapid land redevelopment must be attributed to the institution of LDR. It should be regarded as effective in unshackling the land redevelopment that had been hampered by old institutions during the transition.

Between 1990 and 2014, Jing'an saw its total building floor areas increased by 93.9 percent (from 9.1 to 17.6 million square meters), in which offices were increased from 0.5 to 3.6 million square meters, shops from 0.3 to 1.1 million square meters. But industrial space decreased by 69.1 percent from 2.0 to 0.6 million square meters. Central districts favored by the service and financial sectors see higher intensity of investment than those districts on the periphery and in the suburbs. Investment in the built environment begins to follow the land rent gradient. Driven by market demand, land use efficiency in the central city has been improved significantly.

A total of 52 district-affiliated *danwei* land users were allowed to claim LDR from their land use right, and one municipality-affiliated developer and 69 district-affiliated developers were offered LDR over 70 sites, which were mainly in residential use (see Table 5.5). This is explained by the politics of China's property-led urban development in the 1990s. The district government has an incentive to transfer land under LDR. LDR only requires a nominal payment to the municipal government on top of appropriate compensation to the sitting tenants,[5] and noncompetitive LDR land acquisition ensures that key actors are local district *danwei* and district developers. Local growth coalitions are shaped in the context of political legitimacy, decentralization, and regional competition (Zhu, 1999a, 1999b).

Under the umbrella of growth coalition, the local government and local developers cooperate in a fashion of reciprocity. The district government allows its subordinate development firms and *danwei* land users to carry out land redevelopment in the LDR mode. Land rent derived from underpriced land acquisition, which should otherwise go to the government coffers, is taken by the developers. In return, the beneficiaries have a responsibility to help the government for the benefit of local communities. Therefore, LDR land transfer is regarded as being more beneficial than land leasing in certain circumstances to the locality. This practice is obviously not to the superior central and municipal governments' advantage. Its currency is, however, buttressed by a tacit consent based on a new pro-development ideology, which binds governments at all levels together. Land leasing has only been used so far for land parcels on important locations which are jointly managed by both municipal and district governments and mainly applied to foreign developers.

Performance of the local developmental state is predominantly gauged by economic and physical growth. For the old built-up Jing'an district, large-scale upgrading of dilapidated structures and relocation of residents from substandard housing after many decades of negligence and deterioration to decent

Table 5.5 Land redevelopment under LDR in Jing'an district, Shanghai, 1992–2000

LDR	Developer	Number of projects	Amount of building floor area built (sqm)	Building floor area as % of total
Derived from land use right	Municipality-affiliated *danwei*	138	3,674,677	57.3
Transferred from district government	Municipality-affiliated developer	1	13,500	0.2
	District-affiliated developers	69	1,709,494	26.6
	District-affiliated *danwei*	52	1,017,728	15.9
	Subtotal	122	2,740,722	42.7
Total		260	6,425,399	100.0

Source: author's survey

apartments are the tasks at the top of local government's agenda. The local government's tight budget is nevertheless grossly inadequate for this ambitious development program (Lin, 2000; Wang and Hu, 2001). The emerging real estate market initiated by the commercialization of land and buildings provides a key instrument drawing market capital into urban redevelopment. Different from policy-led government actions, redevelopment decisions by the developers are market driven since the selling prices of new developments are determined by the equilibrium of demand and supply in the real estate market.

A redevelopment project would not be justified if cost-benefit analysis does not anticipate profitability. The cost of acquiring LDR is determined more or less by the compensation to the sitting tenants for their relocation. Many districts, especially those residential quarters in the central city of Shanghai, are of very high density – 80,000 habitants per square kilometer on average in the 1980s. One neighborhood reached a density of 230,000 residents per square kilometer – one of the highest in the world (Fung, Yan, and Ning, 1992). High density and thus high cost of resident relocation make redevelopment costly. These residential quarters would not be considered ripe for redevelopment under current market conditions without government subsidies. In order to push for redevelopment, negotiations between developers and government often lead to alteration of planning parameters under the auspices of a flexible land use planning system in the interests of individual projects. Planning controls are used as a mechanism by which the developmental state negotiates with developers for mutual benefits (Zhu, 1999a, 1999b).

LDR has an implication for land use planning. What can be developed based on LDR is defined by land use planning, which is a system of regulating mechanisms determining how land parcels should be developed. As an essential factor shaping the land and property market, land use planning stabilizes the land market through increased certainty with respect to the future character of a place and reduces or internalizes the impact of negative externalities (Jud, 1980).[6] It has been discovered that discrepancies are overwhelming between what is required by land use planning and the final completed buildings in terms of the planning parameters of land use, plot ratio, site coverage, and building height. LDR gives room for bargaining and negotiation, which often makes the master plan irrelevant, revealed by these discrepancies. There are even two cases of land use change after the Land Use Planning Notes have been issued. The in-depth investigation unveils that development projects of the land-leasing type observe planning requirements, or developers have to pay monetary penalties for building more than what is allowed. Nevertheless, there are no penalties to the developers of cases violating planning requirements in the LDR mode. LDR makes land use control a bargaining regime.

It was found from the survey that one-third of land use control items were not observed and revised after the release of the Land Use Planning Notes.[7] Local government's receptive stance to demand for higher density makes land use planning a collaborative mechanism. As one of the defining elements of LDR, the collaborative planning control is an important tool of the local growth coalition. It is noticeable that the other party of this collaboration is usually

Urban restructuring 107

the district-affiliated *danwei* and developers. A quarter of the total redeveloped building floor area (6.4 million square meters) is undertaken by those local developers on the sites where current land use densities are usually high.

Redevelopment projects may thus become financially feasible after alteration of planning parameters, but a capricious planning regime undermines certainty in the land market. A development control system open to bargaining creates additional uncertainty in the land market. Uncertainty leads to the absence of a predictable and transparent environment, which is essential for market activities. There is land rent generated from changing land use and increasing land use density without internalizing related externalities.[8] Externalities are pronounced in the urban land market (Bowers, 1992). When individuals make decisions to maximize utility, the costs and benefits of the decisions have to be internalized if the whole community is to be sustainable. Bargaining for increases in land use density without bearing arising social costs is thus a pursuit of rent seeking: capture of unearned profits with cost in the form of congestion and strained infrastructure borne by the neighborhood and community. Unchecked rent seeking facilitated by authority's collaborative reception further breeds rent seeking. Aggregation of externalities with no internalization brings the land market to the brink of the commons where land use planning is not observed. A quality-built environment is collectively produced and maintained by order. When market order maintained by the land use planning does not exist, market actors do not have a long-term perspective. Developers would choose to maximize returns within a short time frame. Building at a higher density seems feasible and sensible to recover redevelopment costs sooner than otherwise, knowing that other fellow developers would do the same.

In the development market structured by LDR, it is observed that developers tend to engage more often in lengthy bargaining for favorable land use terms than in pursuing quality development. Based on a survey of eight cases, it is found that developers take between 23 and 52 months, or 36.3 months on average, to bargain for a higher plot ratio. The survey of application processes from initiation to the commencement of construction reveals that land acquisition is not time consuming thanks to the institutions of land leasing and LDR.[9] Finalization of site and building designs for projects under land leasing takes 12.5 months on average, but it costs an average of 29.3 months for projects under LDR. LDR projects tend to have problems in raising development finance in time and in sufficient amounts. It is evident that the developers are engaged in intensive negotiations with authorities and state-owned banks for favorable terms. Suboptimal developments ensue as a result of cutting costs in architectural design and construction due to cost pressure. A comparison between two compatible groups of redevelopments (in similar locations) shows that projects are overall of higher quality in the land-leasing mode than those in LDR mode (see Table 5.6). Developers who have acquired land through land leasing at market prices are under cost pressure to distinguish their products from the competitors of low-priced alternatives. A submarket is created where tenants pay rentals 30–40 percent higher than the alternatives developed in the LDR mode.

Table 5.6 Comparison of the quality of office property developments

	Class A as % of total	Class B as % of total	Class C as % of total
Developments under land leasing	74	26	0
Developments under LDR	23	62	15

Note: Classification of office property is done by the local real estate consultants based on building quality. Class A is the highest and Class C the lowest among the three classes, while Class B is in between. These statistics are based on a sample of 36 cases.
Source: author's survey

Because of its informality and insecurity, LDR induces hasty redevelopment to capitalize the land rent gap, whereas land-leasing projects can wait for the best timing to begin. LDR was one of the main causes of the large oversupply of property in the late 1990s (Zhao, Bao, and Hou, 1998).[10] Shanghai was allegedly facing the biggest property glut in its history in the late 1990s (Jackson, 1997; Lee, 1998; Haila, 1999). High vacancy rates seemed a feature of LDR projects. A separate survey done by the author confirmed that, by the end of 2002, office buildings developed under land leasing had a vacancy rate of 7.1 percent (based on 19 samples) and those developed under LDR had a vacancy rate of 14.1 percent (based on 8 samples).

A survey revealed that during the period 1992–2000, land redevelopment carried out in Jing'an district, Shanghai, amounted to a total area of 135.7 hectares, accounting for 17.8 percent of the total area of the district (762 hectares). Out of 135.7 hectares were there 88.5 hectares (65.2 percent) residential land, 35.7 hectares (26.3 percent) industrial land and 11.5 hectares (8.5 percent) institutional land. The process of land redevelopment was full of bargaining between the sitting land users, developers, and planning authority, resulting in redevelopment at higher density than what zoning had prescribed. According to a sample of 23 cases from a census of 260 redevelopment projects, the incidence of those projects with discrepancies in planning parameters between initial planning requirements and final completion accounted for 53.3 percent of the total! The total building stock was 9.08 million square meters by 1990 in Jing'an, and it grew to 17.5 million square meters by 2012. The gross plot ratio rose from 1.19 (1990) to 2.30 (2012), the district physical density increasing by 93 percent over the period, almost doubling the physical density over the two decades with an astonishingly high population density at 33,600 persons per square kilometer (SMBS,1991b; 2013b).

Redevelopment of the central cities: land markets at work

Prior to 1980, the development of socialist cities was entirely a matter of the state, as the state owned all the means of production. All land and building developments were carried out either by governments on behalf of users or by occupants themselves. Marketization and rapid economic growth in the 1980s at first created a market of user demand for land and buildings from private investments and businesses. The era of economic reforms since 1978 can be divided into three periods with regard to the characteristics of land development: Period I (1978–1987), when land was still a free means of production; Period II (1988–1992), when greenfield land sites were developed extensively under the new regime of land leasehold; and Period III (1993–present), when the built-up areas' land sites were brought into the land market by the sitting land users. According to a sample of five cities, land and building developments occurred in ever-increasing numbers (see Table 5.7). Nationally, on average, the floor areas of buildings under construction in 1995 were 80.3 percent more than those in 1990. An examination of seven provinces/municipalities (Shanghai, Zhejiang, Shandong, Guangdong, Hainan, Guizhou, and Gansu) revealed that there were increments of between 14.6 percent (Gansu) and 127.6 percent (Zhejiang) during the same period (NBSC, 1991, 1996). Shantou, a medium-sized city in Guangdong Province, saw its built-up area expand from 7.8 square kilometers (1979) to 63.7 square kilometers (1999) in a period of just 20 years (STBS, 2000). Dongguan, a county town in the same province, witnessed its urban area increasing from 16.2 square kilometers (1988) to 41.1 square kilometers (1993) (Yeh and Li, 1999).

Rapid urban change has been driven by the two engines of industrialization and urban spatial development. Land and building development at such a substantial scale in Shanghai since 1980, particularly since 1990, should be attributed to the released pent-up demand as a result of severe underinvestment during 1950–1980. Housing privatization puts an end to urban housing provision, which is the sole responsibility of the state. The case of housing supply from 1978 to 2016 demonstrates how fundamentally the housing provision mode has been changed: considerable amounts of capital flowing into private housing and withdrawal of the state from housing provision (see Tables 5.8 and 5.9). As a result, drastic urban physical change has occurred in Shanghai. Between 1992 and 2000, 2,247 hectares of land were leased to developers for redevelopment, accounting for 12.7 percent of the total land area leased in the municipality (SMBS, 1991b–2001b). It was reported that "a fifth of the world's cranes straddle 20,000 building sites, making Shanghai the world's biggest construction

Table 5.7 Development of buildings in floor space, on average per year (million square meters)

	Shanghai	Guangzhou	Wuhan	Xi'an	Chengdu
Period I: 1978–1987	8.35	3.92	2.88	1.88	6.19
Period II: 1988–1992	9.58	6.29	5.36	2.11	10.49
Period III: 1993–2000	21.97	12.62	10.13	4.23	17.95
Increase rate, %, (I–II)	14.7	60.5	86.1	12.2	69.5
Increase rate, %, (II–III)	119.3	100.6	89.0	113.6	71.1

Sources: SMBS, 2002b; GZBS, 2002; WHBS, 2002; XABS, 2002; CDBS, 2002

Table 5.8 Investment in housing in three periods, Shanghai

Period	1951–1978	1979–1988	1989–2016
Investment in housing as % of investment in fixed assets	4.2	10.0	24.7

Source: SMBS, 2001b; 2017b

Table 5.9 Expansion of building stocks from 1949 to 2016, Shanghai (millions square meters)

Year	1949	1978	1988	2016	Annual rate of increment, % (1949–1978)	Annual rate of increment, % (1978–1988)	Annual rate of increment, % (1988–2016)
Housing	23.6	41.2	80.8	654.9	1.9	7.0	7.8
Factory	10.3	25.4	46.7	264.9	3.2	6.3	6.4
Office	2.3	2.3	5.4	81.5	0.0	8.9	10.2
Shop	3.3	2.3	3.6	74.7	−1.2	4.6	11.4

Source: SMBS, 2001b; 2017b

market" (*Business Times*, December 4, 1995). It was probably not an exaggeration. Urban revitalization has been carried out on a great scale. A substantial amount of land area was made available to be redeveloped for higher and better uses, which has transformed the city significantly.

Since the 1980s, many multinational corporations (MNCs) have set up their headquarters in Shanghai for the Chinese market. Well-known MNCs such as AT&T, 3M, Intel, Emerson, Dupont, ICI, Hewlett-Packard, Philips, Nortel, Toshiba, and NTT have established their presence in Shanghai (Rose, 1999).

> By the end of 1997, over 230 of the world's 500 largest industrial firms—as identified by Fortune magazine in 1996, had investments in Shanghai. Among the world's top 100 industrial TNCs, 55 of them were involved in operations in the city.
>
> (Yeung and Li, 1999: 519)

During the transformation, Shanghai is shedding its image of an industrial city and re-establishing itself as the main service center in China. Outputs of manufacturing and services in 1978 accounted for 77.4 percent and 18.6 percent of GDP, respectively. The share of manufacturing decreased to 47.4 percent, and that of services increased to 51.0 percent in 2002 (SMBS, 2003b). The Bund, the waterfront of the Huangpu River, used to be colonial Shanghai's central business district. The imposing classic buildings made the Bund a well-known "Wall Street" of the Far East in the 1930s when there were about 168 banks, including 58 foreign banks, and about 2000 trading firms linking Shanghai with the rest of China and the world (Bank of Communications, 1993). With the market orientation, Shanghai obviously becomes a market choice for financial business, evidenced by an increasing share of contribution of the financial sector to GDP: from 3.8 percent (1981) to 10.8 percent (2002) (SMBS, 2003b). The financial sector is also becoming more international oriented by the participation of foreign banks, financial companies, and insurance companies. In 2002, 128 foreign-owned financial institutions were in operation in Shanghai (SMBS, 2003b).

Since 1981, the Shanghai municipal government had been searching for a location to build a new office center for the incoming international businesses, while redevelopment of the old CBD was blocked by sitting tenants with their socialist land use right. Under the auspices of the 1984 open cities program, a large greenfield site at Hongjiao was identified and designated as the Hongqiao Economic and Technological Development Zone (Hongqiao ETDZ). Planned to comprise of international-standard hotels, offices, and premises for foreign consulates, Hongqiao ETDZ occupies an area of 65.2 hectares. Having been the first planned commercial office cluster developed based on market demand since the opening up of the city, Hongjiao attracted a large amount of both local and foreign real estate investments (see Figure 5.1). Good location (close to the Hongjiao International Airport) and well-planned infrastructure made Hongqiao offices attractive to international firms (Rose, 1999). The aggregation of international standard office buildings subsequently made Hongjiao Shanghai's de facto central business district.

Nevertheless, a new physical entity representing Shanghai as a new financial center was enthusiastically sought by both central and municipal governments. Lujiazui, the core of Pudong to the east of the Bund separated only by the Huangpu River, is designated as the new finance district of Shanghai to accommodate a financial industry, which is expected to expand at an annual rate of 40 percent in terms of its share in GDP (see Figure 5.1; Shanghai Pudong New Area Administration, 1993). Office spaces have increased at a great scale since 1990. However, spatial distribution of new office spaces is intriguing. During the period 1985–1991, development of new offices in the traditional CBD Huangpu district (where the Bund is located) was much less than the central city's average in terms of quantity of floor space, while nontraditional office centers Putuo, Zhabei, and Hongkou districts were more dynamic than expected (see Table 5.10). It was the sitting tenants' socialist land use right that blocked the occupied sites from redevelopment. Office developments had to find vacant sites wherever possible, which resulted in scattering opportunistic constructions.

Since 1992, the enacted Shanghai Municipal Ordinances on Urban Land Management has decentralized the administration of land management from the municipal authority to district governments. Because of local interests and the nature of the developmental state, districts compete with each other in engaging real estate capital with land redevelopment. LDR made land parcels in the central location available, but the local developmental state distorted the land market and disintegrated the office property market along the boundary lines between district jurisdictions. In the period 1993–2002, Huangpu continued to lose

112 *Urban restructuring*

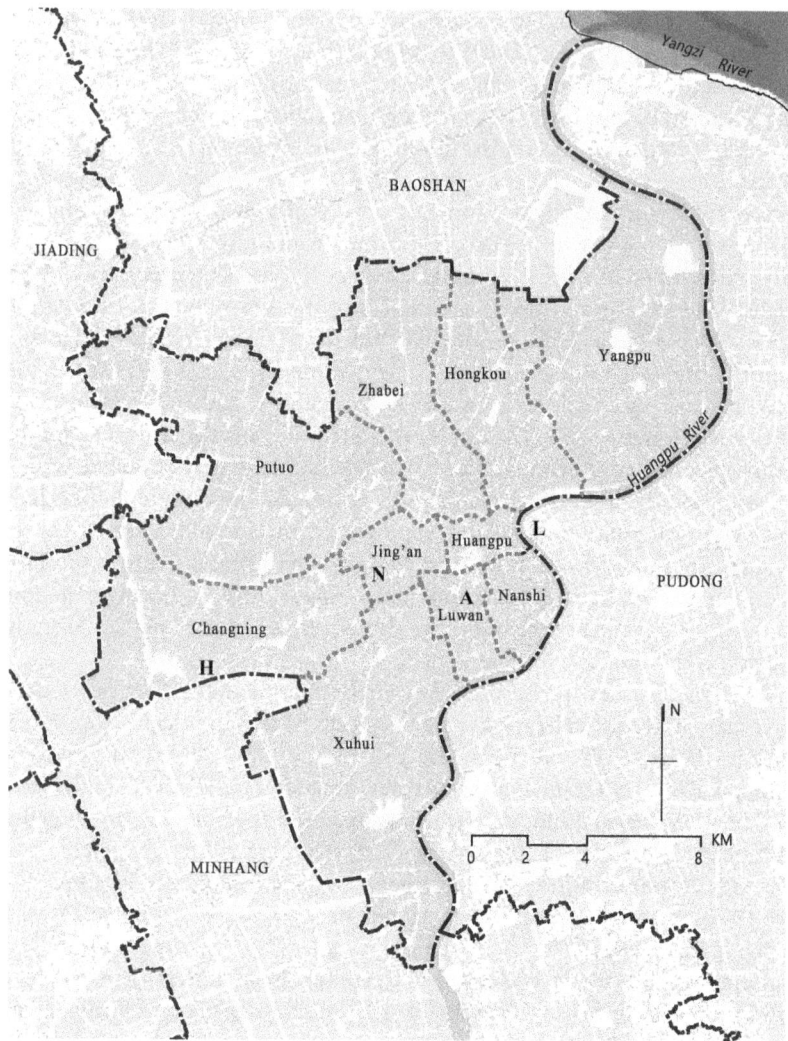

Figure 5.1 Shanghai's urban districts and prime office locations, 1990s.

its dominance, and Putuo, Zhabei, and Hongkou lost their momentum, while Luwan (Huaihai Road East), Changning (Hongjiao), and Jing'an (Nanjing Road West) emerged as new office centers eventually (see Tables 5.10 and 5.11; Figure 5.1). By the end of 2001, there were 2.81 million square meters of Class A[11] office spaces that were distributed as follows: 32.0 percent in Lujiazui, 17.8 percent in Hongjiao, 16.6 percent in Nanjing Road West, and 14.2 percent in Huaihai Road East. Finance services concentrate in Lujiazui, producer services (IT, consultancy, law, accounting, advertisement) in Nanjing Road West and Huaihai

Table 5.10 Distribution of office stock (million square meters) in districts and increase of office stock over periods 1985–1991 and 1993–2002 (%)

District	1985	1991	1985–1991 (%)	1993	2002	1993–2002 (%)
Huangpu	1.27	1.39	9.4	1.22	4.52	270.5
Luwan	0.20	0.32	60.0	0.42	1.91	354.8
Xuhui	0.70	1.06	51.4	1.00	2.62	162.0
Changning	0.39	0.50	28.2	0.60	2.41	301.7
Jing'an	0.28	0.50	78.6	0.53	2.15	305.7
Putuo	0.30	0.66	120.0	0.67	1.37	104.5
Zhabei	0.11	0.36	227.3	0.35	1.28	265.7
Hongkou	0.21	0.67	219.0	0.68	1.15	69.1
Yangpu	0.25	0.33	32.0	0.31	0.78	151.6

Source: SMBS (1986b, 1992b; 1994b; 2003b)

Table 5.11 Distribution of office stock in districts (%)

District	1985	1991	1993	2002
Huangpu	35.0	25.5	21.1	19.0
Luwan	4.9	5.0	6.5	8.0
Xuhui	17.2	16.7	15.4	11.0
Changning	9.6	7.9	9.3	10.1
Jing'an	6.9	7.9	8.2	9.0
Putuo	7.4	10.4	10.3	5.8
Zhabei	2.7	5.7	5.4	5.4
Hongkou	5.1	10.5	10.5	4.8
Yangpu	6.1	5.2	4.8	3.3

Source: SMBS (1986b, 1992b; 1994b; 2003b)

Road East, and manufacturing offices in Hongjiao (http://www.shjagh.gov.cn/seconds/deve_plan/njxl1-2.htm, accessed July 21, 2004).

The new pattern of central business districts illustrates the working of land markets structured by both the equilibrium between demand and supply and the institution of local development state. Being a well-known retail street, Huaihai Road East (HRE) in Luwan district was not a choice for offices, let alone a prime location. The development of Huaihai Road was initiated by French settlers in 1900 when the place was the French Concession. In its prime time, there were 360 shops, of which 250 stores were specialists and 43 had nationwide reputation. A snapshot survey was carried out on September 23, 1990, and found that there were 740,000 shoppers walking on Huaihai Road (Xu, 2003). In the 1986 Municipal Strategic Planning (see Figure 5.2), Huaihai Road was planned to consolidate its retail and commerce functions.

Having seen the underground Mass Rapid Transit planned to pass through Huaihai Road, Luwan district government made a new proposal in 1992 to revise the 1986 Plan. With its autonomy in the urban management, the district

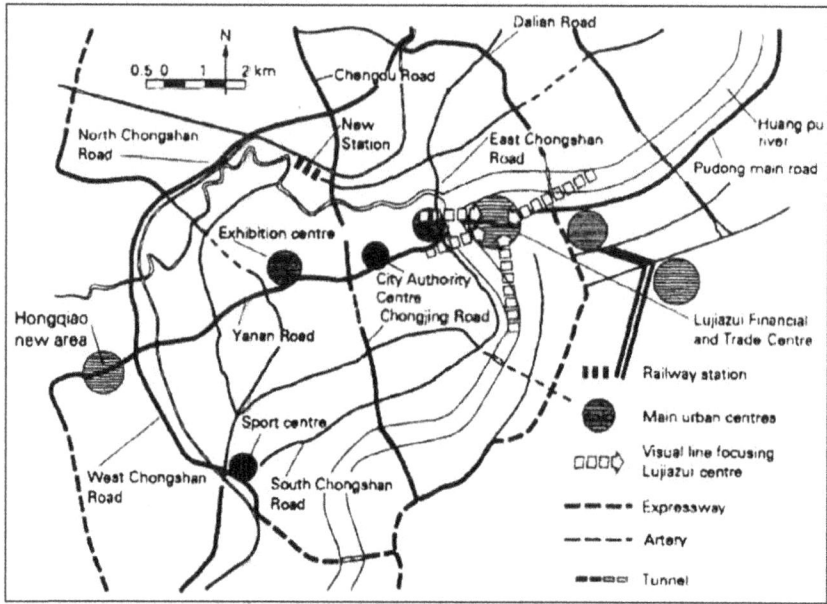

Figure 5.2 Shanghai's strategic planning, 1980s.
Source: Huang, 1991: 92

government finally abandoned what the 1986 Plan had assigned for Huaihai Road, and replaced it with the 1994 Huaihai Road East Redevelopment Plan. Drafted by the District Planning Bureau, the 1994 Plan recommended to intensify HRE land uses and to add office components to its land uses. By the end of 1997, about 165,000 square meters of old retail outlets along the street and dilapidated housing structures behind were demolished. At the turn of the twenty-first century, the profile of the HRE was fundamentally altered (see Figures 5.3 and 5.4). The transformation of a shopping street into a high-rise prestigious office cluster has been significantly achieved with the participation of overseas real estate developers.

Jing'an went through a similar process. The district government hosted the International Symposium on Modernization of Jing'an in October 1992, seeking international advice for redeveloping Jing'an. Large-scale land leasing started immediately in 1993. By 1997, 58 redevelopment projects were under construction (www.shjagh.gov.cn/seconds/deve_plan/njxl1-1.htm, accessed July 21, 2004). Nanjing Road West was dominated by retail and residential land uses prior to the 1980s when the physical idiosyncrasies of the area were of a typical combination of low-plot-ratio and high-site-coverage (see Figure 5.5). The traditional high street shops have given way to shopping malls and office towers since the 1990s, and the fabric of the street has been entirely transformed (see Figure 5.6). Between 1985 and 2014, resident population shrank by

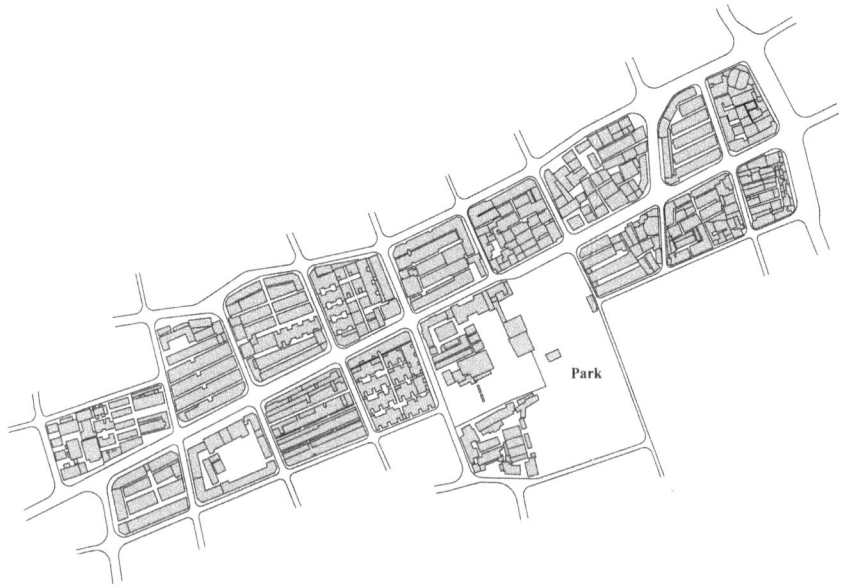

Figure 5.3 Land uses along Huaihai Road East, 1979.

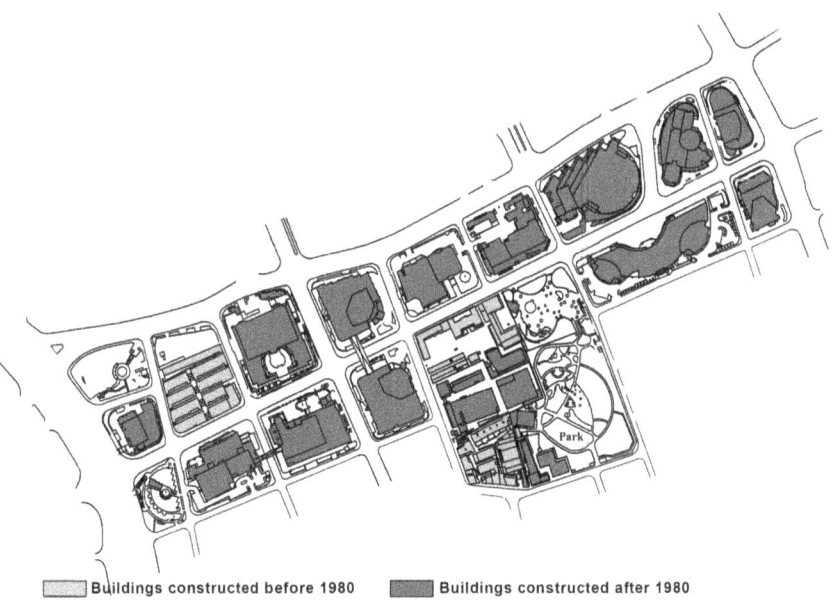

Figure 5.4 Land uses along Huaihai Road East, 2012.

116 *Urban restructuring*

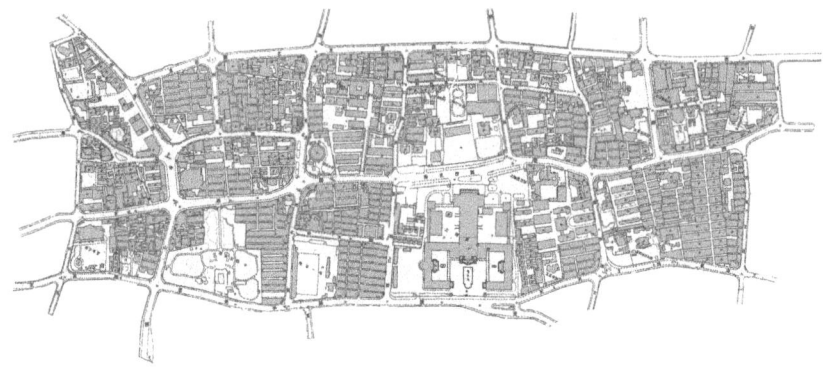

Figure 5.5 Land uses along Nanjing Road, 1980.

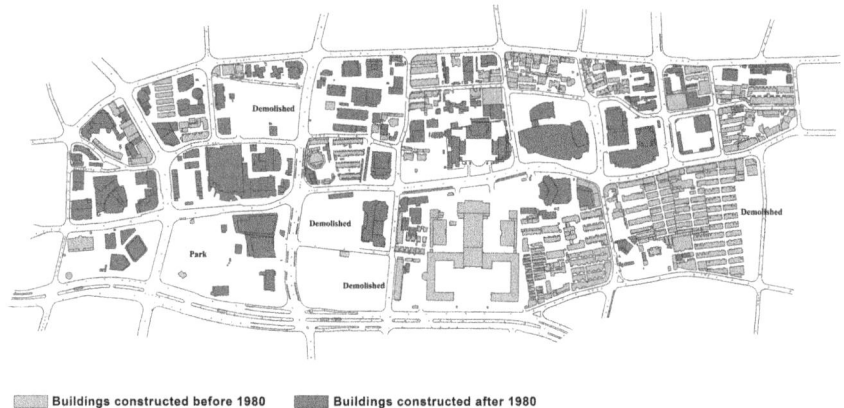

Figure 5.6 Land uses along Nanjing Road, 2012.

half, and office stock as a percentage of the total building stock increased from 3.7 percent to 20.4 percent, while the total building stock increased by 135.7 percent (SMBS, 2015b).

Further institutional change: path-dependent transition

Institutions are generated to cope with pervasive uncertainty in the human world (Heiner, 1983) and institutions "reduce uncertainty by providing a structure to everyday life" (North, 1990: 3). Formation of rules thus aims to reduce complexity and uncertainty and to lower transaction costs (Williamson, 1985). Although providing incentives to land redevelopment, the ambiguous delineation of land rights as unwritten and informal rules does not provide certainty for the emerging real estate market. Therefore, the LDR is a transitional institution. LDR has eliminated the supply-side constraint and thus land redevelopment can be carried out in response to market demand. The institutional change is steered by a compelling desire to capture the land rent gap created by a released pent-up demand for premises. However, under the auspices of the local growth coalition, LDR is characterized as noncompetitive land acquisition with flexible land use planning parameters on the basis of bargaining. In the local growth coalition buttressed by LDR, a reciprocal relationship is demonstrated by a unique 'market provision of public goods' (less profitable redevelopments pushed for, to the benefits of the local communities and thus the local developmental state) and the 'state provision of private goods' (rent seeking allowed, to the benefits of local developers). A very flexible land use planning system subject to bargaining inevitably brings about rent seeking, and prevalent rent seeking makes the land market the commons. Planners' discretionary powers are understandable in the present era of rapid change when inflexible rules often seem too rigid. The balance between discretion and rules is, however, crucial; as Booth (1996: 110) states, "discretion and rules are not merely opposites, they are interdependent". In the transitional Chinese city of Shanghai, the quasi-commons in the land market and lack of competition in land acquisition often give rise to suboptimal urban construction.

Institutional change is fundamentally caused by competition toward a more efficient and productive system. North's notion of path dependence is obvious during incremental change from the socialist central planning to an economy with market orientation, as LDR evolves from the socialist land use right. It is meant to create a land market where land use efficiency can be improved through market mechanisms, while the old actor of the *danwei* are still taken care of during the transition. LDR is, however, deemed a transitional institution because it more often than not brings about a suboptimal utilization of land resources. LDR cannot survive the circumstance of severe premise shortages. When building shortages are alleviated considerably to the extent of oversupply, rapid quantitative growth is no longer warranted as a strategy or a goal for the state to pursue. When given a choice, the customers would weed out the inferior goods. This is demonstrated by the unsold and vacant buildings. Suboptimal utilization of land assets does not add positively to the credibility of the state. Rent seeking breeds corruption.[12] Finally, the central government, as a remote principal whose property rights over urban land have been attenuated by the institution of LDR, has to strengthen its ownership. In 2002, the central government had to strengthen its control of urban landownership by issuing a directive demanding land transfer through land leasing. Land transfer through LDR for property development is ruled out.[13] Since August 1, 2003, urban land leasing through negotiation has been strictly controlled by Decree 21 – Regulations on Land Leasing through Negotiation, issued by the same ministry on June 11, 2003. It appears that the strengthening of state landowner's property rights over urban land has been achieved. Since 2002, there have been nine launches of land sales through transparent public bidding in Shanghai, which are publicized on the government website (see http://www.shanghai.gov.cn; and http://www.shfdz.gov.cn/tdsyqcr/zbgg.asp, accessed October 20, 2003), while during the period 1988–1995, only 9 out of a total of 1303 land plots were allocated through tender (Zhao, Bao, and Hou, 1998). Clarification of land rights, a precondition for efficient resource utilization and optimal production, is therefore the goal for path-dependent institutional change.

For those land parcels still held by the *danwei*-enterprises, the socialist land use right remains valid and valuable. Shanghai's No. 10 Iron and Steel Factory had operated its workshop on a site in Changning district since 1956, until the mid-1990s, when it was closed down as a victim of globalized competition. It became Red Town, a project of conservation of industrial heritage in mid-2000s, which hosted art galleries and exhibitions by the refurbished plants. It had become one of the famous culture-led urban regeneration projects in Shanghai (Wang, 2009). Its landholder, Shanghai's No. 10 Iron and Steel Factory, decided in April 2014 to initiate commercial redevelopment with an approval from the urban planning bureau and acquired land leasehold by incurring ¥1.48 billion. It did not intend to develop the site by itself, and the leasehold was transferred immediately to Rongqiao, a developer, at ¥2.75 billion in December 2014 (see http://house.people.com.cn/n/2014/1209/c164220-26177372.html, accessed January 28, 2019). The difference of ¥1.27 billion is considered the price of the socialist land use right for the land plot of 4.8 hectare.

Further institutional change is propelled by organizational change in the context of market competition. The local developmental state and *danwei*-enterprises, two prominent organizations during the gradual reforms, are given room and time by the LDR to be transformed gradually while market mechanisms develop. The local developmental state adapts itself to fit into the market, and *danwei*-enterprises evolve to become full market players. The SOE reforms have deepened since the mid-1990s when the term 'socialist market economy' was officially coined, indicating the long-term direction of economic reforms. Privatization of small- and medium-sized SOEs and the corporatization of large SOEs began. Many SOEs have since completed the transformation toward shareholding companies and have been listed on the Shanghai and Shenzhen Stock Exchanges (Broadman, 1995; Iskander, 1996). SOE's roles in urban physical development have been diminishing (see Table 5.12). In Guangzhou, SOE developers' share in the real estate development market in 1995 was 46.3 percent in terms of floor space. Their share in 2001 dropped to 13.3 percent (GZBS, 2002). Non-state-owned entities and private firms are taking over SOEs as main actors in the new economy. The *danwei* is fading out and *danwei*-enterprises are discarding their *danwei* responsibilities and becoming independent enterprises. The amount of housing purchased by *danweis* at market prices and then assigned to their employees at subsidized prices was decreasing substantially and would be terminated later. A total of 78.5 percent of all housing units in the market were sold to *danweis* in the period 1991–1993 (SMBS, 1994a). This dropped to 2.8 percent in 2002 (SMBS, 2003a).

Table 5.12 Investment in fixed assets by SOEs as percentage of total in five cities

	Shanghai	Guangzhou	Wuhan	Xi'an	Chengdu
1980	88.6	94.5	96.7	97.2	93.3
1985	80.9	86.4	78.5	88.2	71.8
1990	84.7	89.0	86.6	89.0	70.3
1995	59.8	61.9	59.0	59.8	50.2
2001	38.1	46.4	50.0	58.1	49.3

Sources: SMBS, 2002a; GZBS, 2002; WHBS, 2002; XABS, 2002; CDBS, 2002

Without insulation from the political and social interests of society, China's local developmental state is not a detached and disinterested state. A strong pro-growth position and weak leverage in guiding market forces by local governments and the state often disable their roles of the third party. The local developmental state is not so conducive to the construction of the market mechanisms. The land use planning system is an illustrative case in this regard. Land use planning is intended to reduce or eliminate the impact of negative externalities, and thus it is expected to lead to an efficient and equitable land use structure. Without appropriate land use planning controls, substandard overcrowded 'urban villages' appear in many of southern China's cities (Du, 1999; Jin, 1999; Zhu, 2004). Suboptimal developments are mostly related to the land plots with ambiguous property rights. Market competition exposes the inferiority of these projects, resulting in high vacancy rates in these buildings. Slums in the midst of glittering modern buildings and a large amount of vacant buildings damage the creditability of local developmental states. Moreover, the local developmental state and *danwei*-enterprise coalition is gradually losing its relevance, while *danwei*-enterprises are becoming autonomous enterprises and social responsibilities are increasingly taken over by the state. It is in the best interest of local governments to take the third-party role to provide order to the market where building development is increasingly commoditized (see Table 5.13).

Nevertheless, the ambiguous property rights may still be needed to advance local growth by strengthening local growth coalitions in less-developed regions. Market-driven economic growth has not occurred evenly throughout the whole country (see Table 5.14). The degrees of marketization and commoditization are lower in the central and western regions, where SOEs remain dominant in the economy. There are indications that the new decrees issued by the Ministry of Land Resources may not be strictly observed in less-developed cities. As of 2003, there were 3,837 development zones nation-wide with a total area of 36,000 square kilometers, of which only 232 were approved by the central state council and 1,019 by the provincial governments (see http://www.people.com.cn/GB/14857/22238/28463/28464/2015058.html, accessed September 10, 2002). Most of the development zones without the blessing of upper-level authorities

120 *Urban restructuring*

Table 5.13 Commoditization of building development in Shanghai

Year	Commodity building floor area as % of total building floor area	Commodity housing floor area as % of total housing floor area
1998	46.7	63.3
2000	50.2	80.8
2001	64.0	90.8

Source: SMBS, 1999a; 2001a; 2003a

Table 5.14 Regional disparities in economic growth and marketization, 2000

Region	Population as % of total	Urban population as % of total	GDP as % of total	Development of commodity building as % of total	% of total industrial output contributed by SOEs
Eastern region[1]	42.4	52.2	59.4	62.4	38.0
The rest[2]	57.6	47.8	40.6	37.6	70.1

Notes
1 The Eastern Region comprises Beijing, Tianjin, Hebei, Liaoning, Shanghai, Jiangsu, Zhejiang, Fujian, Shandong, Guangdong, Guanxi, and Hainan, with a land area of 1.3 million square kilometers.
2 The rest (Central and Western regions) consists of remaining 19 provinces with an area of 8.3 million square kilometers.
Source: NBSC, 2001

are set up by localities in the central and western regions. Under the regime of ambiguous property rights, land in development zones has already been conveyed at very low prices to local-government-owned land developers and thus is beyond the jurisdiction of the new decrees which only control land conveyance from local governments. It is perceived that the ambiguous property rights practiced in the developed cities in the 1990s would still be practiced in developing cities in the 2000s, as the institution offers an incentive conducive to local growth in the initial stage of marketization.

China's emerging urban land markets are structured by the new institution of ambiguous property rights, which has evolved from the socialist people's ownership of land in the context of economic reforms characterized by gradualism and dualism. The new institution has helped the local growth coalition between the local developmental state and the *danwei*-enterprises in their endeavor to develop the local economy. It has also facilitated the release of land, formerly locked up by the old socialist institution, to the urban land redevelopment market. Although regarded as a positive change toward the establishment of land markets in a matrix of institutions related to central planning, the ambiguous property rights create land rent. Capitalization of land rent undermines the emerging land market: the distorted equilibrium between demand and supply leads to building booms and oversupplies, and the absence of the state as the third party gives rise to inadequate order in the land development market. The ambiguous property rights do not achieve what an institution should – providing certainty to the market and incentives for the optimal utilization of resources. The institution of ambiguous property rights is deemed transitional as the cost it incurs is increasingly becoming greater than the benefit it brings.

Building effective institutions for markets is a great challenge to many developing countries and transitional economies. In this endeavor, the state is a crucial actor and its capacity is a key factor. A critical test for the transitional economies, which are undergoing a makeover from a centrally controlled system to a market economy, is to build market mechanisms in their economies. Market failures are prevalent in many developing countries, evidenced by shortages of basic private/public goods, such as housing and infrastructure. One of the characteristics of the Third World countries' urbanization is that informal developments dominate in their cities (Brennan, 1993). However, it has been argued that market failures are often caused by government failures (World Bank, 2002). A functional market would not exist without effective market institutions, and building institutions for the market is a challenging task for the state as well as for the community. China's experience in establishing urban land markets has demonstrated that openness, competition, and a capable and responsive government are the critical factors in the process of institutional change toward a market system. The state has a very constructive role to play in the building and managing of functional markets. Functional markets cannot be established instantly, as building market institutions is always a gradual process.

With broadening openness and intensifying competition, local economies of the advanced regions have progressed to a phase where it is quality development, instead of speedy but shoddy growth, that measures the performance of local governments. It is not so necessary for the local government to help SOEs at this stage, as SOEs are increasingly being weaned from state subsidies to stand on their own feet and non-state-owned-enterprises are taking a leading role in the economy. When the shortage of urban premises comes to an end, thanks to the economic reforms, inferior developments brought in by the transitional institution are exposed and discredit, rather than serve, the local developmental state. The continuous decentralization since the reforms has somehow been making the central government a regulatory state playing the role of the third party, while the local developmental state is an active actor in its local economy. Since 2002, the central government has reiterated that it should strengthen its governance of urban land leasing and has stressed its property rights over urban land.[14] Without an effective state serving as the third party, uncertainty could induce disorderly short-term behavior in the market. An orderly invention with measures to spread risks would be a viable option when there are governments maintaining order. Institutional change for the establishment of land markets in urban China is on the path toward a complete system of state land leasehold where the state principal's rights over land are fully in force.

Notes

1 The present capital value of land is "net returns expected to be earned in future years" (Harvey, 1987: 97).
2 The urban reform is a general umbrella under which comprehensive, yet gradual changes have been initiated to install market mechanisms in the process of urbanization, in parallel with the replacement of comprehensive and direct state involvement by interventions via indirect levers such as taxes, subsidies, and macroeconomic policy tools.
3 Shanghai is reemerging as an open city to the world. One of the tallest buildings in Shanghai, Jinmao, exemplifies the internationalness of the city. Its construction involved contractors from seven countries and regions: USA, Japan, France, Germany, Singapore, Hong Kong, and Shanghai itself.
4 In the large cities like Shanghai, there is a hierarchy of central state-owned enterprises (*zhongyang qiye*) and local state-owned enterprises (municipal-affiliated, *shishu qiye*), district-affiliated (*qushu qiye*), and *jiedao*-office-affiliated (*jiedao qiye*). Almost all state-owned enterprises were managed by the central government before 1957 when the reform of the industrial management system was initiated to increase the power of local governments. The decentralization reduced the number of enterprises under central control and changed vertical control into horizontal management. Thus local state-owned enterprises emerged. In 1990, there were 52,058 central state-owned enterprises with 9.93 million employees and 276,758 local state-owned enterprises with 53.85 million employees (NBSC, 1995; Lü and Perry, 1997: 8).
5 Initially, LDR did not require any payment to governments. Since 1995, in order to strengthen its position as one of the landowners, the municipal government has required that a payment must be made to itself to validate the land transfer. The payment is equivalent to five years' land use fee at a rate charged to foreign tenants who use land for production and business. This rate is only a fraction of the prevalent land-leasing prices.
6 According to the Urban Planning Act 1989, prior permissions are required for land and property developments. Development applications are evaluated by the planning authority against the Land Use Master Plan. Thereafter, a Land Use Planning Note will be issued with land use planning parameters attached such as land use, plot ratio, site coverage, and building height. When all the formalities for the land transaction are cleared and the land site details finalized, a Land Development Permit is issued. With the permit, the developer can proceed to commission architects to design the building. After the examination of building designs by the planning bureau, a building permit is granted and the project can proceed to the construction stage. This process of development control is the so-called one-note-and-two-permits system.
7 The finding is derived from a sample of 23 cases that was selected from a census of 260 real estate projects developed during the period 1992–2000.
8 When there is a relative land scarcity, land use zoning often determines the price of a piece of land by regulating its use and use intensity. A change to a more productive use and/or a higher density gives rise to a higher land price, other things being equal. In public land leasing, the price of land leasehold is determined by its land use and density. While zoning takes into consideration the community's environmental and infrastructural capacities, changing land use and raising land use density directly impact on the community. Having higher land use density without paying for it means that these negative externalities are not internalized. Rent is created when individuals gain at the expense of the community.
9 In a case of site clearance, it took 11 months to settle the relocation of 281 households and 16 *danwei* land users on a site of 1.53ha.
10 It has been estimated that the office vacancy rate reached about 40 percent in December 1997 (Jackson, 1997).

11 Class A means the best quality, international-standard office space among the three classes. The other two are Class B and Class C.
12 Rent-seeking inevitably implicates government officials in charge of land allocation. Between 1999 and 2002, there were 549,000 cases of corruption involved with land deals, and 3,800 officials were accused nationwide (http://www.people.com.cn/GB/2014899.html; accessed September 24, 2003). All the costs incurred by the institution of ambiguous property rights are increasingly becoming greater than its benefits.
13 The Ministry of Land Resources has finalized regulations governing public land leasing in its Decree 11 issued on May 9, 2002 (http://www.people.com.cn/GB/14857/15305/25695/25909/25914/1974602.html; accessed July 24, 2003). (http://www.peopledaily.com.cn/GB/shizheng/16/20010531/478475.html; accessed May 31, 2001).
14 Decree 11 [2002] regulates land leasing through auction and bidding. Decree 21 [2003] regulates land leasing through negotiation. Decree 71 [2004] requires that Decree 11 should be applied to all previous land-leasing cases and those outstanding cases should be settled by August 31, 2004. In October 2004, Prime Minister Wen Jiabao spoke to local land bureau cadres on the central government's determination to manage national land assets effectively. The State Council released a document about strict controls over land leasing in December 2004.

References

Bank of Communications (1993) *Practical manual of investment* (2nd ed.). Shanghai: Shanghai Culture Publishing House. (in Chinese).
Bertaud, A. & Renaud, B. (1994) *Cities without land markets: Location and land use in the socialist city*. Policy Research Working Paper 1477. Washington, DC: World Bank.
Booth, P. (1996) *Controlling development: Certainty and discretion in Europe, the USA and Hong Kong*. London: UCL Press.
Bowers, J. (1992) The economics of planning gain: A re-appraisal. *Urban Studies*, 29(8): 1329–1339.
Brennan, E. M. (1993) Urban land and housing issues facing the Third World, in J. D. Kasarda and A. M. Parnell (eds.) *Third world cities: Problems, policies and prospects*, 74–91. Newbury Park, CA: Sage Publications.
Broadman, H. G. (1995) *Meeting the challenge of Chinese enterprise reform*. Washington, DC: World Bank.
Chengdu Bureau of Statistics (CDBS) (2002) *Chengdu Statistical Yearbook, 2001*. Beijing: China Statistics Press. (in Chinese).
Du, J. (1999) The choices faced by urban villages in the new millennium. *City Planning Review*, 23(9): 15–17. (in Chinese).
French, R. A. & Hamilton, F. E. I. (1979) Is there a socialist city? in R. A. French & F. E. I. Hamilton (eds.) *The socialist city – Spatial structure and urban policy*, 1–21. Chichester: John Wiley & Sons.
Fung, K. I. (1981) Urban sprawl in China: Some causative factors, in L. J. C. Ma & E. W. Hanten (eds.) *Urban development in modern China*, 194–221. Boulder, CO: Westview Press.
Fung, K. I., Yan, Z. M. & Ning, Y. M. (1992) Shanghai: China's world city, in Y. M. Yeung & X. W. Hu (eds.) *China's coastal cities: Catalysts for modernization*, 124–152. Honolulu: University of Hawaii Press.
Guangzhou Bureau of Statistics (GZBS) (2002) *Guangzhou Statistical Yearbook, 2001*. Beijing: China Statistics Press. (in Chinese).

Haila, A. (1999) Why is Shanghai building a giant speculative property bubble? *International Journal of Urban and Regional Research*, 23(3): 583–588.
Harvey, J. (1987) *Urban land economics*. London: Macmillan.
Heiner, R. A. (1983) The origin of predictable behaviour. *American Economic Review*, 73: 560–595.
Hu, J. & Zhang, G. H. (2000) Large scale urban redevelopment in the 1990s – Empirical survey of Jing'an District. *Urban Planning Forum*, 4: 47–54. (in Chinese).
Huang, F. X. (1991). Planning in Shanghai. *Habitat International*, 15(3): 87–98.
Huangpu Investment & Development Company (1997) *Investment in Huangpu*, (marketing brochure). Shanghai: Huangpu Investment & Development Company.
Iskander, M. (1996) Improving state-owned enterprise performance: Recent international experience, in H. G. Broadman (ed.) *Policy options for reform of Chinese state-owned enterprises*, 17–86. Washington, DC: World Bank.
Jackson, D. G. (1997) *Asia Pacific property trends: Conditions and forecasts*. New York: McGraw-Hill Books.
Jin, D. (1999) A survey on urban villages. *City Planning Review*, 23(9): 8–14. (in Chinese).
Jud, G. D. (1980) The effects of zoning on single-family residential property values. *Land Economics*, 56: 142–154.
Lee, H. S. (1998) DBS Land's Shanghai bet. *Business Times* (Singapore), 5 May.
Lin, S. (2000) *Too many fees and too many charges: China streamlines its fiscal system*. Background Brief No. 66, East Asian Institute, National University of Singapore.
Lü, X. & Perry, E. J. (1997) Introduction, in X. Lü & E. J. Perry (eds.) *Danwei: The changing Chinese workplace in historical and comparative perspective*, 3–17. Armonk, NY: M. E. Sharpe.
Marcuse, P. (1996) Privatization and its discontents: Property rights in land and housing in the transition in eastern Europe, in G. Andrusz, M. Harloe & I. Szelenyi (eds.) *Cities after socialism: Urban and regional change and conflict in post-socialist societies*, 119–191. Oxford: Blackwell.
National Bureau of Statistics, China (NBSC) (1991, 1995, 1996, 2001) *China statistical yearbook*. Beijing: China Statistics Press. (in Chinese).
North, D. C. (1990) *Institutions, institutional change and economic performance*. Cambridge: Cambridge University Press.
Research Institute of Communist Party's History (2018) *Break through: Oral history of Shanghai's public leasing of urban land*. Shanghai: Shanghai People's Press.
Rose, F. C. (1999) Consideration of urban development paths and processes in China since 1978, with special reference to Shanghai, in G. P. Chapman, A. K. Dutt & R. W. Bradnock (eds.), *Urban growth and development in Asia, making the cities*, Vol. I, 82–107. Hants: Aldershot.
Shanghai Municipal Bureau of Statistics (SMBS) (1989a – 2003a) *Shanghai real estate market, 1988–2002*. Beijing: China Statistics Press. (in Chinese).
Shanghai Municipal Bureau of Statistics (SMBS) (1986b – 2015b) *Shanghai statistical yearbook, 1985–2014*. Beijing: China Statistics Press. (in Chinese).
Shanghai Pudong New Area Administration (1993) *Shanghai Pudong new area handbook*. Shanghai: Shanghai Far East Publishers. (in Chinese).
Shantou Bureau of Statistics (STBS) (2000) *Shantou statistical yearbook, 1999*. Beijing: China Statistics Press. (in Chinese).
Sun, S. W. and Deng, Y. C. (1997) A Study of the role of urban planning in Shanghai. *Urban Planning Forum*, 2: 31–39. (in Chinese).

Tang, Z. L. (1986) Resident relocation in Shanghai central city. *Urban Planning Forum*, 41: 12–21. (in Chinese).
Wang, H. K. & Hung, C. T. (1997) *Shanghai's industrial relocation under land marketization: A case study on Shanghai electrical instrument works*. Paper presented at the International Symposium on Marketization of Land and Housing in Socialist China, organized by Hong Kong Baptist University, October/November. (in Chinese).
Wang, J. (2009) 'Art in capital': Shaping distinctiveness in a culture-led urban regeneration project in Red Town, Shanghai. *Cities*, 26: 318–330.
Wang, S. & Hu, A. (2001) *The Chinese economy in crisis: State capacity and tax reform*. Armonk, NY: M.E. Sharpe.
Williamson, O. E. (1985) *The economic institutions of capitalism: Firms, markets, relational contracting*. New York: The Free Press.
World Bank (1993) *China: Urban land management in an emerging market economy*. Washington, DC: The World Bank.
World Bank (2002) *Building institutions for markets: World Development Report 2002*. New York: Oxford University Press.
Wu, F. L. (2002) China's changing urban governance in the transition towards a more market-oriented economy. *Urban Studies*, 39(7): 1071–1093.
Wuhan Bureau of Statistics (WHBS) (2002) *Wuhan statistical yearbook, 2001*. Beijing: China Statistics Press. (in Chinese).
Xu, H. X. (2003). *Avenue Joffre – Huaihai Lu*. Shanghai: Shanghai Academy of Social Sciences Press (in Chinese).
Yeh, A. G. O. & Li, X. (1999) Economic development and agricultural land loss in the Pearl River Delta, China. *Habitat International*, 23(3): 373–390.
Yeung, Y. M. & Li, X. J. (1999) Bargaining with transnational corporations: The case of Shanghai. *International Journal of Urban and Regional Research*, 23(3): 513–533.
Zhao, M., Bao, G. L. & Hou, L. (1998) *Reforms of land use system and development of cities and the country*. Shanghai: Tongji University Press. (in Chinese).
Zhu, J. M. (1999a) The formation of a market-oriented local property development industry in transitional China: A Shenzhen case study. *Environment and Planning A*, 31(10): 1839–1856.
Zhu, J. M. (1999b) Local growth coalition: The context and implications of China's gradualist urban land reforms. *International Journal of Urban and Regional Research*, 23(3): 534–548.
Zhu, J. M. (2004) Local developmental state and order in China's urban development during transition. *International Journal of Urban and Regional Research*, 28(2): 424–447.

6 Bottom-up rural spatial changes under an uncertain institution of collective land rights

Rural industrialization has been a critical movement for rural development in China. Marketization had provided once-in-a-lifetime opportunities for township-village enterprises to grow and flourish since the late 1970s. Nonagricultural economies are positively correlated to the village incomes, though rural industrialization did not occur evenly in all regions. In situ urbanization becomes phenomenal as rural nonagriculturalizaion takes hold in the two dynamic regions of Yangtze River Delta and Pearl River Delta, where peasants 'leave the fields without leaving the countryside, and enter the factories without entering the city'. Bottom-up rural nonagricultural development shows intriguing patterns of intensive mixture of agricultural and nonagricultural land uses, suggesting highly fragmented in situ urbanization. The collective land rights that are conducive to farming become problematic when the villages are urbanizing as the accentuated land rent differentials are contested between the urban state as a de jure owner and the rural collective as a de facto landholder. With the closure of collectively owned village enterprises, an informal institutional change from below makes autonomous villages a rentier class, relying on extraction of land rent. Environment integrity is worsened by land use fragmentation, which prompts private governance in the face of collective commons in the suburbs.

Rural industrialization

As an old agrarian civilization, China has gone through a long journey in its rural development. Nonagriculturalization has been proved the only option for raising rural incomes that remain stubbornly low in the long China's history so that villages have become a synonym of poverty (Fei, 1939), though cottage industries and household handcraft businesses had been helpful marginally. It is echoed by the experiences of many other land-scarce agricultural regions that have to search for nonfarm income sources (Bryceson, 1996; de Janvry and Sadoulet, 2001; Reardon, Berdegué, and Escobar, 2001; Singh and Dhillon, 2004). Rural-urban divide, which prohibited free migration from the countryside to cities, also contributed to rural poverty. In 1952, agricultural outputs accounted for 50.5 percent of the national GDP, but the farming labors represented 83.5 percent of the labor forces. Even in 1978 did the former decline to 28.1 percent, while the latter still remained as high as 70.5 percent (NBSC, 2000). The high redundancy of farming workers in the agricultural sector had been evident. One of the positive effects of the Great Leap Forward (1958–1960) was the initiation of rural industrialization where 'commune and brigade industries' (*shedui gongye*), using local materials and rural labors, were established to support agricultural production (Byrd and Lin, 1990). 'Walking on two legs' (*liangtiao tui zoulu*) was the policy that advocated parallel development of large, modern manufacturing in cities and small, primitive industrial production in the countryside. According to Marxist ideology, it was believed that rural industrialization could lead to the erasure of three great differences: between the city and the countryside, between industrial and agricultural production, and between manual and mental labors.

The bold new program Household Production Responsibility Scheme,[1] implemented since the early 1980s, constituted a powerful engine for the rural economy and there was, thereafter, significant improvement in farm productivity (Putterman, 1993). However, the problem of surplus labor was exacerbated because of the improvement in farming efficiency. Marketization provided a historical opportunity for the township-village enterprises (TVEs) (*xiangzhen qiye*) to grow and to flourish, and the TVE movement has been officially endorsed as a key strategy for rural development since 1984 (CARD/RUC and SST/NBSC, 2006). In 1976, there were 1.1 million rural enterprises employing 17.9 million workers and producing a total gross income of ¥27 billion (Chang and Kwok, 1990). In 1993, 24.5 million rural enterprises were in operation, and employing 123.5 million workers with industrial product of ¥3,154 billion. In 1994, production of TVEs represented about 38 percent of the nation's total industrial product, whereas it was only 9 percent in 1978 (Chang and Wang, 1994; Wong and Yang, 1995). The contribution of rural industries to the total rural income overtook that of agriculture in 1987 at the national level (Oi, 1999), which should count as the most important hallmark in the long history of agrarian China. Rural industries have become one of the major forces transforming peasants' lives and building up a local social service system. The ratio of nonfarming sectors in the total township economy is clearly positively correlated with GDP per capita in the townships of Jiangsu Province, one of the provinces with most advanced rural economies (see Figure 6.1).

Yonglian village, one of the rising stars of rural industrialization in China, is a case in illustration. Located in the Yangtze River Delta, it was a new settlement built on the reclaimed land of 78.3 hectares from alluvium along the river of Yangtze in 1971, with 766 settlers (192 households) coming to make a living from nearby poor villages. Village population expanded to 820 (227 households) in 1984 when the Household Production Responsibility Scheme was implemented. Subsequently, a total of 650 *mu* farmland was equally distributed to the villagers, and farmland holding per capita was as low as 0.79 *mu*. Needless to say, the village needed to diversify into nonagricultural economies to survive. Eight small TVEs were already in operation by 1984, employing 120-odd villagers. Set up in August 1984, Yonglian Iron and Steel, the

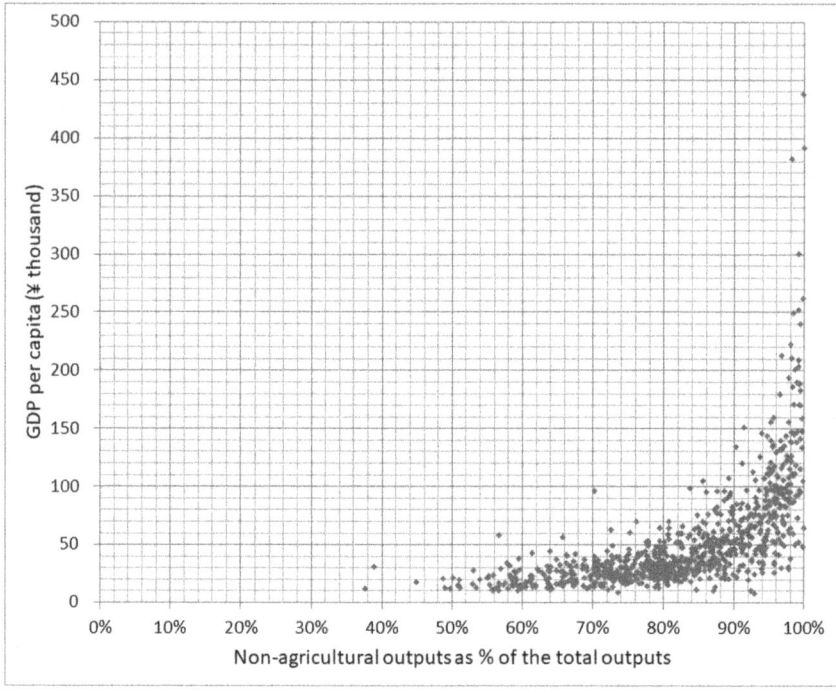

Figure 6.1 Correlation between nonagricultural economies and rural GDP per capita in Jiangsu province, 2014.

firm that has made the village well known for rural development, employed 145 workers initially. By 2012, it hired 13,100 employees, in which 5,906 ones were migrants, while the expanded village had a population of 10,593. The village GDP reached at ¥38 billion in 2016 (http://journal.crnews.net/zgcz/2017n/d4q/zgczsl/60812_20170508024400.html, accessed August 18, 2018), while the village aggregated income was only ¥56,000 in 1978 (Compiling Committee of the History of Yonglian Village, 2015). Established as a collective village firm in the beginning, Yonglian Iron and Steel has been changed to shareholding, with the Yonglian village holding 25 percent of the shares. The enterprise is privatized, but the village collective remains one of the largest owners. Business and shareholding income stood at 84.0 percent of the total income for the village collectives in Nanfeng township, where Yonglian is a subordinate (2015). Only 10.9 percent of village households were still engaged with farming in 2015, full-time or part-time, and agricultural income only accounted for 0.6 percent of the villages' economic incomes (2012) (Bureau of Agriculture, Municipality of Zhangjiagang, 2016).

Market opportunities were abundant, and those villages that could grab the opportunities with their own entrepreneurs and geographical links to the markets developed industries for the village economies. Unfortunately, rural industrialization did not occur evenly to all regions, and a regional disparity was clearly displayed in a similar pattern as national economic development where the east region is the most dynamic and the west region the least sanguine (see Table 6.1). It is observed that there is a positive correlation between urban industrialization and rural nonagricultural development in its jurisdiction. Measured by the interprovincial Gini coefficient, TVE outputs (0.604) were spatially more uneven than GDP (0.408) (1994). It suggested that TVEs were more market driven than the general economy at provincial level. Rural nonagricultural growth is exogenous, depending on regional industrial advantages. Determined by the favorable market conditions and the availability of village entrepreneurship, rural industrialization or bottom-up in-situ urbanization was basically unfolded in the dynamic coastal region (Yangtze River Delta and Pearl River Delta, in particular) and the suburbs around large cities.

In hindsight, the 1980s was the only historical window conducive to rural collective industrialization when urban state-owned enterprises were still shackled by the old central planning regime. The urban reform, led by state-owned-enterprise transformation and inward private firms since the early 1990s, took its toll on the rural collective industrialization. Collective TVEs reached the zenith in the mid-1990s, when the manufacturing became increasingly globalized in China. Rudimentary village enterprises faced increasingly hard competition from inward foreign and private firms which had industrial expertise and modern technologies. Unable to compete in the market, village industries were either bankrupt or privatized consequently (Che and Qian, 1998; Vermeer, 1999). In 2011, production of TVEs only accounted for 1.3 percent of nation's total industrial outputs (NBSC, 2012). Most privatized enterprises stay put in the rural areas as the new owners are mostly village entrepreneurs who are attached to their home locales. Miraculous rise of rural industries has, nevertheless,

Table 6.1 Nonagricultural jobs as a percentage of rural population in China's five regions, 1987, 1996, and 2011

Region	1987	1996	2011
	percent		
East*	13.7	19.0	34.7
Central^	9.6	14.7	14.7
Southwest#	5.9	8.0	10.4
Northwest@	6.8	12.5	9.2
Northeast&	10.9	16.9	12.6

Notes: *Beijing, Tianjin, Hebei, Shandong, Jiangsu, Shanghai, Zhejiang, Fujian, Guangdong, Hainan. ^Shanxi, Henan, Anhui, Hubei, Jiangxi, and Hunan. #Sichuan, Chongqing, Yunnan, Guizhou, and Guangxi. @Xinjiang; Xizang, Qinghai, Neimenggu, Gansu, Ningxia, and Shannxi. &Heilongjiang; Jilin; and Liaoning.
Source: Compiling Committee for Annual Yearbook of China's Township and Village Enterprises, 1988, 1997, 2012

130 *Bottom-up rural spatial changes*

improved the life of numerous peasants significantly. Unexpected fall of rural industries has also led to a search of new forms of rural growth.

In situ urbanization: bottom-up rural development

Since the economic reforms, nonagricultural economies in the rural counties have been growing significantly, though with regional variations (see Figures 6.2 and 6.3), and free rural-urban migration transforming agricultural labors to urban workers. The share of rural population remains, however, relatively high (see Table 6.2). As a very successful county in transforming the economic structure, Kunshan has changed itself from a rural economy to an industrial one. Its rural population still accounted for 45.5 percent of the total (see Table 6.3), but only 8.0 percent of the workforces registered as rural were engaged in farming and 92.0 percent were employed in nonagricultural sectors in 2015. While 30 years earlier in 1985 63.3 percent of rural workforces were tilling the land. Nonagriculturalization in the rural region gives rise to in-situ urbanization that is well pronounced in the two dynamic regions of Yangtze River Delta and Pearl River Delta, where peasants 'leave the fields without leaving the countryside, and enter the factories without entering the city' (*litu bu lixiang, jinchang bu*

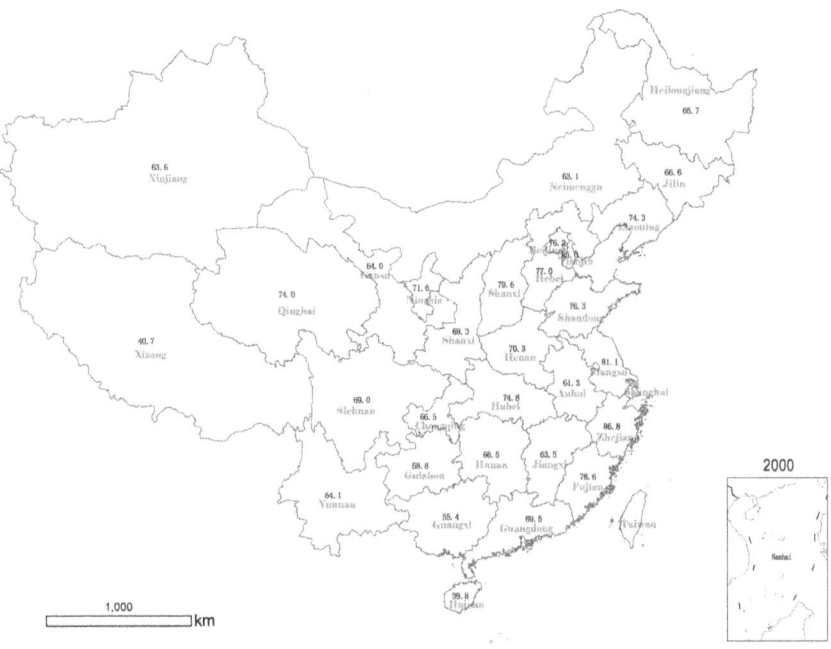

Figure 6.2 Nonagricultural sectors as a percentage of the county's economies at the provincial level, 2000.

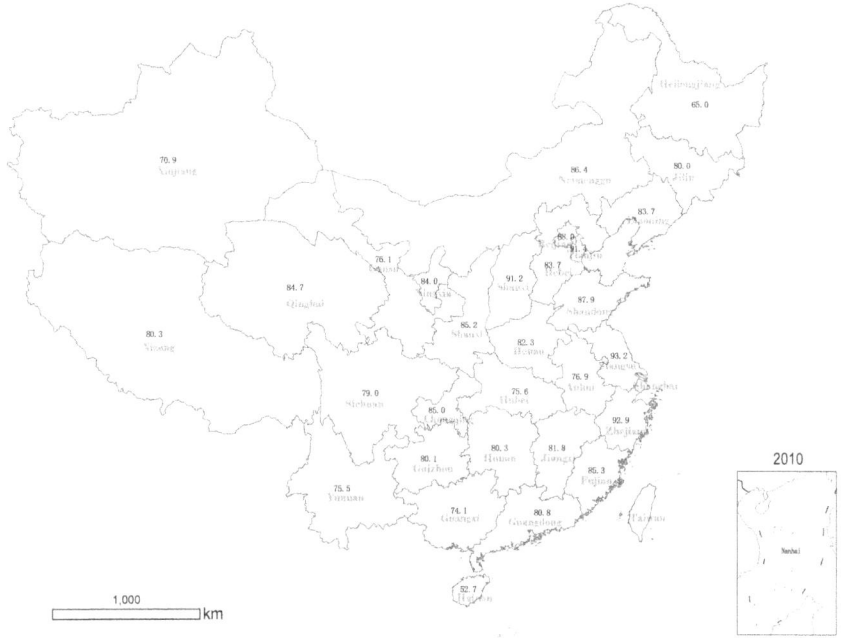

Figure 6.3 Nonagricultural sectors as a percentage of the county's economies at the provincial level, 2010.

Table 6.2 The shares of agricultural outputs, labors, and population in the national total

	1978	1995	2015
Agricultural outputs as % of the national GDP	28.1	19.6	8.8
Agricultural labors as % of the total labor forces	70.5	52.2	28.3
Rural population as % of the total population	82.1	71.0	43.9

Source: NBSC, 2017

Table 6.3 Agricultural outputs and rural population as % of Kunshan's total

	1978	1995	2008	2015
Agricultural outputs as % of GDP	51.4	10.5	1.1	0.9
Rural population as % of the total population	82.0	64.7	64.2	45.5

Source: KSBS, 2017

jincheng). There are two fronts in China's urbanization. One is urban expansion managed by the urban state; the other is rural nonagricultural developments initiated by the village collective. Two quintessential characteristics about rural in-situ urbanization need to be borne in mind. One is that bottom-up nonagricultural developments occur on the collectively owned land, and the other is that rural entities could conduct development projects only within their own jurisdictions.

Townships are at the bottom of the state administration system. Market towns are the places where rural produce is exchanged and industrial products are brought to the rural consumers. Social interactions and commercial transactions convene in the towns where villagers are exposed to outside worlds beyond their daily communal life. Those craftsmen with skills usually settle down in towns to offer their services that are not available in the villages. It is the spirit of contract, rather than clan and lineage, that governs the towns. Considered as the tail of urban societies and the head of rural hinterland (*xiangshou chengwei*), market towns are the nodes linking urban economies to rural villages. There were about 40,000 towns between 3,000 cities and 3.8 million villages in China (NBSC, 2017). Towns are responsible for rural development. TVEs as a significant initiative of the rural development represent two key actors in the rural domain: townships and villages. The organization of villages is conducive to farming, but nonagricultural economies are integrative beyond the boundaries of villages and even townships. Townships are considered more appropriate than villages for the coordination of integrative rural industrialization based on rational choice in the rural domain, and township governments can impose an institution of land use planning on the town jurisdiction across small villages' boundaries to coordinate nonfarming land uses. Thus, nonagricultural economies would be less fragmented than the case managed by the villages. But in reality, interests always prevail over rationality.

Villages in China are a unique geographically tied unit of social organization. Due to farmland resources made increasingly scarce by the burgeoning population growth, resulting in subsistence farming as a principal mode of rural agriculture, villages have developed a keen sense of territoriality in the face of constricted economic opportunities and perennial political disorder (Dong, 1992). Based on clan and lineage, villages had become a basic autonomous socioeconomic unit, increasingly introverted and hostile to migrants. There were solidarity and coordination within the rural community that was managed by the village gentries before the 1949 revolution (Skinner, 1971; Duara, 1988). The People's Commune movement strengthened the nature of China's villages as a basic collective community and transformed villages into a collective economic entity (Li, 2009). Village's social services (health, education, and elderly welfare) and infrastructure were mainly the responsibilities of the village itself (Wong, 1997; Tsai, 2007).

Because of high population density and land scarcity, villages tend to be small in area. The reform of Household Production Responsibility Scheme splits farmland within the village boundary equally between the village families and thus incurs farmland fragmentation. Fragmented farming may not be a great problem as the collective farming of scale has failed disastrously to the extent that peasants cannot even feed themselves. By the same token, village-initiated nonagricultural economic activities have to be conducted on the village's own land parcels if without township's coordination, leading to fragmented industrial land development. Fragmented nonagricultural land uses should not be a cause for concern if population density is low. Various modes of land development actually give rise to diversity in the built-up environment. But it becomes a serious challenge when environmental integrity and optimal utilization of scarce land resources are seriously compromised in the setting of autonomous and compartmentalized village nonagriculturalization.

According to a nationwide survey in 1992, only 8 percent of rural industrial enterprises were located in town areas, while 92 percent were in villages. It seems that villages are in the leading position for managing their nonagricultural economies as use rights over agricultural land are with the villages. Privatization of TVEs since the mid-1990s has changed the locational pattern, and 22 percent of rural industrial enterprises were located in town areas in 2002 (CARD/RUC and SST/NBSC, 2006). However, in the advanced Yangtze River Delta region, it appears that towns are leading the rural industrialization. In Wuxi, Jiangsu province, about 55 percent of rural industries in terms of outputs were situated in the town areas (WBST/IER/CSSA, 1999).

Bottom-up rural nonagricultural development: spatial patterns

Intensified competition for land is well reflected in the areas where the process of urbanization is unfolding in the forms of land development and redevelopment. The process of urbanization, incorporating social, economic, and physical transformations, often takes places in the form of urban activities penetrating into rural areas. Continuous urban expansion creates constant rural-urban interactions, which are conceptualized as suburbanization, urban fringe, edge cities, and so on in various socioeconomic contexts (Adell, 1999). The urban fringe becomes a transitional zone between the city and the countryside, in which urban and rural land uses are often mixed (Thomas, 1974). The term 'edge cities' was coined by Garreau (1991) to refer to urban agglomerations emerging in the urban periphery. The most profound and intriguing changes for many Asian developing countries occur in the suburbs where rural areas located on the urban outskirts become more urban in terms of economic structure, social fabric, and physical appearance, while the areas in question still, by and large, remain as villages. McGee (1991) coined the term '*desakota*', which captures the unique feature of transformation of rural areas in Asian developing countries in the context of high population density – that is, intense mixture of agricultural and nonagricultural land uses in the urban periphery. China's rapid urbanization since 1980 has been a process of transformation of its land and people: rural peasants have been turned into urban residents, and agricultural land to urban land. In China's suburban areas, it also entails institutional transition from the rural collective landownership to the urban state landownership. The land conversion takes place extensively at the peripheries or in the suburbs of metropolises, where competition for land between urban governments and rural villages is explicitly demonstrated. Three cases of Beiqijia, Kunshan and Nanhai are presented as follows to illustrate the interactions.

Being the political capital for many dynasties throughout history, Beijing has become the capital of the People's Republic of China and grown substantially along with socialist industrialization since 1949 (Ding, 2004). The municipality of Beijing was composed of the suburbs of nine counties and the central city of nine districts. In 1999 the administrative status of seven suburban counties was converted to that of city districts. It is believed that this conversion was to enable Beijing central city to annex suburban spaces to its purview of citywide planning and to facilitate city expansion and rural-urban integration (Ma, 2005). As a result, Changping county has become a district. Within the jurisdiction of Changping district, Beiqijia township is located to the north of Beijing city center and consists of 21 administrative villages (see Figure 6.4).

Figure 6.4 Beiqijia in Beijing municipality.

Since the 1990s, Beiqijia has been one of the most dynamic townships in Beijing, experiencing rapid population increase and economic growth. During the period 1990–2002, its GDP rose from ¥123 million to ¥355 million – an average annual growth rate of 9 percent. In 2002 the total population was 232,000, consisting of 26,000 local peasants (11 percent), 128,000 permanent migrants (55 percent), and 78,000 temporary migrants (34 percent) (CAUPD, 2003). Most of the permanent migrants were Beijing residents who had purchased private housing built in Beiqijia and were thus relocated from the central city to the suburbs; migrants mainly came from other provinces to seek temporary jobs in Beijing. In 1997 there were only 34,000 residents; five years later, the total population had increased by 277 percent: the number of local residents grew by 56 percent, and the number of migrants rose by a factor of 11 (CAUPD, 2003). Beiqijia has been subject to a rapid process of urbanization: in 2002, after a decade of socioeconomic transformation, its agricultural sector contributed less than 20 percent to its GDP, and 89 percent of its population were nonlocal and nonagricultural workers.

By the end of 2002, 38.9 percent of the total area of Beiqijia (60.5 square kilometers) was in nonagricultural land use, and only 61.1 percent of land was used for farming (see Table 6.4 and Figure 6.5). The spatial pattern of land uses shows a mixture of agricultural and nonagricultural ones, suggesting an intriguing pattern of development. This mixed land use pattern should be viewed in the perspective that Beiqijia is a high-density township, at 3,800 residents per square kilometer. An intensive mix of urban and rural land uses is conducive to neither urban living nor rural farming, as effective provision of facilities for living and farming requires urban compactness and contiguous farmland.

Kunshan was a county where agriculture predominated until 1989, when it was administratively designated as a county-level municipality with a territory of

Table 6.4 Land uses in Beiqijia township, 2002

Categories of land uses		Area (km^2)	As % of the total area
Total area of Beiqijia Township		60.5	100.0
Nonagricultural land		23.5	38.9
In which:	Collectively owned non-agricultural	10.5	44.4
	land in which: Rural residential land	5.8	
	Industrial land	3.4	
	Expressway (state-owned)	1.9	8.2
	Urban housing land in which: Public	8.1	34.4
	housing	2.7	
	Private housing	5.4	
	State-owned nonagricultural land*	3.0	12.9
Agricultural land		36.9	61.1

Note
* land acquired before the 1990s by state-owned enterprises and institutes.
Source: CAUPD, 2003

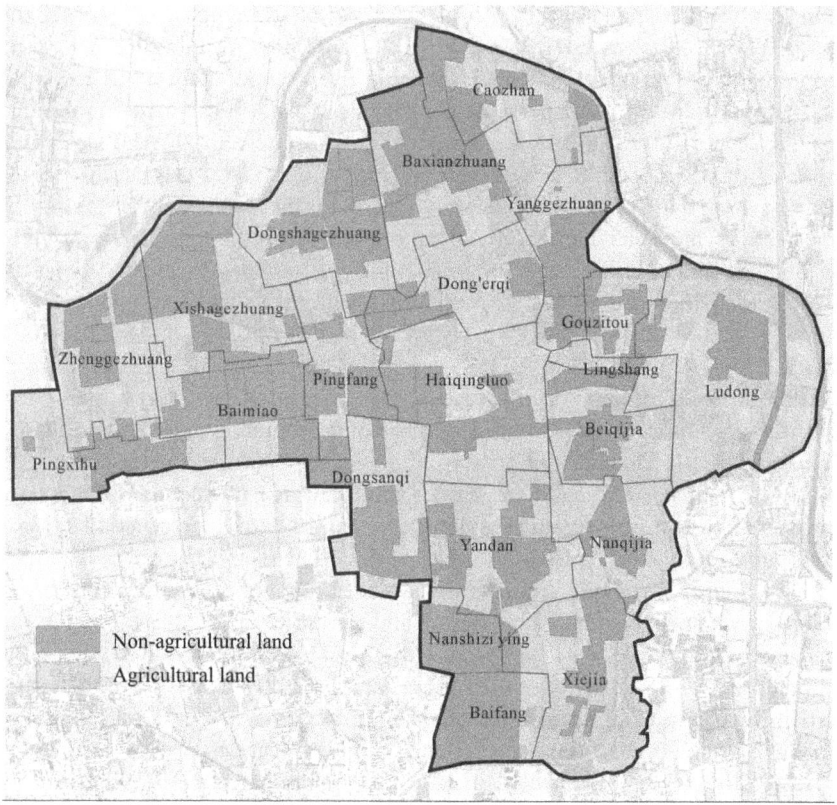

Figure 6.5 Agricultural and nonagricultural land uses in 21 villages, Beiqijia township.

921.3 square kilometers. It is located to the east of Suzhou and to the west of Shanghai, sandwiched between two economic powerhouses in the Yangtze River Delta (see Figure 6.6). Economic and social progress in Kunshan since the 1980s has been one of the great stories of success in the context of economic liberation and globalized production (see Table 6.5). The development of rural industries in Kunshan picked up its pace from the early 1980s. Villages made tremendous bottom-up efforts to bring in industrial expertise from elsewhere (Marton, 2000). The efforts paid off quickly. There were 335 TVEs in operation in 1985, accounting for 67.7 percent of the total 495 industrial firms in Kunshan, and manufacturing contributed 50 percent to the county GDP, while agriculture contributed 31 percent (KSBS, 1985).

Rural industries became the backbone of the county economy. The share in the total industrial output contributed by the TVEs increased from 59.5 percent (1985) to 70.6 percent (1990) and further to 74.9 percent (1995) (KSBS, 1985, 1990, 1995). The rural agricultural county economy has been significantly

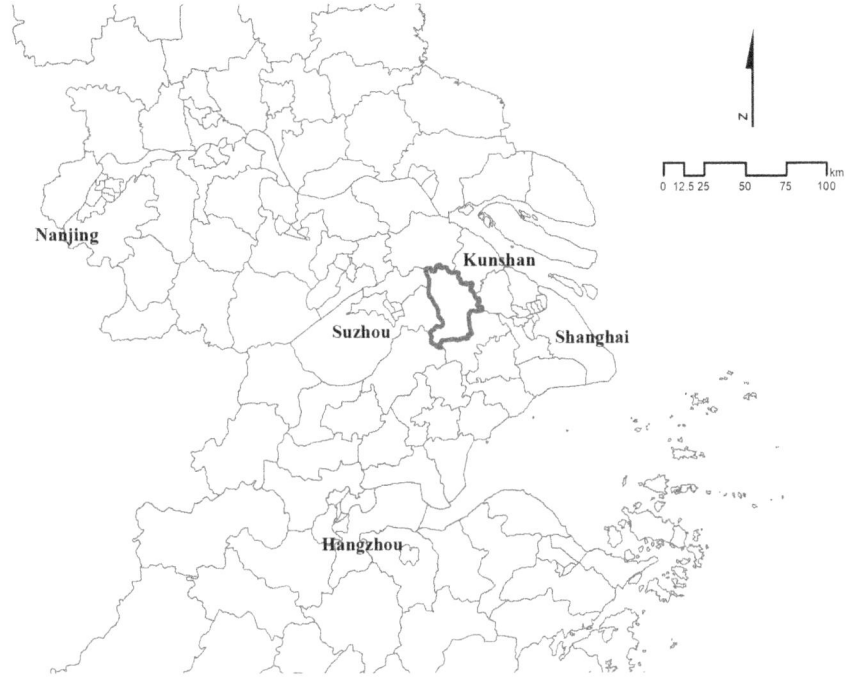

Figure 6.6 Kunshan in the Yangtze River Delta.

Table 6.5 Economic, social, and physical changes over the period 1970–2010, Kunshan

		1970	1980	1990	2000	2010
Locals (with *hukou*, thousand)		483.3	523.5	564.6	594.6	711.3
Migrants (without *hukou*, thousand)		0	0	10.1	131.3	1212.6
GDP (¥ billion)		0.1	0.3	2.0	20.1	210.0
GDP structure (%)	Agriculture	58	44	23	6	1
	Manufacturing	19	42	56	59	64
	Services	23	14	21	35	35
rural *hukou* : urban *hukou*, (%)		90:10	87:13	82:18	53:47	–
built-up land : farmland (%)		–	–	3.2:96.8	11.7:88.3	28.3:72.7

Source: KSBS, 1970–2011

transformed into an industrial economy, with agriculture only accounting for a negligible 1 percent of the city GDP in 2010, while farming was still the main pillar (44 percent) in 1980. The substantially expanded economy as of 2010 not only supported the city's local population of 0.7 million but also accommodated 1.2 million migrant workers. All this drastic economic change started from meager rural industries in the early 1970s.

138 Bottom-up rural spatial changes

It was revealed by 1990 data that an average administrative village in Kunshan, composed of several natural villages, had 1,200 villagers in an area of 200 hectares (KSBS, 1990). Autonomous village development gave rise to piecemeal rural industrialization with factories and workshops scattered all over the countryside (*cuncun dianhuo, chuchu maoyan*) (Pei, 2005; Long et al., 2009). A Fragstats[2] patch[3] analysis reveals that when only accounting for 3.2 percent of the total county territory in 1989, the built-up area of 29.6 square kilometers was split into 598 patches, and the size of each patch was only 4.9 hectares on average (see Figure 6.7). Kunshan achieved an economy of ¥210 billion GDP with a total built-up area of 262.3 square kilometers that accounted for 28.3 percent of the total municipal land area in 2010 (KSBS, 2011). Another Fragstats patch analysis shows that the average size of nonagricultural patches reached 33.0 hectares in 2010 and that the total patch numbers declined from 1384 (2000) to 795 (2010) (see Figure 6.7). Spatial fragmentation seems on the mend: contagion index[4] increasing slightly from 39.1 (2005) to 40.2 (2010).

The Pearl River Delta region has been the pioneer of China's new practice of 'reform and openness', and it has become one of the most dynamic regions in the world, known as the 'world's manufacturing factory' (Vogel, 1989). Rapid urbanization manifested by its unprecedented expansion of built-up land is well pronounced (Weng, 2002). With a total area of 41,690 square kilometers, the Pearl River Delta saw its built-up land area increased by 2.9 times between 1988 and 2008, rising from 1765.1 square kilometers to 6816.0 square kilometers (Yang and Yuan, 2010). While the old central cities are restructured substantially, driven by new equilibrium of demand and supply, the rapid urban expansion is

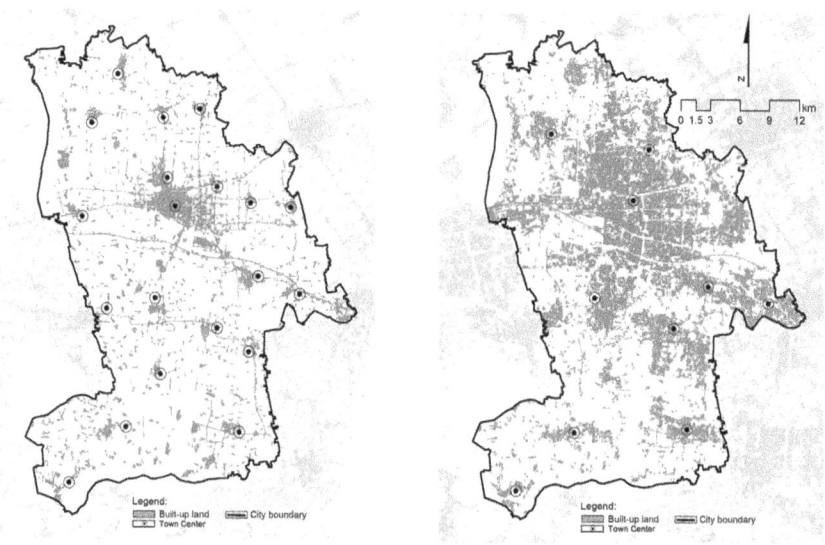

Figure 6.7 Built-up areas in Kunshan, 1989 (L) and 2010 (R).

marked by the extensive land development in the outskirts to accommodate incoming industrial investments and rural-urban migrants. The built environment in the interface between the core cities and traditional rural areas – namely, the peri-urban areas – has been experiencing dramatic change.

Nanhai is located to the immediate west of Guangzhou, the capital city of Guangdong province, and to the north of Foshan central city that is the third-largest city in the Pearl River Delta after Guangzhou and Shenzhen (see Figure 6.8). Nanhai used to be a rural county, and it has become an urban district annexed to Foshan municipality since 2003. Located in the fringe of both central cities, it has been receiving substantial outside investments and becoming a dynamically growing district. From 1982 to 2010, its total gross economic output increased from ¥0.8 billion to ¥179.7 billion (at current prices) at an annual growth rate of 22.2 percent. With the economic development, the total population in 2008 was 2.6 times of that in 1978, reaching 2.1 million, among which 55.8 percent (1.2 million) were local residents with *hukou* and 44.2 percent (0.9 million) were nonresidents working and living temporarily in Nanhai without *hukou* (NHBS, 2011). As a rural county initially, Nanhai has been experiencing rapid urbanization since the 1980s, demonstrated by its extensive and high-speed land conversion from agricultural uses to urban uses. It saw its built-up land area reach 568.8 square kilometers in 2008, rising from 114.5 square kilometers in 1990. The built-up area as a percentage of the total

Figure 6.8 Location of Nanhai in the Pearl River Delta.

140 *Bottom-up rural spatial changes*

land area (1073.9 square kilometers) rose from 10.7 percent in 1990 to 53.0 percent in 2008 (see Figure 6.9).

During the period 1988–2000, 328.3 square kilometers of land, or 30.6 percent of the total territory, was converted from farmland to land for nonagricultural uses, among which 20.8 square kilometers were for rural housing, 153.7 square kilometers for industries, and 60.8 square kilometers for urban and town centers. One phenomenon stands out from the land use statistics in 2008. The bottom-up urbanization is well pronounced as urban built-up land only accounts for one-third of the total, and the remaining two-thirds belong to rural built-up land which is overwhelmingly used by rural housing and industries. The industrial land amounts to 57.0 percent of the total built-up land, and the rural industries take three-quarters of it.

Further analyses reveal that the built-up land has been developed in a spatially dispersed manner. There are 1,776 natural villages in total. On average, each village has an area of about 41 hectares. Village-based industrialization has produced 1,868 industrial land patches spatially dispersed and farmland has been disintegrated into 1,862 patches (see Figure 6.8). A Fragstats patch analysis highlights that farmland has become increasingly fragmented over time, indicated by the gradual fall of the mean patch size from 1,245 hectares to 63 hectares per patch.[5] The continuous dropping off of the contagion index over time from 62.7 to 30.3 shows that Nanhai's landscape is increasingly piecemealed, with farmland and built-up land extensively piecemealed and spatially intermingled. Self-contained development of small villages in terms of land area due to land scarcity and high population density creates, in aggregate, fragmented urbanization.

Institution: the collective land rights

The three cases have shown that rural nonagricultural developments generate a spatial structure of intensive mixture of farming and nonfarming land uses, and it does not seem conducive to either urban living or rural farming. Built

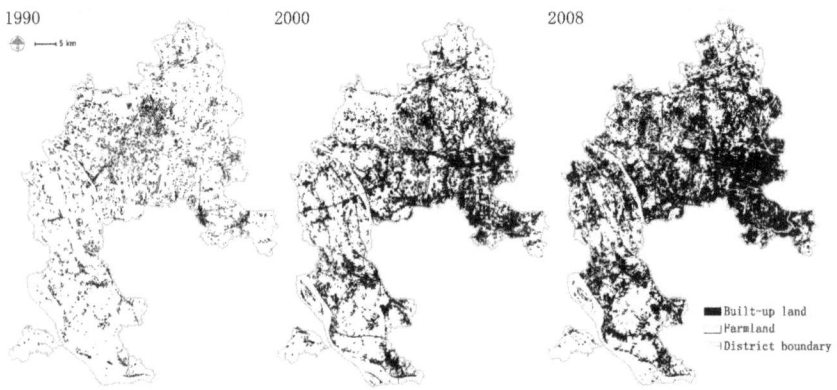

Figure 6.9 Development of the built-up areas in Nanhai, 1990–2008.

environments are created within an institutional structure where land rights in a setting of high population density and acute land scarcity are significantly formative. The Cooperative Movement abolished the private ownership of farmland and replaced it with collective ownership officially in 1956. It has become a defining moment for the villages in the socialist era. According to China's Constitution (1998), urban land is owned by the state, and rural land is collectively owned by rural communities. A survey of land resources in 1996 found that 53 percent of China's territory was owned by the state, and 46 percent by the collectives. The remaining 1 percent is unclear as to whether ownership resides with the state or the collective (Ho and Lin, 2003). However, China's collective land rights are a unique institution. The idiosyncrasy of the collective landownership is that it is based on the Marxist doctrine that land should be treated as a means of production, not an economic asset.[6]

Land is owned by the rural communities on the condition that it is only used for economic production. The rural collective could convert farming land to nonagricultural uses for public facilities (schools, clinics, etc.), village housing, rural industries, retail premises, and so on used by villagers themselves (Byrd and Lin, 1990). Pursuing higher income-yielding activities is in the best interests of the agricultural community (Ho and Lin, 2003). Rural industrialization has thus stimulated growth of nonagricultural land uses, on the one hand. On the other hand, loss of arable land is also aggravated by rapid urbanization driven by the drastic economic transformation. Concerned with potential large-scale agricultural land loss and security for food supply, the central government in its Land Management Law (1986) (see http://www.china.org.cn/english/environment/34345.htm, accessed June 27, 2015) promulgates centralization of the management over rural land development for nonagricultural uses to the government at the county level or above (Ash and Edmonds, 1998; Brown, 1995; Smil, 1999; Lin and Ho, 2005). The greater the area of land conversion, the higher level of the authority from whom the approval should be sought. Moreover, there is a control mechanism of annual quotas set by the central government to limit the amount of land conversion. Annual quotas are distributed downward, from provinces to counties, according to land use plans at various government levels, and the limitation of land lost to nonagricultural uses is hierarchically centralized. Collective landownership is thus emphasized as the collective has neither the right to derive income from land by letting it out nor the right to change its form and substance by developing it for nonagricultural activities without approval from the government at the county level or above. The right to develop rural land for village industries should be granted by the urban state (Byrd and Lin, 1990). The right to alienate collective land is restricted to the situation where the other party in the transaction should be the state (Lin and Ho, 2005).

Rural China is managed by a three-tiered governance system, which was composed of commune, brigade, and team. This has become a cornerstone for the rural collective landownership system. Since collective farming was replaced by the Household Production Responsibility Scheme after the demise of the People's Commune in the early 1980s, the collective landownership has remained vested with the three entities, with only the names being changed: communes, brigades, and teams were replaced by townships (*xiang/zhen*), administrative villages, (*xingzhengcun*), and natural villages (*zirancun*), respectively (Ho, 2001). Ownership of rural land is vested with the collective entities at three hierarchical levels as well. An official maxim describes owners of the collective land as *sanji suoyou, dui wei jichu* (collective ownership belonging to three entities – the commune, the brigade, and the team – and with the team being the basic holder).[7] Thus, the collective landownership is ambiguous to its nominal owners, as how much each entity is entitled to has never been clearly delineated. A nationwide investigation of 271 villages in the late 1990s revealed the perception of collective ownership among the stakeholders: 45 percent of the respondents believed that villages should be the main owners; 40 percent reckoned that administrative villages should be the owners; and 15 percent thought that the owners should be both villages and administrative villages (Cai, 2003). The distribution of compensation fees among the collective owners can reveal empirically the share of each owner. However, it is always obscure, secretive, and ad hoc, and there is no formal formula for application and reference.[8] It is a matter of negotiation and competition. Moreover, demographic boundaries and structures of the natural villages change continuously as new members (through births and marriages) join and existing members drop out (through deaths and emigration). Landowners themselves are a constantly changing variable (Rozelle and Li, 1998).

The collective land rights are also incomplete in that the collective landowners do not autonomously possess the right to develop land or change its agricultural uses to nonagricultural uses unless the urban state grants this right to the collective. Incomplete land rights are reflected in the governance over land use changes as well. As land is a special property because of its intrinsic attributes of location fixity and resultant externalities, land use and development rights have to be defined by land use planning in order to internalize detrimental externalities which may be caused by individual land developments against other land users in the neighborhood. Ex ante designation of land uses and development parameters maintains the landed interests in relation to the neighborhood spatial structure. Land utilization in the rural jurisdiction is autonomously managed by the collective, according to the Land Management Law (1998) (see http://www.china.org.cn/english/environment/34345.htm, accessed June 27, 2015). Although land use planning for villages and market towns, coordinated by the township government, is recommended by the central government in its "Regulations on Management of Village and Market Town Planning and Development" issued on June 29, 1993 (see http://www.jincao.com/fa/law19.20.htm, accessed on June 27, 2015), the proposed land use coordination at the township level is often resisted by villages, which autonomously manage their land resources. As a matter of fact, a statutory land use planning system, considered as an urban institution, has not been established formally in the rural jurisdiction, and land utilization is practically at the discretion of the village heads or villagers themselves. If development control is highly discretionary without necessary certainty, or it does not exist at all, land users and residents do not have the right not to

Bottom-up rural spatial changes 143

be affected by negative externalities generated in the neighborhood, especially when residential density and land use intensity are on the rise.

The villagers as members of the collective owners are explicitly entitled to: the use right over farmland allocated to them under the Household Production Responsibility Scheme and the right to residual income of farming, the use right over a small plot of land to build housing for the household, and the right to benefit from land held under a three-tier hierarchy of management of the rural communities. The collective land rights are not problematic when the collective is mainly engaged in farming and cottage industries. When the locality where the collective is situated is urbanizing, the collective landownership becomes problematic as the accentuated land rent differentials are contested between the urban state as a de jure owner and the rural collective as a de facto landholder. The term 'collective landownership' connotes full property rights instead of 'a means of production'. Overt challenges to the urban government's farmland acquisition are abundant on the one hand. Covert (nominally illegal) land developments for nonagricultural activities by the collectives themselves are rampant on the other hand, as the official policy to rural bottom-up, nonfarming economies is generally supportive. Ambiguity and ambivalence breed rent seeking.

Fragmented urbanization: competition between the urban state and rural collectives

Rapid urbanization in the Pearl River Delta is manifested by its unprecedented expansion of the built-up areas. Guangzhou, the capital city of Guangdong province, saw its urban built-up area increase from 980 square kilometers (1996) to 1,237 square kilometers (2017). The urban built-up area as a proportion of the total territory of the municipality (7,434 square kilometers) reached 16.6 percent in 2017 (see Figure 6.10; GZBS, 2005). Guangzhou's population rose from 5.0 million to 14.5 million during the period 1980–2017. In 2017 the population density stood as high as 19,600 residents per square kilometer in its central area (280 square kilometers, consisting of four districts) (GZBS, 2018).

Rapid urbanization is noticeably unfolding in the suburbs between the central city and the near countryside. Panyu district in Guangzhou is the case in illustration (see Figure 6.11). Located to the immediate south of Guangzhou central city, Panyu had a territory of 774 square kilometers, with 999,200 *hukou* residents and 1,023,300 temporary migrants (without *hukou*) in 2009 (PYBS, 2010). In spite of Panyu becoming an urban district in its administrative status, 45.5 percent of its *hukou* residents were still categorized as rural residents, living mainly in the villages. According to the statistics of the Panyu's economy, where agricultural farming accounted for only 5.3 percent of its annual GDP in 2009, it could be inferred that only a fraction of villagers was working in the fields. Most of them, together with a great deal of temporary migrants, worked in the manufacturing and service industries.

As a suburban unit, Panyu consists of 19 rural townships and urban *jiedaos*[9] as of 2011. Further down in the hierarchy there are 247 rural administrative

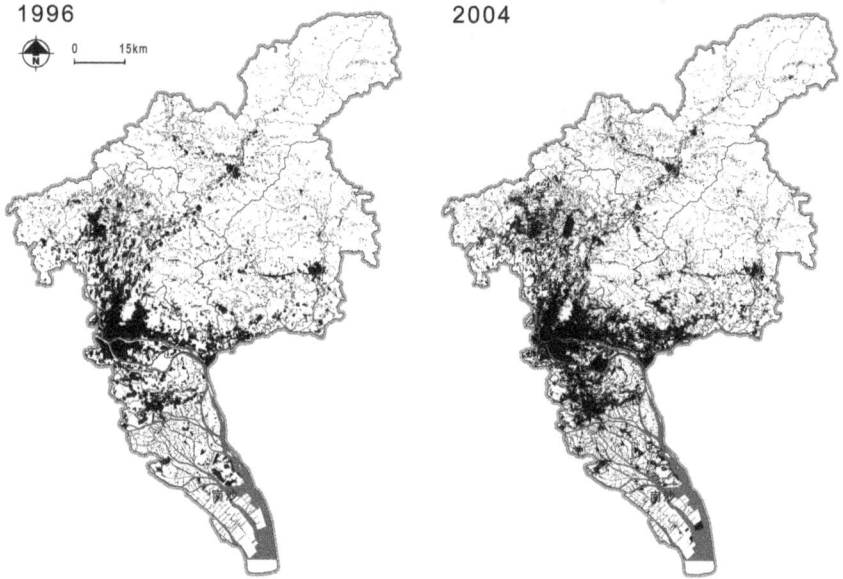

Figure 6.10 Urban built-up areas in Guangzhou Metropolitan Region, 1996 and 2004.

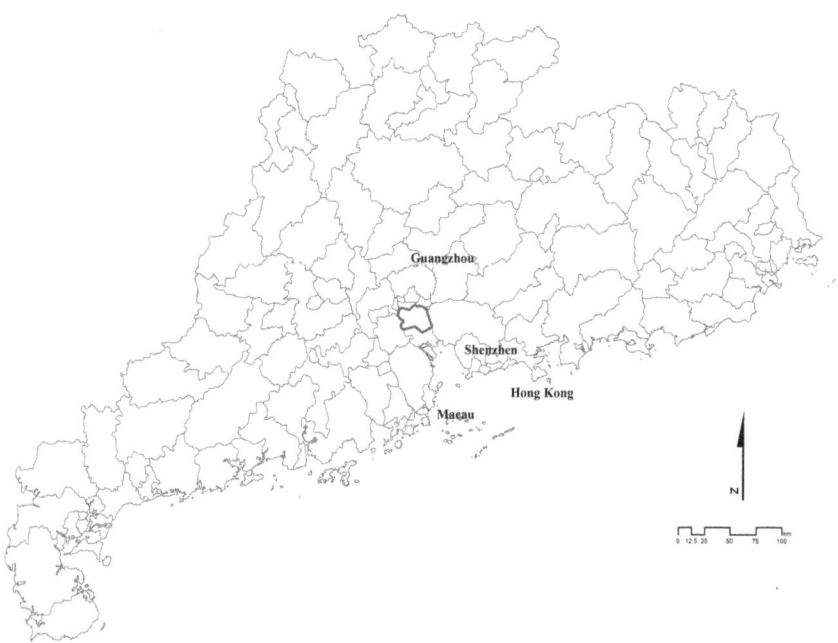

Figure 6.11 Panyu district in the Pearl River Delta.

Bottom-up rural spatial changes 145

villages and 2,352 natural villages in the rural domain, and 92 urban neighborhood units in the urban domain. With 69.4 percent of its total area in agricultural uses and 30.6 percent in nonagricultural uses, Panyu as rural suburbs is rapidly urbanizing in the periphery of Guangzhou central city. A Fragstats patch analysis reveals that there are 1,287 patches of farmland and 4,352 patches of built-up land in total, and patch densities (number of patches/square kilometer) of 1.7 for farmland and 5.6 for built-up land, respectively. Land development during the process of urbanization appears to have created a fragmented landscape (see Figure 6.12), which seems to have resulted from inadequate governance over the transformation from rural to urban.

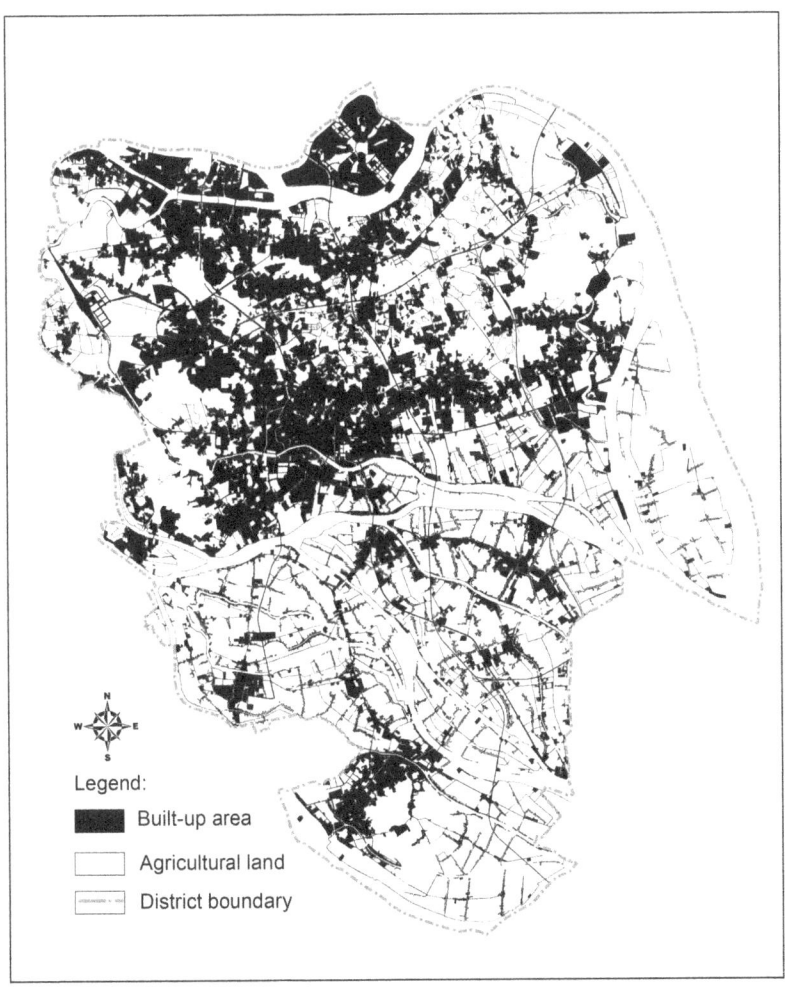

Figure 6.12 Agricultural and nonagricultural land uses in Panyu district.

146　*Bottom-up rural spatial changes*

It is observed that there are two types of urbanization spatially intermingled. One is the top-down penetration of urban projects sponsored by the city state (49.2 percent); the other is the bottom-up rural industrialization and other constructions initiated by the village collective (50.8 percent) (see Figure 6.13). The former entails change of landownership from the collective to the state, while the latter does not change the nature of landownership, as the land is still held by the collective community. Overt competition and covert negotiation between the urban state and rural collectives are clearly demonstrated by

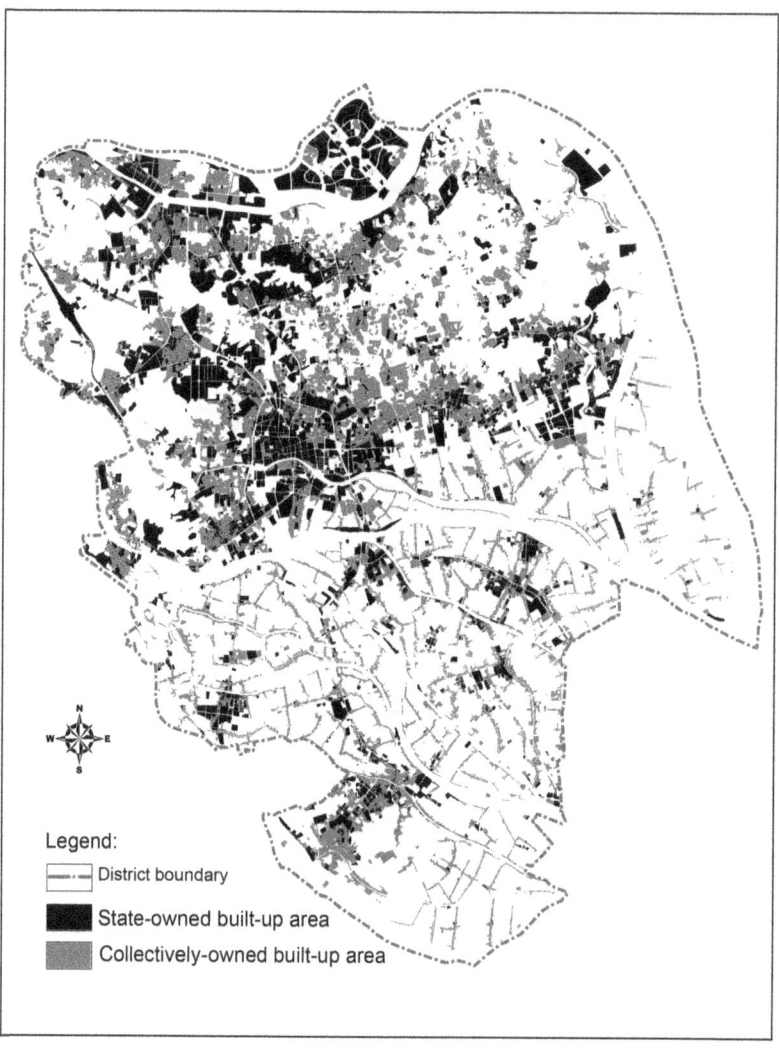

Figure 6.13 State-sponsored and collective-initiated land development in Panyu.

the even distribution of industrial land patches developed by both the parties among the villages. Villages could conduct land development for nonagricultural uses within their own territories, while the urban state needs to negotiate with every village for land acquisition so that each village has its 'fair' share of land acquired. Usually ill-conceived and hastily executed, these developments are often not carried out in the best interests of long-term sustainability. The taking of land rent differentials has direct impact on the mode of land development. Disordered land rent competition is one of the key factors responsible for a spatially disorganized mixture of agricultural and nonagricultural land uses. Uncontrolled externalities accumulate and worsen the quality of social and ecological environments.

Buttressed by the Land Management Law (1986), agricultural land can be legally acquired by the city government in the course of urbanization before its leasehold is sold to developer for a land lease premium based on the new land use. Conversion of collective land ownership to the state requires compensation paid to the collective owners based on the land value under existing land uses – that is, agricultural farming instead of the potential value derived from the new urban land use. One investigation of a case in Nanhai, Guangdong, by Wen and Zhu (1996) unveils that compensation price is ¥28,000 per *mu* (1992) for the land acquired in the village of Zhoubiao. It is hard to judge whether the compensation price of ¥28,000 per *mu* is fair, because there is no formal market for agricultural land transactions as trading is forbidden. However, it is obvious that this practice of land acquisition and compensation has not been perceived as 'fair' and acceptable by the affected peasants (Guo, 2001). It is reported that about 65 percent of peasant demonstrations, unrests, and even riots were caused by land acquisition disputes (see http://www.zaobao.com/gi/zg060223 504.html). At the center of disputes is the land rent differential – that is the gap between the compensation fee (the actual land rent) and the land lease premium (the potential land rent). Land rent differentials are often substantial – reported as between 10 and 20 times the compensation fees (http://news.sina.com.cn/c/2006-06-21/233910217416.shtml, accessed May 28, 2019).[10] Capturing the land rent differential intensifies competition between the urban state and rural collectives. Unfolding in the transition zone between urbanized areas and agricultural regions, China's urbanization produces a physical form of fragmented land development caused by diverse interests in land and thus various modes of land development.

The urban state has been made the dominant actor in the conversion of rural land for urban use in the progressive economic reform. As the local developmental state, local governments place highest priorities on economic development, productivity, and local competitiveness (White and Wade, 1988; Woo-Cumings, 1999; Qian, 2000; Zhu, 2005). Advancing developmental strategies, which can stimulate local growth, and expanding fiscal capacity are two essential goals of local governments (Wong, 1987; 1992). However, in the same vein, the rural collective also seeks local development and revenues of its own. Land rent is thus keenly sought after in the context of the twofold competition between the rural collective and the urban state, and among the joint owners of the rural community. There are four stakeholders in the competition: three (peasants, village committees, and township governments) in the rural domain, and the state in the urban domain. The competition for land rent differentials between the rural collective and the urban state creates a fertile ground for conflicts and confrontation and also cultivates dubious strategies for rural land development on the part of the collective actors.

In the name of stimulating village economies, some land development projects are carried out under the disguise of legitimate provision of premises for village economic activities. As a matter of fact, many land parcels are developed to be rented to outside industrialists. Thus, the real motivation of land development is to capture the coveted land rent, which makes land development a pure real estate business. Using land as assets, rather than as 'a means of production' is not considered legitimate by the state, and thus land development for the purpose of rent taking is clandestine, informal, and opportunistic. Though the state-sanctioned land management rules require that land for village housing should be used for owner occupation only, and villagers cannot rent out housing space to earn rental income, it is a common practice that villagers ignore the rules by building their family houses much larger than their households actually need. As those extra spaces are leased out, land rent differentials are taken by the villagers.

Thus, urbanization in the suburbs where a substantial amount of land is converted has caused confusion and conflict over landed interests among stakeholders. Demsetz (1967) believes that property rights should be clarified when externalities have to be internalized, if the gain of internalization becomes greater than its cost. The problematic definition of land rights over rural land during transition generates externalities, which constitutes a problem for governance. The overall gains of internalization may be greater than its total cost. However, the key issue unaddressed is who receives the gains and who bears the costs. This is the critical incentive structure driving the institutional change.

Who has actually captured the land rent differential? The municipal government as the agent of the state is in the best position to capture the lion's share of it, and thus acquisition of agricultural land has become a means of consolidating municipal revenue sources. It is estimated that 60–70 percent of land rent go to governments at various levels (township and above), 25–30 percent are taken by the village collective, and only 5–10 percent are given to the peasants (Wen and Zhu, 1996). It is evident that the rural collective does not benefit from the formal land development as much as it believes it should do – the urban state is the main beneficiary.

The rural collective does not receive what it perceives to be a fair share of compensation from the formal land conversion. Conflicts and confrontations give rise to devious strategies for the competition over land rent differentials with the urban state. Informal land developments, orchestrated by rural actors, emerge in parallel to the formal land developments dominated by the urban actors. Such development is regarded as 'informal', as the land development is carried out without sanction of the urban state.[11] Beiqijia's TVEs have ventured into land-related businesses since the 1990s. Joint ventures between external capital and local land and labor are a legitimate business mode. However, the line between land development for legal owner occupation and for illegal commercial gain is blurred. Where land is developed for legal owner occupation, the collective uses the land as the holder of land use rights, whereas in illegal commercial gain, the collective captures the land rent differentials in the process of land development for 'highest and best' uses, at the expense of the urban state.

Hongfu Enterprise Park in Zhenggezhuang village, Beiqijia, was set up in 2000 and had 13 manufacturing firms in 2003. It was built by the Hongfu Group, which was, initially, a village enterprise. It was later privatized, detached from the management of the village committee which held a 16.6 percent share of the company assets. As an independent shareholding enterprise, the Hongfu Group did not have the use rights over the collective land; therefore, the Hongfu Group had to rent land parcels from the village collective. As a result, Zhenggezhuang village collective captured the land rent differential, which was deemed 'informal' or 'illegal' as the collective did not have the right to rent out land for commercial undertakings. In a similar way, Dongsanqi villagers rented out spare rooms in their houses to migrants who were working temporarily in Beiqijia although the housing was supposed to be used only by the villagers themselves and not for commercial gain. These cases show that there is a two-tiered competition for land rent differentials: between the urban state and the rural collective; and between the township government, villages, and peasants.

The informal development of commodity housing by the indigenous developers did not have ownership certificates issued by the urban state for the housing units, and thus the housing units could not be legally transacted in the market. The township government invented the notion of 'township property rights', or *xiangchanquan* (Hsing, 2006), which was not legally recognized by the state. The wily invention of 'township property rights' was entrepreneurial, invoking the outgoing socialist institution of 'people's use rights' over public resources.[12] Township household registration certificates were strategically offered by the township office to the owners of housing with *xiangchanquan* to make them local residents entitled to 'people's use rights'. With only the right to use, but not full ownership rights, those housing units are only worth about 50 percent of the value of housing with formal ownership certificates (http://www.focus.cn/news/2005-11-09/164295.html, accessed December 1, 2005).

In a functional neoclassical land market, competition should enhance quality, and thus land resources should be utilized efficiently. Land rent differentials should go to the landowners or the state, or be shared between the two, depending on the ideology of the time and place. Open competition for land rent differentials should be a matter of national or local politics (Goodchild and Munton, 1985). Ambiguous and incomplete property rights of collective owners over rural land generate a land development market in which covert and disorderly competition for land rent differentials prevails, evidenced by the informal developments. Disordered land rent competition is one of the key factors that has been responsible for the disorganized mixtures of agricultural

Table 6.6 Land development by the two competitors in Beiqijia

Nonagricultural land	Rural collective	Urban state
2352.0 ha	1095.5 ha	1256.5 ha
	46.6%	53.4%

Sources: Author's survey; CAUPD, 2003

and nonagricultural land uses. Resentful because of having been deprived of land development rights, the rural collective launched a covert operation, in defiance of the urban state, to seize the rights in the name of the promotion of local growth. The rural collective and the urban state captured almost equal shares of land rent differentials, after the 'entrepreneurial' endeavor of the rural collective (see Table 6.6).

Development becomes a preemptive measure taken against potential rent taking by other joint nominal owners, resulting in land development for the sake of rent taking. Those lands are often not used for the 'highest and best' purpose, for example, having no formal deeds to the private apartments with 'township property rights' halves the housing value as well as the land value, and thus land rent dissipates. The intense mix of agricultural and nonagricultural land uses along the boundary lines of village units demonstrates that villages are the basic unit of land use management. Villages remain a key actor with which the urban state has to negotiate for land acquisition and conversion in most localities.

Autonomous village-led nonagricultural development: from village enterprises to a rentier class

Because of a large rural population against a limited availability of arable land, scarcity of farmland is prevalent in China's villages. The Household Production Responsibility Scheme since 1983 has incentivized farmers to improve agricultural productivity, but land fragmentation has deteriorated as limited farmland is further divided among village households (Nguyen, Cheng, and Findlay, 1996; Hu, 1997). Numerous irregular and piecemeal farmland plots make installation of farming infrastructure, such as irrigation, difficult and costly. Fragmented farmland holdings make agricultural economies underproductive (Wan and Cheng, 1996). Nonagricultural development initiated by rural industrialization has changed the destiny of many villages that are trapped in subsistence farming. However, because of low landholdings per village and thus small-area villages, village-based industrialization has generated dreadful problems of industrial sprawl in the form of piecemeal industrial sites and farming lands, which compromises the environmental integrity as well as industrial and agricultural productivity.

Since the implementation of the Household Production Responsibility Scheme, farmland has been let to village households equally in terms of land quality and quantity based on the egalitarian principle (Kung, 1995, 2000). As a result of land allocation based on the household, further improvement in agricultural productivity was seriously hampered by the extremely piecemeal land subdivisions that do not allow economies of scale. Meanwhile, off-farm jobs have become abundant in the Pearl River Delta, which has been rapidly urbanizing since the 1980s. Instead of tilling the meager landholding, young peasants went to the cities for better remuneration. Twenty percent of the rural laborers were already engaged in nonagricultural employment by 1990 (Hou and Zeng, 1991). With the closure of mostly collectively owned village enterprises, village economies were in peril in the face of market competition, which prompted an informal institutional change from below. Aspiring to lead the way of industrializing villages, villages gradually took the role of 'landlords' leasing land to private enterprises so as to live on land rent.[13]

Village land shareholding cooperatives have emerged since the early 1990s in the course of deepening rural transformation (Fu and Davis, 1998). For those villages voluntarily adopt the cooperative, all landholdings except household housing parcels are re-collectivized so as to carry out nonagricultural development. The beckoning rural collective industrialization needs consolidated large land parcels. Farmland lots need to be pooled to enable agricultural production with economies of scale when some villagers have abandoned household farming and migrated to cities to seek urban jobs. Village members are given landholding shares and become shareholders. Since villagers are the natural members of the cooperatives, cooperatives are reckoned as both social and economic autonomous organizations, not controlled by professional managers as are urban shareholding corporations. Incomes from village enterprises and properties are distributed among cooperative members according to their shares, albeit about 40 percent of the collective incomes are supposedly held by the cooperative organization for future collective development.

While the official doctrines of collective landownership remain unchanged, cooperatives manage to strengthen their holding of the collective land by stipulating that an agreement from two-thirds of the cooperative members should be required in the case of alteration of cooperative resources where land stock is the major component. It is most significant to the villages as the power of the urban state in land acquisition is effectively curbed. Cooperatives cannot lease their land resources to renters openly to earn land rentals, as regulated by the collective landownership. Only recently has agricultural land leasing been allowed to overcome the problem of farmland fragmentation. Thus, leasing of nonagricultural land without the urban authority's approval is an informal institution. The fact that cooperatives cannot place their land parcels as collateral for bank loans is a clear testament that collective land is not an asset. Nevertheless, informal institutional change is not formally recognized by the state, and there is no existence of long-term certainty and security of the informally acquired land rights. When uncertainty occurs, it prevents one from making rational and long-term planning.

Instead, uncertainty can induce short-term behavior. It is observed that most industrial sites in the cooperatives are developed opportunistically in a piecemeal and casual manner. Because of the status of informality, or strictly speaking, illegality of land conversion, cooperatives are unable to raise loans from the financial market for the industrial property development. It explains the low standard of industrial buildings and nonexistent services for the industrial sites that therefore only attract low-end industrial tenants.

A cooperative is "an autonomous association of persons united voluntarily to meet their common economic, social, and cultural needs and aspirations through a jointly-owned and democratically-controlled enterprise" (The International Cooperative Alliance, http://www.ica.coop, cited by Ortmann and King, 2007: 41). As an organizational arrangement, cooperatives are characterized as voluntary and open membership, autonomous management, and members' active participation in the economic management (Hendrikse and Veerman, 2001). A cooperative may be able to serve its members' economic needs in a certain social context, but as an organization, it has intrinsic problems breeding members' short-termism. Short-termism is caused by the problems of free-riders, horizon, and transaction costs in decision-making (Cook, 1995; Royer, 1995). When property rights are not transferable and not clearly delineated in the open membership cooperatives, free-rider problems occur. Having the same rights as the existing members, new members without prior contribution to the cooperative can obtain the rights to residual claims, which causes dilution of returns to the existing members. The horizon problem arises when the productive life of collective resources is longer than the time-span a shareholder can claim on the dividends generated, as the shareholder may leave or die (Vitaliano, 1983; Porter and Scully, 1987). The horizon problem is derived from the problem of restrictions on transferability of residual claimant rights. Therefore, there is a disincentive for members to contribute to the long-term investment and an incentive for members to maximize the short-term dividends.

Because of the democratic member-controlled system (one-member-one-vote), there could be high transaction costs in reaching management decisions, and the cost of group decision-making increases with the size and diversity of the cooperative (Staatz, 1987). Cooperative management may not be able to react to market opportunities in a timely manner, likely leading to management inaction. Ostrom (1990) advocates management of common pool resources with neither centralized government control nor privatization. However, contextual variables such as the relative scarcity of the resource and the size of the collective involved are emphasized as critical for effective collective self-governance (Ostrom, 2000). High population density and land scarcity challenge collective governance over common land resources. Autonomous village-based cooperatives in high-density land-scarce regions in China are made spatially small and fragmented. Preferring short-term gain to long-term investment, village land shareholding cooperatives without economies of scale will gradually become underproductive in the environment of intense market competition, and diminishing returns will make village cooperatives economically unsustainable in the long term.

Land shareholding cooperatives are intended as economic organizations and expected to operate like normal shareholding corporations. The shareholding structure was fixed initially, that is, a closed membership system, as collective revenues were expected to be used chiefly for village welfare and development, and only a very small percentage was for dividends. Since cooperatives are increasingly relying on incomes from land rent, the initial fixed cooperative membership system based on collective enterprises is challenged. There are no reasons why only existing members could claim the land benefits, as village population change is still dynamic. The closed membership structure gives rise to an equity problem, as new village members brought in by birth and marriage are not entitled to cooperative shares, while those members having left villages because of death or migration could still claim village revenues. Equity in village members is a legitimate concern. An open membership has been adopted since the early 2000s after abandonment of the closed membership system.

As a result, the number of shareholders has been on the rise. Rural *hukou* becomes valuable, which is unprecedented in the post-1949 Chinese history, as urban *hukou* has always been a more coveted entitlement than the rural *hukou* (Unger and Chan, 1999). Fifty-three percent of Nanhai's areas had been urbanized by 2008, but residents with rural *hukou* still accounted for 64 percent, while urban residents represented the remaining 36 percent of the total (NHBS, 2011). Village equity may have triumphed, but the free-rider problem looms large. The number of shares has been increasing every year, and it is beyond the control of existing members. The future returns per capita become uncertain. Cooperative shares cannot be transacted in the open market, and thus the shares do not have market value. Though shares could be bought back in the case of member's departure, or shares could be sold to other members in the same cooperative, the share prices, comparing with annual dividends, are relatively low. Therefore, cooperative members do not have a long-term perspective, which constitutes the horizon problem (Cook, 1995). Shares are treated as a certificate of entitlement only, rather than an investment.

Because land leasing is the major pillar of the cooperative economy and land resource per capita is meager, cooperative members do not have confidence in the long-term future of cooperatives, coupled with general cooperative free-rider and horizon problems. Short-term returns and welfare are preferred over long-term economic productivity. The primary concern of the village managers is the maximization of revenues for distribution, and no one seems to care about sustainability of the collective economy. The statistics show that cooperatives' revenues retained for investment were only 6.3 percent and 6.6 percent of the total on average in 2007 and 2008, respectively (Nanhai Department of Rural Work, 2008). Under the pressure of maintaining ever-growing dividends, cooperatives have to convert more farmland and lease it to industrial tenants in order to increase the cooperative incomes. Agricultural land was converted to industrial land at a rate of 1,280.3 hectares per year during 1988–2000, and this rate increased to 1,941.5 hectares per year during 2000–2008 (Nanhai Land and Resource Bureau, 2008). An influx of migrant workers comes with a rapid increase of labor-intensive factories. Serious environmental problems in the high-density villages are imaginable. In the whole of Nanhai, 65.1 percent of the total collectively owned built-up area was used for manufacturing, while rural village residential land uses only accounted for 28.9 percent in 2008 (Nanhai Land and Resource Bureau, 2008). It is extraordinary and excessive that almost half of village land resources are used by and leased to manufacturing, and villages have virtually been occupied by the industrial plants.

Moreover, in order to raise annual dividends, many cooperatives have adopted a policy of direct leasing of raw land without services and premises, so as not to spend on capital investment. Raw land leasing usually does not incur expenses on facilities and infrastructure and allows tenants to build their own premises. Despite the fact known to the cooperatives that land productivity of premises leasing could be as much as six times of that of raw land leasing, three-quarters of the industrial land resources are still used unproductively (Nanhai Department of Rural Work, 2008). It seems that cooperative members are unwilling to sacrifice short-term dividends at all for a more productive long-term return. Cooperatives, initially intended as a collective economic corporation, have been sliding into a welfare organization.

Disordered competition for land rent results in problematic suburban sprawling (see Figure 6.14 and Table 6.7). It is exacerbated in more urbanized areas, illustrated by an area comprising six towns in Panyu (see Table 6.8). The built-up land accounts for 59.5 percent of the total and the rest is farm land (40.5 percent) in the area. One-fifth of the area is developed for rural and urban manufacturing and another one-fifth for rural and urban housing. Farmland is split into 455 patches within the area of 139 square kilometers with a total of 479 villages. The scattered industrial land parcels seriously compromise the environmental quality, and segregation between residential and pollution-prone industrial land uses becomes urgent for habitations where population density is high.[14]

It shows the detrimental effects of villages, instead of townships or the district, as the basic autonomous units managing rural nonagricultural development in the context of ambiguous land rights, while the district government does not and cannot impose zoning regulations on rural jurisdictions. 'Self-contained' village informal development and bargaining negotiation for land acquisition between the urban state and the rural collective inevitably generate unproductive land utilization. Polluting and hazardous factories are widely spatially dispersed in Panyu. This spatially haphazard pattern of urbanization has been found elsewhere in Guangdong, corroborated by empirical investigation (Jiang and Liu, 2003; Yang and Liu, 2004; Yuan, Yi and Wang, 2005; Yuan et al., 2009). As a result, the neighborhood environment deteriorates, demonstrated convincingly by haphazardly located and extensively spreading industrial factories built by both the urban government and the rural villages.

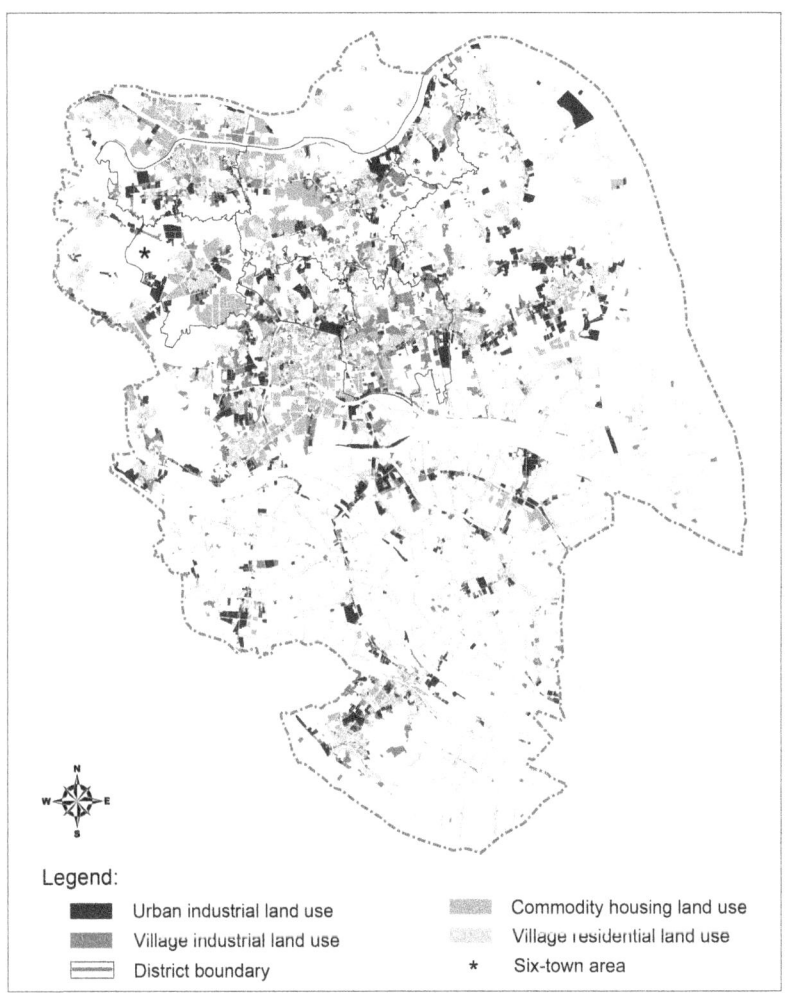

Figure 6.14 Extensive mixture of residential and industrial land uses in Panyu. A full-color version of this image can be found at http:// www.routledge.com/9780367 358037.

Table 6.7 Fragmentation of urban and rural housing and industrial land uses in Panyu

Land use	As % of total built-up area	Number of patches
Village housing	14.8	594
Rural industries	16.8	1,142
Urban private housing	14.4	360
Urban industries	25.6	1,391

Source: Panyu Planning Bureau

156 *Bottom-up rural spatial changes*

Table 6.8 Patch analysis of industrial and agricultural land uses in the six-township area

Township	Number of nature villages	Number of patches in industrial land use			Number of industrial patches per km²	Number of farmland patches	Average size of farm patches (ha)
		Rural	Urban	Total			
Dalong	92	157	71	228	8.9	93	9.3
Dashi	85	118	57	175	8.8	91	7.4
Dongkuan	41	56	27	83	6.9	38	9.9
Nancun	147	225	89	314	7.1	147	11.7
Xinzao	44	44	27	71	5.1	23	40.1
Zhongcun	70	57	39	96	4.1	63	17.3
Total	479	657	310	967	7.0	455	12.4

Source: Panyu Planning Bureau

Rising private governance in the face of collective commons

In the absence of effective governance by the state or orchestrated collective action, private governance emerges from the market in the form of suburban gated super-housing-estates with well-defined property rights over the fenced-off quarters. Chaotic and disorganized rural nonagricultural development prompts first-of-its-kind suburbanization with Chinese characteristics. Though private gated communities meet the aspiration of a rising middle-income class for a decent living environment, social segregation inevitably arises. The urbanization characterized by the dotted gated super-communities in the suburbs and environmental deterioration in the suburban areas is not deemed environmentally, socially, and economically sustainable.

Resulting from an absence of the regulatory state in the midst of changing governance, spatial deterioration caused by ambiguous and incomplete land rights is a sign of deficient state governance, exacerbated in the setting of high population density. China, as an ancient nation with a large population, has long been run according to Confucianism as a cultural cornerstone, which regards the state as the only credible institution that can manage society. Stability of the nation was interrupted only periodically by chaotic anarchy followed by the decay of dynasties. The market as a mechanism of provision and allocation had never been fully nurtured. Pursuit of economic growth since the reform has inevitably forced the state to discharge its role of the absolute provider and to give room for bottom-up initiatives. Owing to path dependency, the socialist, authoritarian state is changing from its preoccupation with political ideologies to the active pursuit of economic development in order to legitimize itself by improving the livelihood of its citizens.

Intimately involved in economic production, the pro-growth local developmental state has not possessed, intentionally or unintentionally, adequate regulatory capacity for the management of the economy and society. An absence of land use planning may not be a serious problem to the usually low-density and low-intensity rural communities. For the low-income developing countries with high population density, urbanization is made unsustainable by disorderly competition and uncoordinated development. Sprawling of substandard developments ensues as a result. When a planned urban housing quarter with required public goods and amenities is in the vicinity of a crowded village with a paucity of open space as a result of uncontrolled development, trespassing is inevitable by the village residents into the housing estate to seek the enjoyment of environmental amenities (see Figure 6.15).

When public governance by the state fails, private governance by the market arises to fill the void. The gated community as private governance is a well-known phenomenon in both developed and developing countries (Glasze, Webster, and Frantz, 2006). Worsening public security and inadequate urban amenities as public goods are considered as two primary causes for the rising momentum of gated communities. Gated housing estates are fenced off, and property rights over the residential environment are well defined and managed by developers initially and subsequently by homeowner associations. If public goods are underprovided and amenities overconsumed in the public domain, exclusionary collective goods and amenities can be protected by the clear property rights in the private domain (Webster, 2002; see Figure 6.16).

Figure 6.15 Potential spillover of externalities from a crowded village into a planned housing estate, Panyu.

158 *Bottom-up rural spatial changes*

Figure 6.16 Two kinds of governance: open village settlement versus gated housing estate.

Because of well-defined and ascertained property rights, privately planned gated housing estates are able to use land more efficiently and offer a better living environment than spontaneously urbanized areas without collective planning. In Figure 6.16, the village settlement, next to a site of village industries, reaches a plot ratio of 0.49 and site coverage of 34.7 percent, while the planned housing estate achieves a plot ratio of 1.7 and site coverage of 23.9 percent. On the one hand, the village is still urbanizing, and its open space is not protected and will be encroached upon under the pressure of high population density. This trajectory is clearly seen in many urbanizing villages in the Pearl River Delta (Tian, 2008). On the other hand, environmental amenities in the urban housing estate are under control, protected by the condominium property rights. The mode of high plot ratio with low site coverage is considered more efficient and sustainable in terms of land utilization than the mode of low plot ratio with high site coverage for an urbanizing region with high population density, as the former offers more housing and open green spaces than the latter. In view of the ongoing dynamic urbanization, the development mode of the village represents only the interests of the status quo (existing residents), as the village's capacity of accommodating migrant newcomers is much less than a planned housing estate.

Being a global phenomenon, gated communities are not unfamiliar to China's urban middle classes. Gated communities are associated with exclusion and coveted privileges derived therefrom. Almost all newly built urban housing estates are gated in China. Nevertheless, gated housing estates in the suburbs were unheard of in China up to the late 1990s. China has been a predominantly agrarian society up to now, as about 50 percent of its populace is still engaged in the agricultural sector. Rural living has a connotation of backwardness in China, rather than the romance and peace related with country living in the developed countries. Living in the suburbs, or suburbanization, is not perceived to be related to modern life. It is in the people's psyche that city living means modernity and quality. Central locations are always sought after, demonstrated by much higher housing prices in the city center. Therefore, it was phenomenal, even revolutionary, that Chinese-styled suburbanization occurred in Guangzhou in the late 1990s for the first time in history, when the idea of suburban living was still associated with peasantry and car ownership was still low.[15] Gated super-housing-estates leapfrogged to locales further away from the urban periphery and emerged in the far suburbs in Panyu, where greenfields lay undeveloped and the environment was wholesome (see Figure 6.17 and Table 6.9). Although the demand for decent living environments was evident from a rising middle class, this risky but measured undertaking (as against normal-size gated communities in the city) was to provide potential residents with another option against the existing suburban environment. It is a choice between the places without effective state governance and the ones under effective private governance.

Exploiting the advantage of economies of scale, those gated super-housing-estates can provide a variety of services and facilities as club goods which are not found elsewhere. The first gated super-housing-estate, Clifford Estates, was initiated in 1991 by a Hong Kong developer returning to his hometown. It had developed about 50,000 housing units by 2006 with private schools (primary, secondary, and international), a private hospital, and estate shuttle buses serving residents commuting between the Clifford Estates and the central city of Guangzhou. The developer effectively assumes the role of mayorship, serving about 150,000 residents, albeit his 'constituency' is composed of customers who are middle-class homeowners. Land rent dissipation and consequent environmental deterioration in the villages are prevented within the Clifford Estates by the private governance. However, social segregation and inequality are exacerbated, as low-income residents are excluded from gated housing estates as private cities and increasingly concentrated in ever-deteriorating villages. This social dichotomy is clearly created by the land development market without effective public governance.

Figure 6.17 Gated super-housing-estates in Panyu district.

Table 6.9 Gated super-housing-estates in Panyu

No.	housing estates	size (ha)	No.	housing estates	size (ha)
1	Clifford Estates	390.2	4	Yajule Garden	311.9
2	Jingxiu Xiangjiang Garden	87.6	5	Huanan Newtown	202.5
3	Huanan Bigui Garden	69.2	6	Xinghe Bay	80.0

Source: Panyu Planning Bureau

Notes

1 The household production responsibility scheme, introduced by the economic reforms of 1978, contracts the use rights of agricultural land to individual farm households for a period of thirty years. It terminated the collective farming system which had been in existence since 1953. Replacing the people's commune, farm households become production units making decisions on what to grow and to sell at market price after fulfilling the required planned output quotas.
2 Fragstats is a computer software programme for spatial pattern analysis (see http://www.umass.edu/landeco/research/fragstats/fragstats.html, accessed 27 June 2015).
3 Patch is a terminology in the discipline of landscape ecology, defined as spatially consistent areas with similar thematic features as basic homogeneous entities, in describing or representing a landscape (McGarigal and Marks, 1994).

4 The contagion index (0 – 100) measures the extent to which land uses are aggregated or fragmented. The landscape is aggregated at high values, and dissected into small patches at low values (O'Neil et al., 1988).
5 A farmland patch is defined as a complete plot of farmland without spatial separation.
6 If land is an asset, its owner has the property rights over land. Land rights are primarily a bundle of rights associated with ownership which consists of the right to use land, the right to derive income from it, the right to change its form and substance, and the right to transfer these rights to another party at a price mutually agreed upon (Pejovich, 1990).
7 Although this official definition was made known in 1962 (Tang, 2009), it has become a cornerstone for the collective landownership ever since.
8 The following case of empirical investigation is a reference only, and it does not mean a universal rule. Wen and Zhu (1996) investigated a case in Nanhai, Guangdong, and discovered that compensation fees of ¥28,000 per *mu* (1992) for a piece of land acquired in the village of Zhoubiao were distributed to four parties which made up the collective: Pingzhou Township (10.7 percent); Xiabei Administrative Village (17.9 percent); Zhoubiao Village (50.0 percent); and individual peasants in the village, as the 'owners' nearest to the land (21.4 percent).
9 *Jiedao* is the urban equivalent to the rural township.
10 Part of the land rent differential is used for servicing the raw land with infrastructure and public facilities, though. The same investigation by Wen and Zhu (1996) indicated that the total cost incurred before the land could be leased for urban uses was about ¥127 000 per mu (1994) on average – four to five times the compensation fees.
11 Many developing countries are characterized by the informal economy, usually emerging from the circumstances where the formal economy cannot offer sufficient employment to working adults in the cities. It is noted that "the lower the level of development of a country, the larger its informal sector" (Charmes, 1990: 17). It should be pointed out that the informal sector is not economically efficient and thus may not be sustainable for developing countries where low productivity has already dragged economies down (Hugon, 1990). Likewise, housing which violates building codes or for which there are no planning permits is also known euphemistically as 'informal housing'; it is commonplace in developing countries. It is estimated that about 50 percent of the inhabitants of large developing cities live in these informal shelters (United Nations Centre for Human Settlement, 1987). 'Informal land developments' in China's villages refer to the projects built without permission issued by the competent authorities in the urban state. It is thus technically illegal.
12 In the socialist system in which the means of production are in public ownership, although it is clear that the state is the de jure owner of urban land, people's use rights over state land are somehow perceived in a higher position than the ownership rights, and thus make land users de facto owners (Marcuse, 1996; Zhu, 2002).
13 Land rent is the value of land appropriated in economic transactions, as the market price of land is interpreted as capitalised land rent. The rental value of a land site is largely determined by the equilibrium of demand for and supply of land as a commodity with its use designated by zoning (agricultural, residential, commercial and so on). The potential land rent represents the amount of rent that can be capitalised under the 'highest and best use'. The gap between the potential land rent and actual land rent capitalised under the present land use is the land rent differential.
14 It was reported that a chemical plant located between two villages in Panyu exploded in 24 November 2011. Toxic hydrogen chloride gas was detected in the air following the explosion, and about 6000 residents had to be evacuated (Mo, Zhang and Zhang, 2011).
15 Actually, the estate management offices of gated super-housing-estates provide estate shuttle buses for residents to commute between their residence and the central city of Guangzhou.

References

Adell, G. (1999) *Theories and models of the peri-urban interface: A changing conceptual landscape*. Unpublished report by Development Planning Unit, University College London, London.

Ash, R. F. & Edmonds, R. L. (1998) China's land resources, environment and agricultural production. *The China Quarterly*, 156: 836–79.

Brown, L. (1995) *Who will feed China? Wake-up call for a small planet*. New York: Norton.

Bryceson, D. F. (1996) Deagrarianization and rural employment in sub-Saharan Africa: A sectoral perspective. *World Development*, 24: 97–111.

Bureau of Agriculture, Municipality of Zhangjiagang (2016) *Economic statistics of villages, Nanfeng Township*. Unpublished report.

Byrd, W. A. & Lin, Q. (1990) *China's rural industry: Structure, development, and reform*. New York: Oxford University Press.

Cai, Y. S. (2003) Collective ownership or cadres' ownership? The non-agricultural use of farmland in China. *The China Quarterly*, 175: 662–680.

Chang, C. & Wang, Y. (1994) The nature of the township enterprise. *Journal of Comparative Economics*, 19: 434–52.

Chang, S.D. & Kwok, R.Y.W. (eds.) (1990) *The urbanization of rural China*. London: M.E. Sharpe.

Charmes, J. (1990) A critical review of concepts, definitions and studies in the informal sector, in D. Turnham, B. Salome & A. Schwarz (eds.) *The informal sector revisited*, 10–48. Paris: OECD.

Che, J. and Qian, Y. Y. (1998) Insecure property rights and government ownership of firms. *Quarterly Journal of Economics*, 113(2): 467–496.

China Academy of Urban Planning and Design (CAUPD) (2003) *Land use planning of Beiqijia*. Unpublished report.

College of Agriculture and Rural Development, Renmin University of China (CARD/RUC) & Socioeconomic Survey Team, National Bureau of Statistics, China (SST/NBSC) (2006) *Development report of China's small cities and towns, 2005/06*. Beijing: China Agricultural Press. (in Chinese).

Compiling Committee for Annual Yearbook of China's Township and Village Enterprises (1988, 1997, 2012) *Annual yearbook of China's township and village enterprises, 1987, 1996, 2011*. Beijing: China's Press of Agriculture. (in Chinese).

Compiling Committee of the History of Yonglian Village (2015) *The history of Yonglian Village*. Nanjing: Phoenix Press.

Cook, M. L. (1995) The future of US agricultural cooperatives: A neo-institutional approach. *American Journal of Agricultural Economics*, 77(5): 1153–1159.

de Janvry, A. & Sadoulet, E. (2001) Income strategies among rural households in Mexico: The role of off-farm activities. *World Development*, 29: 467–480.

Demsetz, H. (1967) Toward a theory of property rights. *The American Economic Review*, 57(2): 347–359.

Ding, C. R. (2004) Urban spatial development in the land policy reform era: Evidence from Beijing. *Urban Studies*, 41(10): 1889–1907.

Dong, F. R. (1992) *Industrialization and China's rural modernization*. New York: St. Martin's Press.

Duara, P. (1988) *Culture, power, and the state: Rural North China, 1900–1942*. California: Stanford University Press.

Fei, H. T. (1939) *Peasant life in China: A field study of country life in the Yangtze Valley*. London: G. Routledge and Sons.

Fu, C. & Davis, J. (1998) Land reform in rural China since the mid-1980s. *Land Reform*, 2: 122–137.
Garreau, J. (1991) *Edge city: Life on the new frontier.* New York: Doubleday.
Glasze, G., Webster, C. & Frantz, K. (eds.) (2006) *Private cities: Global and local perspectives.* New York: Routledge.
Goodchild, R. & Munton, R. (1985) *Development and the landowner: An analysis of the British experience.* London: George Allen & Unwin.
Guangzhou Bureau of Statistics (GZBS) (2005, 2018) *Guangzhou statistical yearbook, 2004, 2017.* Beijing: China Statistics Press. (in Chinese).
Guo, X. L. (2001) Land expropriation and rural conflicts in China. *The China Quarterly*, 166: 422–39.
Hendrikse, G. W. J. and Veerman, C. P. (2001) Marketing cooperatives and financial structure: A transaction costs economics analysis. *Agricultural Economics*, 26(3): 205–216.
Ho, P. (2001) Who owns China's land? Property rights and deliberate institutional ambiguity. *The China Quarterly*, 166: 394–421.
Ho, P. & Lin, G.C.S. (2003) Emerging land markets in rural and urban china: Policies and practices. *The China Quarterly*, 175: 681–707.
Hou, W. Y. & Zeng, J. M. (1991) A survey report of agricultural workers' employment structure. *High Education Exploration*, 2: 34–38. (in Chinese).
Hsing, Y. T. (2006) Brokering power and property in China's townships. *The Pacific Review*, 19(1): 103–124.
Hu, W. (1997) Household land tenure reform in China: Its impact on farming land use and agro-environment. *Land Use Policy*, 14: 175–186.
Hugon, P. (1990) The informal sector revisited (in Africa), in D. Turnham, B. Salome & A. Schwarz (eds.) *The informal sector revisited*, 70–87. Paris: OECD.
Jiang, S. S. & Liu, S. Y. (2003) Land capitalization and rural industrialization: A survey of economic development in Nanhai, Fushan, Guangdong. *Management World*, 11: 87–97. (in Chinese).
Kung, J. K. S. (1995) Equal entitlement versus tenure security under a regime of collective property rights: Peasants' preference for institutions in post-reform Chinese agriculture. *Journal of Comparative Economics*, 21(1): 82–111.
Kung, J. K. S. (2000) Common property rights and land reallocations in rural China: Evidence form a village survey. *World Development*, 28(4): 701–719.
Kunshan Bureau of Statistics (KSBS) (1970–2017) *Kunshan statistical yearbook.* Beijing: China Statistics Press. (in Chinese).
Li, H. Y. (2009) *Village China under socialism and reform: A micro history, 1948–2008.* Stanford, CA: Stanford University Press.
Lin, G. C. S. & Ho, S. P. S. (2005) The state, land system, and land development processes in contemporary China. *Annals of the Association of American Geographers*, 95(2): 411–436.
Long, H. L., Liu, Y. S., Wu, X. Q. & Dong, G. H. (2009) Spatio-temporal dynamic patterns of farmland and rural settlements in Su–Xi–Chang region: Implications for building a new countryside in coastal China. *Land Use Policy*, 26: 322–333.
Ma, L. J. C. (2005) Urban administrative restructuring, changing scale relations and local economic development in China. *Political Geography*, 24(4): 477–497.
Marcuse, P. (1996) Privatization and its discontents: Property rights in land and housing in the transition in eastern Europe, in G. Andrusz, M. Harloe & I. Szelenyi (eds.) *Cities after socialism: Urban and regional change and conflict in post-socialist societies*, 119–191. Oxford: Blackwell.

Marton, A. M. (2000) *China's spatial economic development: Restless landscapes in the Lower Yangzi Delta.* London and New York: Routledge.

McGarigal, L. & Marks, B. J. (1994) *FRAGSTATS manual: Spatial pattern analysis program for quantifying landscape structure.* http://ftp.fsl.orst.edu/pub/fragstats.2.0.

McGee, T. G. (1991) The emergence of *desakota* regions in Asia: Expanding a hypothesis, in N. Ginsburg, B. Koppel & T. G. McGee (eds.) *The extended metropolis: Settlement transition in Asia,* 3–25. Honolulu: University of Hawaii Press.

Mo, F., Zhang, Q. L. & Zhang, X. F. (2011) Explosion of a chemical plant in Panyu, http://news.sina.com.cn/c/2011-11-24/190223520398.shtml. (in Chinese).

Nanhai Bureau of Statistics (NHBS) (2011) *Nanhai statistical yearbook, 2010.* Beijing: China Statistics Press. (in Chinese).

Nanhai Department of Rural Work (2008) *Nanhai's rural economic statistic yearbook, 2008.* Foshan: Nanhai Press. (in Chinese).

Nanhai Land and Resource Bureau (2008) *Research report on big issues: The preliminary work of the remaking of Nanhai's land use plan.* unpublished report.

National Bureau of Statistics, China (NBSC) (2000, 2012, 2017) *China statistical yearbook, 1999, 2011, 2016.* Beijing: China Statistics Press. (in Chinese).

Nguyen, T., Cheng, E. & Findlay, C. (1996) Land fragmentation and farm productivity in China in the 1990s. *China Economic Review,* 7: 169–180.

Oi, J. C. (1999) *Rural China takes off: Institutional foundations of economic reform.* Berkeley and Los Angeles: University of California Press.

O'Neill, R. V., Krummel, J. R., Gardner, R. H., Sugihara, G., Jackson, B., DeAngelis, D. L., Milne, B. T., Turner, M. G., Zygmunt, B., Christensen, S. W., Dale, V. H. & Graham, R. L. (1988) Indices of landscape pattern. *Landscape Ecology,* 1(3): 153–162.

Ortmann, G. F. & King, R. P. (2007) Agricultural cooperatives I: History, theory and problems. *Agrekon,* 46 (1): 28.

Ostrom, E. (1990) *Governing the commons: The evolution of institutions for collective action.* Cambridge: Cambridge University Press.

Ostrom, E. (2000) Collective action and the evolution of social norms. *The Journal of Economic Perspectives,* 14(3): 137–158.

Panyu Bureau of Statistics (PYBS) (2010) *Panyu statistical yearbook, 2009.* Beijing: China Statistics Press. (in Chinese).

Pei, X. L. (2005) Collective landownership and its role in rural industrialization, in P. Ho (ed.) *Developmental dilemmas: Land reform and institutional change in China,* 203–226. London: Routledge.

Pejovich, S. (1990) *The economics of property rights: Towards a theory of comparative systems.* Dordrecht, the Netherlands: Kluwer Academic Publishers.

Porter, P. K. & Scully, G. W. (1987) Economic efficiency in cooperatives. *Journal of Law & Economics,* 30 (2): 489–512.

Putterman, L. (1993) *Continuity and change in China's rural development – Collective and reform eras in perspective.* New York: Oxford University Press.

Qian, Y. Y. (2000) The process of China's market transition (1978–1998): The evolutionary, historical, and comparative perspectives. *Journal of Institutional and Theoretical Economics,* 156(1): 151–171.

Reardon, T., Berdegué, J. & Escobar, G. (2001) Rural nonfarm employment and incomes in Latin America: Overview and policy implications. *World Development,* 29: 395–409.

Royer, J. S. (1995) Potential for cooperative involvement in vertical coordination and value-added activities. *Agribusiness: An International Journal,* 11(5): 473–481.

Rozelle, S. & Li, G. (1998) Village leaders and land-rights formation in China. *The American Economic Review*, 88: 433–438.

Singh, J. & Dhillon, S. S. (2004) *Agricultural geography*, 3rd Edition. Delhi, India: Tata McGraw-Hill.

Skinner, G. W. (1971) Chinese peasants and the closed community: An open and shut case. *Comparative Studies in Society and History*, 13(3): 270–281.

Smil, V. (1999) China's agricultural land. *The China Quarterly*, 158: 414–429.

Staatz, J. M. (ed.) (1987) *The structural characteristics of farmer cooperatives and their behavioral consequences*: ACS Service Report 18 (July). Washington, DC: U.S. Department of Agriculture.

Tang, J. J. (2009) Collective ownership belonging to three entities [the commune, the brigade, and the team], and with the team being the basic holder. *Archives World*, 4: 17–21. (in Chinese).

Thomas, D. (1974) The urban fringe: approaches and attitudes, in J. H. Johnson (ed.) *Suburban growth: Geographical process at the edge of the Western City*, 17–30. London: Wiley.

Tian, L. (2008) The chengzhongcun land market in China: Boon or bane? A perspective on property rights. *International Journal of Urban and Regional Research*, 32: 282–304.

Tsai, L. L. (2007) Solidary groups, informal accountability, and local public goods provision in rural China. *American Political Science Review*, 101(2): 355–372.

Unger, J. and Chan, A. (1999) *Inheritors of the boom: Private enterprise and the role of local government in a rural South China township*, Working paper, 89.

United Nations Centre for Human Settlements (1987) *Global report on human settlements, 1986*. Oxford: Oxford University Press.

Vermeer, E. B. (1999) Shareholding cooperatives: A property rights analysis, in J. C. Oi and A. G. Walder (eds.) *Property rights and economic reform in China*, 123–144. Stanford, CA: Stanford University Press.

Vitaliano, P. (1983) Cooperative enterprise: An alternative conceptual basis for analyzing a complex institution. *American Journal of Agricultural Economics*, 65(5): 1078–1083.

Vogel, E. F. (1989) *One step ahead in China: Guangdong under reform*. Cambridge, MA: Harvard University Press.

Wan, G. H. & Cheng, E. J. (1996) Economies of scale, farmland fragmentation and production of crops in China. *Observation of China's Country*, 3: 31–36, 64. (in Chinese).

Webster, C. (2002) Property rights and the public realm: Gates, green belts, and Gemeinschaft. *Environment and Planning B: Planning and Design*, 29: 397–412.

Wen, T. J. & Zhu, S. Y. (1996) Governments' capital accumulation and conversion of farmland to non-agricultural land. *Management World*, 5: 161–169. (in Chinese).

Weng, Q. (2002) Land use change analysis in Zhujiang Delta of China using satellite remote sensing, GIS and stochastic modelling. *Journal of Environmental Management*, 64: 273–284.

White, G. & Wade, R. (eds.) (1988) *Developmental state in East Asia*. New York: St. Martin's.

Wong, C. P. W. (1987) Between plan and market: The role of the local sector in post-Mao China. *Journal of Comparative Economics*, 11: 385–398.

Wong, C. P. W. (1992) Fiscal reform and local industrialization: The problematic sequencing of reform in post-Mao China. *Modern China*, 18 (2): 197–227.

Wong, C. P. W. (1997) Rural public finance, in C. P. W. Wong (ed.) *Financing local government in the People's Republic of China*, 167–212. Hong Kong: Oxford University Press.

Wong, J. & Yang, M. (eds.) (1995) *The making of TVE miracle*. Singapore: Times Academic Press.

Woo-Cumings, M. (ed.) (1999) *The developmental state*. Ithaca, NY and London: Cornell University Press.

'Wu-Bao' Survey Team, Institute of Economic Research, China Social Sciences Academy (WBST/IER/CSSA) (1999) *China's village economies: Report of 22 villages in Wuxi and Baoding (1997–1998)*. Beijing: China Financial and Economic Press.

Yang, L. & Yuan, Q. F. (2010) Land integration models of the 'shanjiu' redevelopment in PRD. *Urban Planning Forum*, 2: 14–20. (in Chinese).

Yang, M. H. & Liu, Y. X. (2004) Suppression and struggle: A theoretical framework for rural land development rights. *Finance and Economics*, 6: 24–28. (in Chinese).

Yuan, Q. F., Yang, L., Qiu, J. S., Wei, L. H. & Wang, H. (2009) Rural land development in urban–rural integrated planning. *Planner*, 4: 5–13. (in Chinese).

Yuan, Q. F., Yi, X. F. & Wang, X. (2005) From urban–rural integration to real urbanization: Review of Nanhai development. *Urban Planning Forum*, 1: 63–67. (in Chinese).

Zhu, J. M. (2002) Urban development under ambiguous property rights. *International Journal of Urban and Regional Research*, 26(1): 41–57.

Zhu, J. M. (2005) A transitional institution for the emerging land market in urban China. *Urban Studies*, 42(8): 1369–1390.

7 From rural fragmentation to urban integration
Governance over spatial change

Compact city is a necessity instead of a choice for high-density low-income countries. The absence of the state in the land development market generates symmetric and interrelated land rights situations of the anticommons and commons, leading to locked-in unsustainable urban forms. Villages as basic agricultural units are autonomous and self-contained, but governance for nonagricultural development bifurcates into two: either villages or townships. Economic disparities between villages in the same region with similar natural endowments are not great as long as landholdings do not vary substantively, but significant rural-rural inequality between villages and between peasant migrants and local villagers are created by land rent enhanced by urbanization besides the long-existent rural-urban divide. Autonomous villages in the urbanizing suburbs become a rentier class. The Renewal and Refurbishment Program implemented in the Pearl River Delta unveils that the collective has been entrenched amid the urbanized metropolis so as to extract land rent perpetually. Whereas township-led rural development in the Yangtze River Delta shows a promising trajectory toward industrial advancement, ecological integrity, and rural equality, rural communities have been in transition to urban ones, facilitated by land rent distributed evenly by the coordination of urban state. According to the subsidiarity principles, the coordination level for high density urbanization should be appropriately chosen.

Urbanization for compact city

For high-density China's urbanization, optimal land utilization is necessary in order to maximize the provision of building spaces for enormous demand with limited land resources. Suboptimal land utilization either exacerbates building shortage or consumes additional land resources to meet building needs driven by the rapid urbanization and thus worsens land scarcity. The compact city is considered one of the effective measures for making cities sustainable (Jenks, Burton, and Williams, 1996; Jabareen, 2006), though there is a counterproposition that it is the process of city building, not the physical urban forms, that makes cities sustainable (Neuman, 2005). It also appears that in certain socioeconomic circumstances, high density breeds crime, vandalism, and social irresponsibility (Fuerst and Petty, 1991), and high density is even unpopular in the United States, where most American people prefer low-density living (Gordon and Richardson, 1997). Despite those concerns, the compact city approach has several qualities that contribute to urban sustainability.

Urban sprawl in the form of low-density scattered development is defined as 'uncoordinated growth' or growth coordinated at the individual development level (Batty, Besussi, and Chin, 2003). Containing urban sprawl helps conserve the countryside, save natural and agricultural land for future generations, and reduce energy consumption and greenhouse gas emissions through shorter travel distances (Elkin, McLaren, and Hillman, 1991; Ewing, 1997; Cervero, 1998; Buxton, 2000). High density supports effective public transport modes and efficient provision of utilities and infrastructure, and thus it is conducive to social interactions and social equity (Burton, 2000). As a result of high efficiency in land use, which is crucial for the land-scarce high population density cities, additional open and green spaces can be created to enhance biodiversity (Swanwick, Dunnett, and Woolley, 2003).

It is nearly universally accepted that sustainable urbanization should be considered one of the most important tasks facing the world community. While sustainability is a responsibility for every country, developed or developing, it is well recognized that sustainable urbanization is a formidable challenge in low-income developing countries, as pursuing economic growth and improving social welfare are still the top priorities for their government agendas and aspirations of their citizens. It is indisputable that sustainability for the developing countries hinges on their economic sustainability, which, in turn, relies to a large extent on the efficiency of their economic development. Inefficient economic development wastes resources unnecessarily, which adds to tension in social relations and heightens pressure on the environment. Deficiency of wealth often leads to social injustice and environmental unsustainability.

High population density makes compact city a necessity rather than a choice. Social and economic developments are, to a great extent, equivalent to industrialization and urbanization. China's cities are still expanding, while a great magnitude of rural-urban migration is expected. Expanding urban spatial capacity is critical for cities to accommodate rapidly growing urban economies and new incoming migrants with supporting infrastructure and physical structures. Densification and urban compaction can be measured by two parameters related to land use, namely, plot-ratio (total building floor area divided by site area) and site-coverage (the land area covered by buildings divided by site area, or building footprint), and can be increased by raising the value of the two variables. Among the four combinations of two parameters, low-plot-ratio with low-site-coverage is not a possible option as it is not feasible for cities with high population density. The option of high-plot-ratio with high-site-coverage is highly undesirable because it is a built environment with unhealthily poor ventilation and poor exposure to natural sunlight. Open space deficiency makes the place dangerous in case of fires or natural disasters. This is exemplified by Hong Kong's notorious Kowloon Walled City (Pullinger, 1989; Girard and Lambot, 1993) and China's urbanizing villages. The remaining are two practical types of compact cities:

high/medium-plot-ratio with low-site-coverage (see Figure 7.1) and low-plot-ratio with high-site-coverage (see Figure 7.2).[1] The critical question is which one of the two makes cities more sustainable in terms of environmental amenities and land use efficiency.

In the early stage of urbanization, spontaneous settlements usually take the form of low-plot-ratio with low-site-coverage, when there is land aplenty. In the course of urban population growth without an effective mechanism of land assembly, rising land scarcity due to rapidly growing urban population gives existing owners of land parcels enough monetary incentives to have land plots subdivided and sold to new migrants or incoming residents to encroach upon vacant open space for building additional housing spaces (Marcussen, 1990; Mahtab-uz-Zaman and Lau, 2000).[2] Being socially spontaneous and full of individual initiatives, this development mode should emerge endogenously by default without top-down regulation in the form of land use planning. Under the heavy pressure of burgeoning urban population, urban construction by this mode would maintain its momentum and encroach upon open spaces both horizontally and vertically. As a result, areas with initial low-plot-ratio and low-site-coverage may evolve further to become high-plot-ratio and high-site-coverage slums as the environmental quality deteriorates quickly and landholding becomes increasingly fragmented (see Figure 7.3).

The high-plot-ratio with low-site-coverage mode should be generated exogenously by design with imposed order, nevertheless. Land development in this mode represented by the case in Figure 7.1 produces a total building floor area as many as two times of the site area (plot ratio 2.0) with a site-coverage of 24 percent (about a quarter of the site area being occupied by buildings and the rest, 76 percent, being open space and access roads), while land development in the mode represented by the case in Figure 7.2 generates an amount of floor

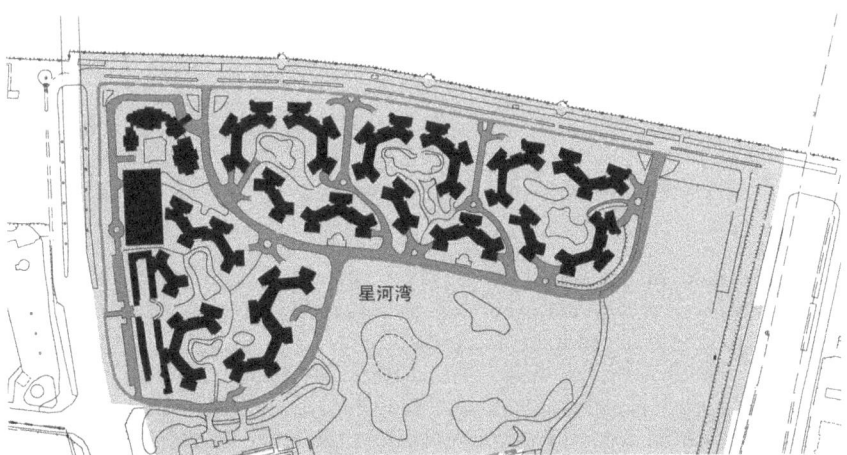

Figure 7.1 A high-plot-ratio with low-site-coverage housing estate.

170 *From rural fragmentation to urban integration*

Figure 7.2 A low-plot-ratio with high-site-coverage street block.

areas less than the site area (plot ratio less than 1.0) with a site-coverage as high as 85 percent. Although the mode represented by Figure 7.2 can be more community-oriented, spontaneous, and probably more favorable to the existing residents than that by the mode demonstrated by Figure 7.1, the former has less housing space per unit area of land and thus is less capable of accommodating ever-increasing rural-urban migrants than the latter. In view of a dynamic process of urbanization that China is experiencing, housing equity between the current residents and newcomers hinges on the adequate provision of housing space through efficient land utilization.

From rural fragmentation to urban integration 171

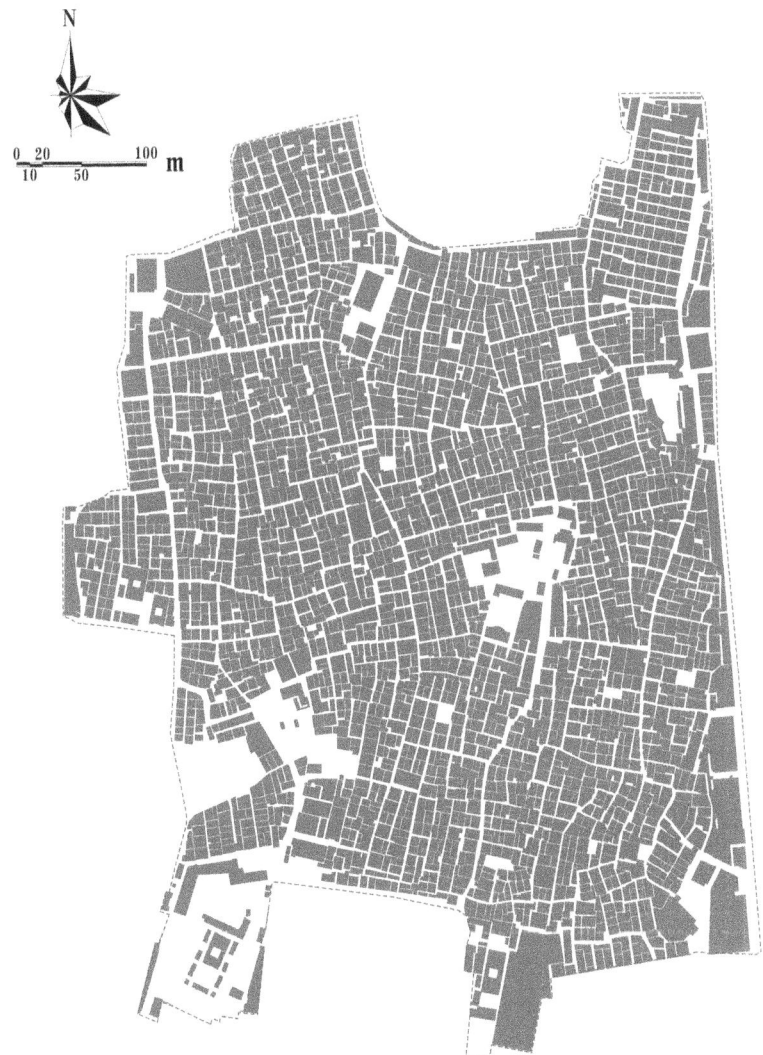

Figure 7.3 Plan of Shipai urbanizing village, Guangzhou, China.

The choice between the two land development modes is facilitated or constrained by the institutions of land rights imbedded in the land development process. Amalgamation of small land lots into a large parcel, required by economies of scale, is onerous, if not impossible, because of prohibitive transaction costs incurred in obtaining consensus from all landholders. In this circumstance, land scarcity is further exacerbated by the underutilization of a significant amount of existing urban built-up areas held by the interest of the status quo. This is the property rights situation known as *the anticommons*, or practically known as 'hold-out' problems, where multiple owners have effective rights excluding each other from efficient utilization of resources (Heller, 1998; Buchanan and Yoon, 2000).

Driven by the heavy demand from migrants and young generations who need shelters, individual landholders carry out intensification of land use by themselves on their small land plots in order to materialize the enhanced land asset value. In order to maximize the building floor areas, individual builders often ignore building codes and zoning, if there are any, thereby imposing negative externalities on the neighborhood. Individual gains (maximization of building floor areas) leads to neighborhood losses (loss of open and green spaces) (see Figure 7.3). Negative externalities are aggregated, and neighborhood environment deteriorates. The neighborhood becomes *the commons*, another property rights situation, where environmental amenities are overconsumed and land utilization becomes suboptimal. In contrast to the anticommons, the commons is the case of *open access to resources*. Individuals seeking personal gain leads to depletion of resources as a result of overconsumption and underinvestment, which harm the collective benefit, the so-called 'tragedy of the commons' (Hardin, 1968). The absence of planning control constitutes the commons, which essentially deprives rights to residents not to be adversely affected by developments in the neighborhood. Uncontrolled developments in the setting of high density result in substandard and inferior habitations.

The commons and anticommons in the land development market reveal the absence of the state as the regulator in the provision of built environment. At this juncture, the state is deemed essential for achieving sustainable urban forms. Clear land rights and effective development controls can contain the commons. Government regulations over land rights to curtail individual interests can eliminate the anticommons for the sake of collective benefits. The state failures in securing both social equity and economic efficiency deprive the state of the legitimacy and moral capital needed to strengthen its regulatory power in the land development market, as demolishing illegal construction means forcing its inhabitants into homelessness. A vicious cycle of poor economic performance and incompetent state management traps the developing countries in an unsustainable process of urbanization (see Loop in Figure 7.4). Inefficiency exacerbates inequity. For high-density low-income China, the symmetric and interrelated land rights situations of the anticommons and commons lead to locked-in unsustainable urban forms (see Figure 7.4).

Autonomous rural development

China's villages are a traditional social organization having existed for a prolonged and enduring history. Villages have become basic, autonomous, and self-contained socioeconomic units. New members are only either born or married into a village, where there is almost no room for outside migrants. Villages, unlike cities, are traditionally egalitarian but not open to nonmembers. Considered as 'self-governing' bodies (Gao, 1999), villages are responsible for

From rural fragmentation to urban integration 173

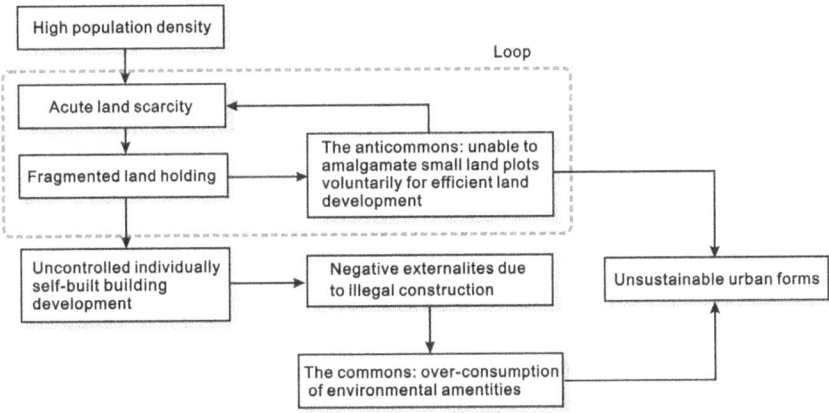

Figure 7.4 Vicious cycle in the land development market leading to unsustainable urban forms.

their own social services (health, primary education, and elderly welfare) and infrastructure construction (Wong, 1997; Tsai, 2007). Villages have also become the basic collective economic organization in rural China through People's Commune movement since the 1949 revolution.

Though the dismantling of People's Communes in the early 1980s decentralized collective agriculture to individual household farming, rural industrialization, a new stimulus for the agrarian development, bolstered the collective nature of villages. Nevertheless, village-led rural industrialization had ground to a halt since the mid-1990s while private enterprises and joint ventures gradually took over (Che and Qian, 1998). The prospects of villages' economies were dampened by the demise of collective industrialization, but another opportunity soon emerged as collective land became potentially valuable when urbanization penetrated into rural areas adjacent to the urban peripheries. Farmland can be converted to nonagricultural land that can be let to inward manufacturing, and thus extracted land rent becomes villages' collective revenues.

Rural China is managed by a three-tiered governance system. Villages remain as autonomous units for agricultural production and social development. The township government is at the top of the rural collective hierarchical governance and at the bottom of the urban-state governance system, an interface between the urban and rural societies. Serving villages and managing rural development, townships are members of the collective. For rural nonagricultural development, extraction of collective land rent is a contentious and competitive matter due to ambiguity in relation to the peculiar collective land ownership, which has further implication for the mode of rural industrialization. It is observed that, in general, clans are rooted more deeply in the villages of Southern China than in those of Northern China because of differences in geography, regional politics, and local culture (Qin, 1998, 2003; Zhou, 1998). It is usual in the Pearl River Delta that clan-based natural villages are the basic units holding collective land for rural development. In the Yangtze River Delta, it is the norm that administrative villages instead of natural villages are the basic units managing agricultural production. In the era of post-TVE nonagricultural development, natural villages remain the leading force in the Pearl River Delta, while it is often the township that coordinates industrialization led by private firms and inward investments in the Yangtze River Delta (Lin, 2015). Collective land for nonagricultural growth is managed by townships, and township industrial zones remain collectively owned.

In the era of rural nonagricultural development, townships in the Yangtze River Delta as a unit in the municipal governance system are the least stable entities in relation to the municipality and villages. The boundaries of the municipality and villages cannot be easily altered, as these entities have strong senses of territoriality. The jurisdiction of townships, especially of those urbanizing townships, can be conveniently adjusted, and thus townships tend not to become independent stakeholders with place-based vested interests. Townships do not have their own fiscal bases from which fees and taxes are collected, either. Therefore, townships are not a political entity. They serve villages and have responsibility for rural development; they also have to convey the central policies downward and ensure coordinated municipal development.

Rural-rural inequality induced by land rent

Social inequality and spatial segregation are long-standing phenomena in the world's cities (Hamnett, 2001). In the contemporary Western cities, new processes relating to the new international division of labor are deemed as underlying causes (Friedmann and Wolff, 1982). Economic transition from manufacturing to services has "brought about the changes in organization of work which are reflected in the social polarization in the income and occupational distribution of workers" (Sassen, 1991: 9). However, as White (1998) highlights, processes of social, economic, and political restructuring may all be part of general forces operating throughout the world, but their actual mechanisms are locally specific. China's transition from a socialist planned system to the market-driven economy suggests dramatic sociospatial restructuring during its rapid urbanization.

The country is categorized into urban and rural societies by the unique urban and rural household registration systems, known as *hukou* (Chan, 2009). It is believed that inequality between urban and rural people, under the general rubric of urban-rural divide, is reinforced by the binary *hukou* system, that is agricultural and nonagricultural residence registration institutionalized in 1958 (Cheng and Selden, 1994). Under the central planning regime, *hukou* served as a means to ensure fair distribution of very limited entitlements and social welfare (including promised universal public housing or land for housing and means for living) among the people by registering them to places. Inequality arose when entitlements given to people with nonagricultural, or urban, *hukou* were far superior to those received by people with agricultural, or rural, *hukou* (Solinger, 1999). The former are of an array of urban benefits (such as medical care, education, retirement pensions, etc.), and the latter are basically of self-sufficiency without those benefits enjoyed by urban fellow citizens. Inequality was exacerbated by the effective curtailment of free movement of people between rural and urban locales, that is, rural-urban migration (Whyte, 2010). The path to improvement of living conditions by migrating to cities was blocked by the 'invisible walls' (Chan, 1994).

The economic reforms since 1978 have softened the dual-*hukou* rigidity, and the rural reforms (de-collectivization of agriculture and decontrolled rural-urban migration) have improved quality of life of many villagers. With the gradual relaxation of constraints over free migration, China has witnessed an unprecedentedly great scale of rural-urban migration and interregional population movement, which is mainly from the central and west regions to the east coastal cities. The influx of migrants has contributed greatly to the sociospatial restructuring of these dynamically urbanizing regions. On the one hand, market-oriented reforms have altered the equality bases constructed under Chinese socialism, leading to urban social stratification along with the changing socioeconomic statuses of people (Tang and Parish, 2000; Li and Wu, 2006). Urban-rural divide has been alleviated to certain extent and urban-rural difference in entitlement has been mitigated during recent years (Chan, 2014). On the other hand, without local urban *hukou*, migrant workers often live in the bottom of urban society, experiencing dire discrimination and social injustice in the city (Meng and Zhang, 2001; Liang and Ma, 2004; Wu, 2004; Li and Wu, 2008).

Organizations, whether they are political, economic, or social, behave and perform as collective actors within a framework defined by institutions (Knight, 1992). China's villages are a unique social organization and a collective economic entity. Collective ownership of rural land, established by the People's Commune movement, has become a defining moment for the villages in the socialist era. Entitlement to village's provisions is based upon village membership, which is not open to outsiders. Therefore, autonomous and exclusionary villages are a unique institution in rural China. Autonomous villages are pertinent to the independent and self-reliant economy of agriculture. In the same region with similar natural endowments, agricultural productivity tends to be equal between villages as long as landholdings do not vary substantively. Villages as autonomous units for the agricultural economy work effectively according to the principle of subsidiarity.

Villagers in the less dynamic regions and less accessible locations remain in farming as they have been laboring for hundreds of years, while villages close to cities in the dynamically urbanizing regions have been diversified into nonagricultural economies. Rural industrialization has not only created jobs for the local villagers but also enhanced the value of collective land. With the unexpected decline and demise of rural collective industries, village economies in the urbanizing regions have increasingly changed to a new form of rural growth that relies on land rent. A new mode of collective economies in the form of land shareholding cooperatives has emerged (Sun, Luo, and Zhao, 2010). These cooperatives are essentially for villages to capitalize on land rent that is enhanced. Land-leasing businesses have become villages' new collective economy. Led by the global capital, private plants have become more vibrant by creating many more jobs than what usually inward-looking TVEs did. In the progressive rural development, villagers are transformed from agricultural producers to industrial producers and further to 'landlords'. Land rent is driven up substantially by industrialization and urbanization and constitutes a handsome source of economic benefits only shared within the village community. Villages can become a rentier class.

An intriguing sociospatial differentiation in the rural setting has occurred. Rising nonfarming land rent is not spatially distributed evenly across villages. Those villages in good locations capitalize on land rent much more than those in not-so-good locations. Reliance on land rent enhanced by the progressive urbanization during the transition to nonagricultural economies creates inequality between villages, reinforced by rural autonomy (Shi, 2000). Those in urbanizing locations are more favored than those still in rural locations. In 2012, 37.1 percent and 32.8 percent of the total annual village collective revenues for the villages in central Yushan and Zhangpu townships, Kunshan, were derived from land rentals, respectively, while only 17.1 percent and 2.0 percent for the villages in faraway Dianshanhu and Jingxi townships, respectively (ORW/KMG, 2013). The gaps between the former and latter are substantial, which gives rise to inequality between village communities because of the degree of nonagriculturalization. The statistics of 162 administrative villages in Kunshan reveal a great deal of disparity in collective revenues from land rentals between villages, the highest being more than 800 times of the lowest. The Gini coefficient measuring inequality between villages' income of land rentals reached 0.593. The total collective revenues show a disparity between villages to a lesser extent (0.420) as other sources of village revenues do not enjoy location-specific advantages (ORG/KMG, 2013) (see Table 7.1). Data from villages in Shishan township, Nanhai, display a similar pattern. The Gini coefficient measuring disparity in village land rental income (0.707) is much more unequal than the disparity in the total village revenues (0.608), as the latter is moderated by the subsidies transferred by the town government to those low-income villages (Shishan Township Government, 2013). It seems land rental income is more pronounced in Nanhai than in Kunshan. In addition to the urban-rural inequality, which is a persistent feature over a long history in China (Whyte, 2010), rural-rural income gaps are widening between those villages in the urban peripheries and those in remote locations, even within the boundary of the same municipality.

TVEs are small enterprises using local labors and local materials, but those globally connected inward and outside industrial investments tend to be more competitive than TVEs and create more jobs than what the local villagers can absorb. Those vacancies have to find migrants to fill in. Industrialization within the village and township territories has significantly attracted a large number of migrant workers into the villages. In 1982 when Nanhai was still a rural county,

Table 7.1 Statistical characteristics of the total collective income and land rental income of 162 villages, Kunshan, 2012 (¥ thousand)

	Mean	Minimum	Maximum	Gini coefficient
Land rental income	1,665	20	16,530	0.593
Total collective income	3,780	526	41,710	0.420
Total collective income with municipal fiscal transfers	5,791	1,577	42,909	0.303

Note: Gini coefficient is a measure of statistical dispersion of a set of data. It is between one and zero. Zero stands for perfect equality, while one denotes absolute inequality.
Source: ORW/KMG, 2013

Table 7.2 Demographic structure by the residence status in Nanhai, 1982–2010

year	Total number of residents	Local villagers as % of the total	Migrants as % of the total
1982	826,100	100.0	0.0
1990	1,022,400	91.3	8.7
2000*	2,133,700	51.3	48.7
2010#	2,591,000	45.9	54.1

Source: NHAB, 1982 and 1990; *NHPCO, 2002; #NHBS, 2011

Table 7.3 Demographic structure by the residence status in Kunshan, 1980–2010

year	Total number of residents	Local villagers as % of the total	Migrants as % of the total
1980	523,500	100.0	0.0
1990	574,700	98.2	1.8
2000	725,900	81.9	18.1
2010	1,923,900	37.0	63.0

Source: KSBS, 1980–2011

there were no migrants at all. The nonlocals have now outnumbered the locals (see Table 7.2). It shows that 71.0 percent of Nanhai's residents were registered in the villages in 2010, including 757,600 local villagers and 1,083,200 migrants. Those migrants living in villages account for 77.3 percent of the total migrants in Nanhai (NHPCO, 2002). Similarly, Kunshan has seen its demographic structure transformed from a typical rural homogenous aggregation to a highly heterogeneous composition since 1980. In three decades (1980–2010), the proportion of migrants in the total grew from nil to 63.0 percent (see Table 7.3). Its economy not only supported local residents of 0.7 million but also accommodated 1.2 million migrant workers.

Hukou and its entitlement are linked to places where people are registered. Place-based entitlement is what *hukou* constitutes, and it is still one of key features in China's urbanization. As described by Chan (2009), the place-based *hukou* registration defines one's rights to locality-specific facilities and services of which the levels and availability vary from place to place, and the division between locals and nonlocals still matters. Though both the local villagers and migrant workers are peasants with rural *hukou*, the only difference is the places of their *hukou*: the former are in the urbanizing regions, and the latter come from agricultural regions where nonagricultural development remains weak. Local villages in the dynamic urbanizing regions have successful, nonagricultural development and thus can provide better village benefits as entitlement to their members than what the villages where migrant workers come from can offer. Landed benefits and rental income are the important entitlements determined by the location of villages.

Villagers are entitled to free provision of land lots for building their family houses. According to Land Management Law, 1988, land for housing is allocated on a per-household basis, one household one housing lot at a size commensurate with the local conditions of land availability (http://www.law-lib.com/LAW/law_view.asp?id=95544, accessed March 5, 2014). Village housing lots are meant for own use, not considered as assets for lease or sale (Ministry of Construction, People's Republic of China, 2008). In comparison with urban households, rural households have an affordable housing option. However, in the poor rural villages, building a proper house is still one of the greatest burdens on the peasant families. According to Gao (1999), a simple single-story house with a wooden frame structure and mud clay walls would cost ten years' income of a male adult peasant in Gao's village in the 1980s, and even the house did not have the housing facilities that urban residents took for granted.

In 1982, there were 2,310 villagers living in a compact housing cluster surrounded by green paddy fields in administrative village X, which is composed of eight nature villages in Nanhai. Industrial land only accounted for 2.7 percent of the total village area in 1994. Considerable conversion of village agricultural land to industrial uses has been relentless in order to increase the collective incomes from land rent, and industrial land reached 22.6 percent of the total in 2008. Those factories were mainly of low-value-added and labor-intensive production, such as printing, paper making, plastic processing, hardware and electric appliance, furniture, and garments. A large inflow of industrial firms, accompanied by an influx of migrant workers, means that the villages are effectively urbanizing drastically. In 2010, there were 2,740 villagers, but the number of migrants increased to 4,620. The revenues of the village land shareholding cooperative were on the rise, so did the demand for village housing space.

In comparison with village X, administrative village L is a much more urbanized village in Nanhai. Only 7.6 percent of its territory remained as farmland, and industrial land accounted for at an astonishingly high level of 41.1 percent of the total in 2008. In 2012, village L hosted 469 small industrial plants, 1,490 retail and wholesale shops, 25,000 migrant workers, and 5,180 own villagers (interviews conducted in 2013). The concentration of such a large number of residents in a relatively small area creates a lucrative market of housing leasing. Shuibu is a nature village within village L, without any farmland unconverted.

There are only industrial land uses (61.7 percent) and residential land uses (38.3 percent) in the village (interviews conducted in 2013). The 'old village' was once inhabited by 106 local households in 1982 (NHAB, 1982). Later, villagers moved to 'new village' in 1994, and to ten six-story apartment buildings in 2000 when severe land scarcity forced the village to shift to apartment living for newly created households. Building apartments, rather than houses, for new village households seems a rational collective decision. The 'old village' has been since mainly rented to and occupied by migrant workers.

Rental incomes from industrial and residential land leasing are taken by the local villagers only, determined by the institution of autonomous village. Those villagers in favorable locations earn additional incomes derived from land rent on top of nonagricultural wages, while those migrants cannot claim any benefits. The quantum of land rent is determined by the extent of farmland converted to industrial uses and density of 'old villages' that have been intensively built up. Land rent accounts for 23.6 percent of the total household incomes on average for Gaoqiao villagers, while land rent represents 51.0 percent of the total in more urbanized Shuibu. Income difference is widening in the course of continuing urbanization. In Gaoqiao, local households' total annual incomes (¥81,179) are 48.8 percent more than that of migrant workers (¥54,550) on average. In more urbanized Shuibu, local villagers (¥150,035) are better off than migrant workers (¥66,146) by 126.8 percent. Although both the locals and migrants are excluded from urban welfare, the former are provided with a variety of social welfares by their village organization, such as pension for the elderly, medical care insurance, education allowance, and so on. Almost all the migrant respondents expressed that they did not receive any social welfare provided by their hometown villages because of the poor collective economies.

Migrant workers only receive wages from industrial employment, while local villagers can claim industrial and housing land rent on top of wages. The growing village 'landlord' economy widens the gap in income and local welfare between the two peasant groups. Moreover, as villages are autonomous and exclusionary organizations, migrants are treated as guest workers who can never settle permanently in the host village, no matter how long they have worked there. The territory of the village belongs to local villagers like 'gated communities'. Discrimination against migrant workers living in this locale is institutionalized, while the village is urbanizing in situ. Therefore, it is the place-based entitlement, not the *hukou* per se, which induces inequality between the locals and nonlocals in the rural setting. Successful nonagricultural development of some villages in the dynamic urbanizing regions has provided better village entitlement to their members than urban provisions cities have offered. As Chan and Buckingham (2008) discovered, many villagers refuse to convert their rural *hukou* to urban one, because of better rural benefits provided by the villages. The dichotomy of rural-urban *hukou* system remains the same, but the urban-rural differentiation has reversed in the dynamic urbanizing regions due to the changed place-based entitlement. In contrast to the old urban-rural divide and inequality based on the dichotomous urban-rural *hukou* system that prohibited free migration between the two domains, a new breed of inequality of rural (urbanizing)-rural (agricultural) divide along with the place dimension also emerges in the context of exclusionary village nonagricultural development during rapid urbanization.

As long as the existing landlord economy is maintained, villages do not have incentives to improve industrial productivity. Wages remain low, while land rent increases due to increasing land scarcity and rising demand for land from nonagricultural activities and housing from migrant workers. Villagers' incomes may be maximized in the short-term, but migrant workers' welfare and long-term future are adversely affected and unpromising. The reliance on land rent makes villages a rentier class that is only interested in land rent taking. The overall social progress brought about by progressive urbanization is compromised. American social reformer Henry George (1879/1938) advocates that increment in land values should be retained by society, as increase in land rent is caused by public investment in infrastructure and facilities as well as rising demand for land due to progressive urbanization. Enhanced infrastructure and provided social and public goods are beneficial and accessible to all members of society. As the betterment in land values resulting from local economic growth and urbanization is solely appropriated by the villages, the fiscal capacity of township and city governments for the provision of public and social goods is weakened. Henry George's Single Tax may be too radical and impractical, certain taxes on land rent should be necessary. It is clear that the convention of land rent taken wholly by the locals is not conducive to inclusive urbanization at all (World Bank, 2008). If infrastructure can be improved and social and public goods provided, it is beneficial and accessible to all members of society.

Ostrom (1990) advocates management of common-pool resources by the community, with neither centralized government control nor market mechanism. One of the eight 'design principles' of effective management of common-pool resources (or collective communities) is to have clearly defined boundaries for forcible exclusion of external unentitled members (Ostrom, 2000). Ostrom's theories seem only applicable to closed and homogenous communities, usually in a rural setting. When China's rural villages are industrializing, discriminative community management of collective land resources during supposedly inclusive urbanization becomes a challenging issue of social justice.

The entrenched collective perpetuated by land rent amid the urbanized metropolis

With a total land area of 57,378 square kilometers, the Pearl River Delta saw its total built-up area increase by 5.9 times during 1990–2012, growing from 1,067 square kilometers (1990) to 7,409 square kilometers (2012). The built-up area as a percentage of the total land area rose from 1.9 percent (1990) to 12.9 percent (2012) in 22 years. One of the striking characteristics is that the built-up areas developed by the villages account for as much as 42 percent of the total built-up areas due to the dynamic, rural, bottom-up, nonagricultural development (The Pearl River Delta Region Planning, retrieved from http://www.gdupi.com/

prd2014/index.asp, accessed May 29, 2017). A binary urbanization led by both the urban state and rural collective has been a prominent feature of the Pearl River Delta development since the economic reform. Moreover, the Pearl River Delta, as the reform pioneer, is one of the regions in rural China where autonomous rural collective-led urbanization has been most dynamic and significant (Shen, Wong, and Feng, 2002).

Nevertheless, village-led nonagricultural development gives rise to problems of spatial fragmentation, ecological deterioration, exclusion of migrants, and underutilized land resources. Villages hold on to their collective land for land rent extraction, which holds off progressive development of villages in the course of urbanization. Tackling those developmental problems entails institutional change to the collective land rights under the competition for land rent between the urban state and rural collective. In the wake of renewal and refurbishment, a village's use right to the collective land proves an effective holding power that gives villages a strong bargaining position against the urban state's attempt to phase out collective land ownership. As a result, path-dependent institutional change to the collective land rights leads to the collective entrenched in the urbanizing Guangzhou metropolis.

Aiming to make the built environment integrative and inclusive, the Renewal and Refurbishment Program (RRP) chiefly incorporates redeveloping underused industrial land parcels, refurbishing deteriorating villages, and renewing dilapidated town areas (*sanjiu gaizao*). It was officially initiated and launched by the Guangzhou municipal government in 2009. Holders of land parcels as concerned stakeholders showed great interest and responded voluntarily and enthusiastically by registering as many as 2,048 land parcels with the Panyu Bureau of Urban Renewal. Industrial land parcels and villages are the main participants, representing 91.4 percent of the total in terms of land area. Collective land accounts for 72.2 percent of the total, and almost half of them (47.4 percent) were illegitimately converted previously to nonagricultural uses, in which three quarters (74.9 percent) of rural industrial land is not legitimate. This demonstrates clearly that the RRP is aiming at the problematic, underproductive built environment created by rural industrialization. Villages also intend to seek formalization of illegitimate lands through the RRP. The built-up area developed by the villages registered in the RRP is as astonishingly high as 79.9 percent of the total collective-owned areas. It is assumed that the substandard built environment is caused by rural industrialization without coordination of land use planning. An urban land use zoning system will be installed in the realm of collective villages via the RRP as well.

Consequently, only 22 registered cases went through out of a total of 2,048 during the period 2009–2014, and yet only 11 cases entered into final implementation. The success rate was disappointingly low at 0.7 percent (60.9 ha) of the total in terms of land areas. Ten out of 11 cases were state-owned sites pursuing upgrading from industrial to commercial land use. As collective land parcels were expected to be converted to state ownership after renewal and refurbishment, a clear message was conveyed that the holders of collective land were not interested in giving up existing ownership by taking one-off benefits of generous land rent differentials. It seems that only those illegitimate collective land parcels are keen to seek formalization by joining in the RRP. It can be inferred that it is more difficult to engage collective land than state land for renewal, possibly due to the fact that a large number of village stakeholders have escalated the transaction cost. Little progress in village renewal suggests that villages are not willing to be parted from their collective-owned land, despite being offered one-off, unprecedentedly handsome land rent differentials. Land for continuous income yielding, though diminishing over time, to the collective community is still considered essential. Villages were adamant that autonomy for collective land resources should be maintained.

The implementation rate of RRP was very low because the collective did not find out that it was to their benefits. A decree issued by the Guangzhou government on December 1, 2015, announced new policies that give more leeway to villages in managing their renewal and refurbishment (Government of Guangzhou Municipality, 2015), in view of the strong bargaining position of the collective. Our field reconnaissance has found that villagers are convinced that the collective should remain as a way of life though the area is totally urbanized. Villagers should actively take part in the redevelopment process of their habitats. The new policies agree to formalize spontaneously developed, illegitimate lands as long as the urban government can take a share of 30 percent and villages retain 70 percent. Villages can keep their collective landownership intact if village members prefer. A special partnership between the collective village and urban government is meant to entice participation of the collective that is keen on securing as much land rent benefit as possible from the RRP and to ensure instillation of land use planning in the collective realm by the urban government. In addition to collective goods that are a gain to the villages, public and social goods provided in place are considered a gain to general urbanites.

Leasing village land to inward private industrial firms with a tacit agreement from the urban government since the economic reform launched in 1978 is an informal institutional change that should be attributed to the phenomenal rural industrialization. It helps significantly to make the Pearl River Delta one of the most dynamic regions in the world, lifting many villages out of rural poverty by nonagricultural economies. As a result, rural collectives are urbanizing economically. However, uncertainty induced by informal institutions breeds short-termism that brings about excessive conversion of farmland for industrial uses. Land adjustment and amalgamation across villages are virtually impossible because of prohibitive transaction costs incurred in obtaining consensus from villages in question. Land scarcity is further exacerbated by the underutilization of a significant amount of land areas held by the villages as the status quo interests. The collective use right constitutes an effective holding power, a gridlock hampering progressive rural change. The power to extract land rent is too good for the collective to relinquish, given the fact that land rent is enhanced by urbanization, and it is an effortless source of collective revenues. The impasse remains unchanged.

The local land reform of 2015 legalizes the illegitimate land with a split between the rural collective (70 percent) and urban state (30 percent), so that 30 percent of illegitimate collective land is decollectivized, while villages retain a larger share of 70 percent. Formalizing illegitimate land is the most enticing measure that is appealing to villages. The RRP evolves from one dominated by the state to one participated in by villages under competition between the two. The latest institutional change to collective land rights seems to be well received by the collective. A partnership between the two works for both parties. The rural collective maintains the collective land, and the urban state ensures a municipal infrastructure and public amenities in the erstwhile realm of villages. With the coexistence of state land and collective land, communities endeavor to make urbanization integrative and inclusive.

The rural collective survives urbanization and is entrenched in the urbanizing landscape. Competition for land rent determines the path-dependent institutional change to the unique collective land. Persistent land rent taking has to be in the name of collectives, so that collectives have to go through the transforming urbanization by holding onto their rural village *hukou* that is the defining factor for a collective. Collective land as a means of production has become a collective asset that is imbedded in the urban society. Land use planning is installed to ensure the provision of infrastructure and social facilities that help to deal with the rural deficiency of fragmentation and exclusion. Collective land as an inadvertent design for socialist rural villages evolves ceaselessly along with rural development and urbanization and has finally become an urban fixture. The rentier class continues its existence along with progressive urbanization. As a result, the collective is perpetuated by land rent in the urbanizing metropolis.

Township-led rural development

There is tension between bottom-up autonomy and top-down integration, which are two significant issues to urbanization. The tension goes up when land scarcity is exacerbated by the rapid urbanization. The differences between urban and rural communities lie in that the former are voluntary, open, and interest-based, whereas the latter are involuntary, close, and place-based. A village is usually autonomous and homogeneous in its social composition, and members are often bound by kinship and lineage. Urbanites are heterogeneous, making cities a mosaic of social worlds (Wirth, 1938). Urban places are interconnected, and a city with multiple functions works as a whole. Thus, cities built by autonomous communities and developers as entities are integrative. Without appropriate planning coordination, city building tends to yield informal and chaotic settlements as a result of disordered competition (Duany, Plater-Zyberk, and Speck, 2000; Roy and AlSayyad, 2004). Fierce competition for limited land resources in developing countries by autonomous actors without effective urban governance often results in spatial fragmentation (McGee, 1991; Firman, 1997; Leaf, 1999; Tian and Zhu, 2013; Zhu and Guo, 2014).

Township-led rural industrialization tends to be more spatially integrative than village-coordinated development. Kunshan in the Yangtze River Delta was designated as a county in the country's administrative structure. More than 85 percent of its people were tilling the soil during the period 1950–1980 (KSBS, 1980). Like the whole country, its villagers were very poor as the peasants were mainly engaged in subsistence agricultural farming, producing barely enough for survival. Over the period of 25 years (1950–1975), its agricultural output per capita only increased 3.0 percent per annum (inflation included) (KSBS, 1980). One peasant only produced an annual agricultural output worth of ¥93.3 in monetary value in 1950, equivalent to ¥0.26 a day.[3] Rural poverty was striking. After 25 years of rural development during which the history witnessed the Rural Land Reform, revolutionary collectivization of the People's Commune, disastrous Great Leap Forward, and Cultural Revolution, agricultural outputs per capita increased merely to ¥195.3 in 1975 (KSBS, 1980).

Agriculture and services accounted for 58 percent and 23 percent of the Kunshan county GDP in 1970, respectively, a typical agrarian entity (KSBS, 1970). The development of rural industries picked up its pace from the early 1980s when the problem of surplus rural laborers became a crisis. Villages and townships made tremendous bottom-up efforts to bring in industrial expertise from elsewhere (Marton, 2000). The efforts paid off quickly. There were 335 TVEs in operation in 1985, accounting for 67.7 percent of the total 495 industrial firms in Kunshan, and manufacturing share in the county GDP rose to 50 percent, while agriculture declined to 31 percent (KSBS, 1985).

Rural industries became the backbone of the county economy. The share in the total industrial output contributed by the TVEs increased from 59.5 percent (1985) to 70.6 percent (1990) and further to 74.9 percent (1995) (KSBS, 1985, 1990, 1995). An important pattern was noteworthy that, over the period 1985–1995, in the rural industrialization led by the township and village industries, the share of village industries in the total industrial output decreased continuously (from 25.2 percent to 19.8 percent), while the share of township industries increased consistently (from 34.3 percent to 55.1 percent) (KSBS, 1985–1995). It was not unusual for townships to preside over villages in coordinating rural industrialization in the Yangtze River Delta (Lin, 2015). A few explanations are available. The sense of clanship has not been particularly entrenched in the Yangtze River Delta villages (Zhou, 1998). 'The fate of a nation being the responsibility of every ordinary people' (*tianxia xingwang, pifu youze*) is the famous motto, becoming a well-known proverb later, coined by one of the country gentries Gu Yanwu (1613–1682) who lived in Kunshan in the late Ming dynasty. It clearly advocates a sort of citizenry beyond clan solidarity. Nonagricultural economies have not been necessarily village-centered. A network of small market towns connected by rivers and canals has been specialized on transaction of agricultural produce and manufacturing of cottage industries' products since Ming dynasty in the Tai Lake region. Setting up plants needed external industrial expertise and serviced sites, which was better coordinated at township level. It was clear that Kunshan townships took the leading role in rural industrialization from the beginning. The other two significant shifts identified were an irreversible decline of village industries relatively (before 1995) and absolutely (after 1995) and the emergence of industrial zones managed by municipal and town governments.

Not being able to face the competition from reformed urban enterprises, the number of collectively owned factories as a percentage of total industrial firms in Kunshan county dropped significantly over the period 1985–2010: from 67.7 percent (1985) to 5.0 percent (2000) and further to 0.2 percent (2010) (KSBS, 1985–2010). Industrialization has been shifted predominantly to inward foreign direct investments and joint ventures (71.3 percent in 2000; 90.0 percent in 2010) ever since (KSBS, 2001–2011). Village enterprises scattered in the countryside were closed down, while inward and private investments were located in industrial zones planned and built by the county and township governments. The Kunshan Economic and Technological Development Zone (KETDZ) was developed adventurously and covertly by the county government initially in 1984 in Yushan, the urban downtown core of the county. It was named the New Industrial Zone (*gongye xinqu*) in the beginning, at a size of 3.75 square kilometers (Chien, 2007). Its development zone status was only recognized ex-post by the provincial government in 1990 and the central government in 1992 when KETDZ began to enjoy preferential open-door policies (Wei, 2010). With the status of special development zone, foreign investments flooded in. KETDZ expanded its size to 6.18 square kilometers in 1991 and 10.38 square kilometers in 1992. Subsequently, all 20 townships within Kunshan municipality designated their own town industrial zones (*gongye xiaoqu*) in the mid-1990s (Marton, 2000). The mode of rural industrialization has clearly shifted from that initiated by the village collectives to that coordinated by the county/townships.

The industrial landscape has evolved from scattered village factories to concentrated city industrial zones (KETDZ) and town industrial zones. Factories are agglomerated to the industrial zones. Further industrial agglomeration occurred as KETDZ gathered strength and grew unabated because of favorable industrial policies and infrastructure. By 2011, KETDZ accounted for 60.3 percent of total industrial output in Kunshan, and village industries had lost their competitiveness completely (0.2 percent), while the former was 43.2 percent and the latter 2.1 percent in 2001, respectively (KSBS, 2002–2012).

The agglomeration of industrial space improves economies of scale for industrial production, which is also critical to the economic and effective provision of infrastructure. It facilitates the structural upgrading of manufacturing. Structural change of manufacturing is defined as a process where some sectors flourish and others decline. It can be attributed to the factors of economies of scale, technological innovation, industrial linkage, and government policies. Since 1998, Kunshan's manufacturing structure has undergone drastic changes as low-value-added labor-intensive sectors[4] decline continuously while high-value-added technology-intensive sectors[5] expand consistently. As a percentage of the total industrial output, the labor-intensive sectors declined from 59.7 percent (1998) to 16.6 percent (2010); the technology-intensive sectors increased from

13.9 percent (1998) to 63.5 percent (2010) (KSBS, 1998–2011). This favorable change shows that the advancement has made manufacturing increasingly productive. Enhanced productivity helps to increase wages to workers. Industrial output per worker was ¥215,800 in 2000, and it grew drastically to ¥664,900 in 2010, achieving an annual increase rate of 11.9 percent on average (KSBS, 1990–2011).

Collectively owned factories in the villages were gradually closed down during the industrial restructuring, and inward private firms preferred industrial zones where quality infrastructure was provided. Yet, there were still too many industrial zones for a small municipality, as there were 22 townships in Kunshan prior to 1990, and each town had at least one industrial zone (Marton, 2000). Restructuring of township jurisdiction was carried out in 1990 when 22 townships were consolidated to 20, and then to 15 in 2001 and further to 10 in 2004 (KSBS, 1985, 1990, 2002, 2006). It is noted that the jurisdiction of three townships in the south (which is more rural in nature in comparison to the rest of the county) remained unchanged over the same period, and drastic restructuring occurred to those urbanizing townships around the county central area. It shows the administration system changing from rural to urban in nature, as decentralization suits rural agriculture and centralization does for urban industries. The changing share of industrial output in each township as a percentage of the total municipal industrial output demonstrates that consolidation of townships has facilitated industrial agglomeration remarkably. The gap between the lowest and the highest township industrial outputs was widening over the period 1995–2011 (see Table 7.4). The spatial division of agricultural and industrial townships has become distinctive.

The important contribution of the spatial agglomeration of industries to sustainable urbanization is that it helps enhance environmental integrity. Rapid industrialization and urbanization inevitably consume a large amount of farmland and open fields. Industrial agglomeration makes a city compact and thus converts less farmland into urban built-up land than would otherwise be the case. Productive industrialization creates quality jobs so as to improve workers' well-being and minimizes usage of valuable land resources that can be retained for ecological quality. With 262.3 square kilometers of built-up land, Kunshan sustains a compact city with densities of 7200 residents/square kilometers, and

Table 7.4 Statistical characteristics of township's industrial output as % of total municipal industrial output, 1995 and 2011

	Mean	Minimum	Maximum	Dispersion index
1995, 20 townships	3.9	1.2	16.4	0.362
2011, 10 townships	9.1	0.3	60.3	0.666

Note: Dispersion index is a measure of statistical dispersion of a set of data. It is between one and zero. Zero stands for perfect dispersion, each township having an equal share of industrial output. One denotes absolute agglomeration, one township having all industrial output.
Source: KSBS, 1995–2012

¥0.8 billion GDP economy/square kilometers (2010) (KSBS, 2011). Kunshan, a typical county-level city in the Yangtze River Delta, should serve as a good model to China, especially to its coastal region, where judicious use of scarce land resources is critical for its sustainable urbanization. Urbanization, which enhances land rent, gives a new lifeline to the declining collective village economy after the collapse of TVEs. But the resultant inequality has become a new social problem, demanding coordination at a level higher than the village to deal with fair distribution of land rent, which is fundamentally created by local economic growth. The fiscal capacity of the urban state is the crucial factor for making urbanization equitable.

A municipal-level coordination seems necessary to mitigate the impact of uneven distribution of land rent. Kunshan municipal government has adopted a fiscal transfer policy to help those rural townships. As a local representative of the state, Kunshan city government has captured a substantial amount of land rent in the conversion of rural collective land to urban state land. Based on the data available, land sale proceeds as a percentage of municipal fiscal revenues were 6.3 percent during 2001–2003, and the percentage rose to 14.8 percent during 2004–2006 (JPCD, 2002–2007; KSBS, 2002–2007). Sharing urbanization benefits in the form of fiscal transfer to rural villages seems just and fair. The size of fiscal transfer reached a substantial amount of 34.7 percent of the total annual village collective revenues in 2012 on average. It accounted for as much as 56.1 percent for the villages in Jingxi (a rural town), while only 8.5 percent for the villages in Huaqiao (an urban town) (ORW/KMG, 2013). Fiscal transfers have mitigated village inequality to a great extent, demonstrated by a Gini coefficient 0.303, improved from 0.420 before the fiscal transfers.

Transition of villages toward urban communities

There is perennial tension between community endeavors managed by the collectives and individual pursuits based on bottom-up initiatives when the scarcity of land as a production means is exacerbated. Collectivity preserves community cooperation, preventing villages from falling into fragmented physical and social entities. Village resilience in the difficult times relies on community's collectivity as social capital. The capacity of making decisions at the individual or household level is equally crucial for economic productivity. The survival of rural villages as community during de-agriculturalization is an intriguing question. At this juncture comes the well-known dichotomy: *gemeinschaft* (rural community) versus *gesellschaft* (urban society) coined by Tönnies (1957). Although the distinction is not so clear-cut in reality, many urban collectivities, or urban tribes as suggested by Maffesoli (1996), are constructed intentionally or unintentionally on the basis of hobby, religion, ethnicity, politics, and so on (Parsons, 2007). As an urban community is created based on certain social order and by people who have a sense of membership of that social order, urban collectivities are usually interest-based and inclusive to those who want to voluntarily join. Rural villages are area-based and exclusionary to outsiders as membership is often hereditary and marital. It is not wrong to claim that there are more individuality and competition in cities than villages, where collectivity and cooperation dominate, as Wirth (1938) suggests primary associations of intimacy and trust give way to contractual and instrumental affiliations because of urbanization (Amit and Rapport, 2002).

Villages in China as a basic rural socioeconomic community are on the brink of disintegration under household farming and village members' individual migration to cities for nonagricultural jobs. Individuality seems to have taken over collectivity. A gradual, instead of a blunt, transition of rural villages to urban communities should be helpful to mitigate transitional hardship inflicted on rural peasants who either have to leave their villages to find jobs in cities or are left behind to take care of household farming alone. The strengthened local economies due to urbanization offer a new opportunity for village collectivity. Village communities are progressively transformed along with the nonagricultural development from agriculture to industrialization and to urbanization. This grassroots economic initiative led by villages tended to be socially inclusive within the village. Being social enterprises, TVEs created industrial jobs for the village peasants and initiated the rural employment shift. The Gini coefficient for uneven distribution of rural population across 20 townships only increased slightly from 0.242 (1975) to 0.268 (1985), suggesting little permanent migration out of own townships (KSBS, 1990). Rural labors engaged in industries accounted for 30.7 percent of the total workforce in 1985, rising from 7.5 percent in 1978 (Jin, 2010). The de-agriculturization of rural employment has become irreversible. Sixty-three percent of rural laborers were engaged in agriculture in 1985, and the percentage declined to 9 percent in 2010 (KSBS, 1985–2010). Many peasants gave up farming and shifted to the manufacturing and service sectors, though most of them still lived in the villages so that they could 'leave the fields without leaving the countryside, and enter the factories without entering the city' (*litu bu lixiang, jinchang bu jincheng*). It was convenient, as factory jobs were in the village, and villagers could still do part-time farming in the busy crop sowing and harvesting seasons.

Since the closure of village factories from the mid-1990s onward, industrialization driven by the KETDZ and town industrial zones has greatly speeded up the pace of urbanization. TVEs are meant as part and parcel of the self-contained village economy, providing jobs chiefly to the villagers. With ambitious business strategies, inward manufacturing firms aim to expand their enterprises and reach out to the global market for their products. Jobs are offered to those who are the most competitive in the labor market, and Kunshan's successful industrialization has brought in a large number of qualified migrant workers who have even outnumbered the locals since 2005 (see Table 7.2). Though many more nonagricultural jobs are provided by the modern industrial firms than were by TVEs earlier, competition in the job market has become keener as workers are more mobile now than in the 1980s. Only the young and energetic can secure placements in the firms. Under open competition, some villagers may find it hard to join the urban workforce. The significant economic change from agricultural to nonagricultural work brings drastic social change to the villages. In the villages, the right to work for every capable member was guaranteed, and there was no competition between village members. Without choices, some unwilling villagers are pushed into urbanization without their consents and may find it hard to adapt themselves to urban living, especially those aging members. Hence, the traditional function of villages as social safety nets needs to be maintained during urbanization in order to help those who cannot cope with the economic change. The collective village economy remains crucial during the transition.

Village collective economies have been withering after collective farming was replaced by household farming and the collapse of TVEs. Villages as a traditional rural social entity are in danger of disintegration without social supports buttressed by a collective economy. Rural industrialization was not promising in helping the villages, but urbanization provides new opportunities to the village collective. Because of urbanization, which generates substantial nonagricultural demand for land, land rent in those villages close to town and city centers has been enhanced by the economic growth. Of the total Kunshan village economic revenues in 2012, land-related rental income accounted for 42.8 percent, while the income contributed by village enterprises only represented 14.4 percent on average (ORW/KMG, 2013). A new mode of collective economies in the form of shareholding cooperatives comes to the aid of transition (Zhao et al., 2009; Sun, Luo, and Zhao, 2010).

Three types of village land shareholding cooperatives have been set up in the Kunshan villages since the early 2000s. Only villagers are eligible to become members of these cooperatives, and the cooperatives are essentially for villages to capitalize on enhanced land rent, so that they can benefit from urbanization. The first is the Farmland Shareholding Cooperatives (FSCs),[6] where willing village households pool their farmland and lease it to growers, who pay rentals in return. These households are no longer tilling the land, as their able family members may have been working in the nonagricultural sectors. The second is the Community Property Shareholding Cooperatives (CPSCs).[7] Accumulated over the eras of People's Commune and rural industrialization, community properties are composed of collectively owned land and properties used for nonagricultural purposes. Village-owned enterprises may have died, but land underneath and buildings above are rented out as valuable assets. The third is the Real Estate Investment Cooperatives (REICs)[8] with the participation of private members (villagers) as well as collective members (villages). The investment vehicles are usually industrial premises, dormitories for migrant workers, commercial buildings, and so on. Villages with surplus revenues and funds from compensation for farmland acquisition can invest in those urban properties for steady rental income. By the end of 2011, there were 147 REICs, 132 CPSCs, and 119 FSCs.

A survey of 375 farming households in Kunshan revealed that the average age of these household heads were 54.3 with an average household size at 4.7 persons. The numbers of those doing farming were 1.9 persons per household. It was clear that only those aged members were engaged in tilling, while their young offspring were working off-farm (Liang, Xie, and Zhu, 2015). In three rural townships (Dianshanhu, Zhouzhuang, Jinxi), 83.6 percent of their total rural households joined the farmland shareholding cooperatives. Overall, 92 percent of the total sown land in Kunshan was in the FSCs (ORW/KMG, 2013). CPSCs and village-involved REICs are the continuity of rural collectivity after the failure of collective farming and industries. Interestingly, it is the urbanization in general, and the enhanced land rent in particular, that helps the village community to survive. In Yushan township (2012), the number of villagers who were eligible of receiving CPSC dividends reached 65.4 percent, and 21.6 percent of the village households participated in REICs (Yushan Town Government, 2012).

Of the Kunshan's total annual village collective revenues in 2012, the income from village enterprises only accounted for 9.4 percent, while the rental incomes from CPSCs reached 24.8 percent and REICs 16.8 percent, respectively (ORW/KMG, 2013). CPSC and REIC rentals constituted a substantial component (41.6 percent in total) to the village revenues, which were used mainly for village social services and social welfares (pensions, medical insurances, unemployment benefits). These social services and welfares are crucial for those elderly and unemployable who are becoming urbanites. Yushan's statistics showed that 84.8 percent of the villagers were shielded by medical insurance and 56.0 percent by social security (Yushan Town Government, 2012). Making up for the loss of TVEs, land rent derived from village lands becomes the new backbone of the village collective economy. By the end of 2011, the shareholders of REICs accounted for 19.8 percent of the total rural households, and almost all rural households benefited from CPSCs.

Land rent: facilitating spatial compactness

Land rent is also harnessed to expedite the process of agglomeration of dispersed village houses into compact urban residential quarters. An influx of migrant workers has created great demand for housing, urban services, and facilities, which constitutes a significant force driving urbanization. City and town centers have been expanding with nonagricultural jobs and new incoming residents. More than three quarters of migrant workers concentrated in tiers I and II towns in 2011; 53.7 percent in tier I and 24.3 percent in tier II, respectively. Only one in five migrant workers lived in tiers III and IV towns; 15.2 percent in tier III and 6.7 percent in tier IV, respectively (see Figure 7.5). Following industrial agglomeration and migrant workers to the town centers, the local villagers find the mode 'leaving the fields without leaving the countryside and entering the factories without entering the city' increasingly obsolete. It calls for the spatial restructuring of rural village living. Village living is naturally dispersed and decentralized because of traditional household farming. Land scarcity in Kunshan has created a high density of village settlements at 2.26 villages per square kilometer (2007), or 44 hectares per village. Being common in the countryside with high population density, rural sprawl in the form of fragmented farmland and village settlements tends to compromise ecological integrity and impede the

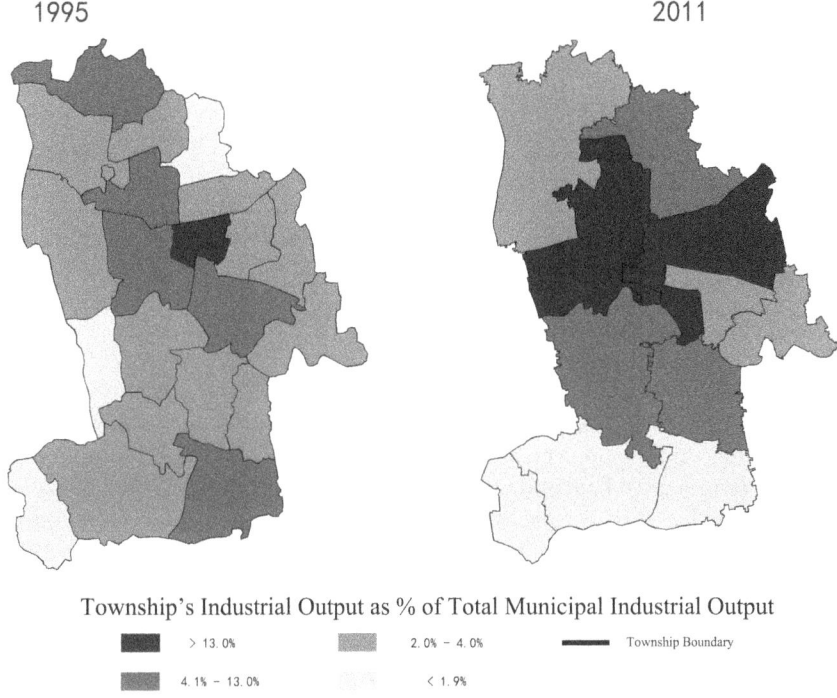

Figure 7.5 Industrial agglomeration from rural factories to industrial zones.

efficient and sufficient provision of village infrastructure. As a result, rural living quality has not been able to improve because of small-scale subsistence farming.

Town industrial zones and KETDZ made industrialization spatially compact, but disparities between centrally located industrial jobs and dispersed and evenly distributed rural industrial workers in the whole municipality revealed that rural workers were commuting long distances for daily working (see Table 7.5). Most rural workers still lived in their village houses because they did not have an additional place to stay in the town. In comparison with urban households, rural households actually have an affordable housing option as they are entitled to free land lots for building their family houses. Strong urban economies and healthy government fiscal revenues allow the municipal government to offer villagers an option for exchanging their rural houses for urban apartments on the basis of equal floor areas. Villagers do not have full property rights over their rural houses as they cannot lease and sell the houses, and thus rural houses do not have explicit market value. Conversely, there are full property rights over urban apartments and urban housing can be transacted in the open market. The exchange proposal has been well received as a fair deal. Rural houses tend to be spacious. One spacious rural house can usually exchange for three compact

Table 7.5 Agglomerated industrial jobs and dispersed rural industrial workers

	Mean	Minimum	Maximum	Dispersion index
Industrial output as % of the total in each township (2003)	6.5	1.0	56.3	0.669
Rural industrial labours as % of the total labour force in each township (2000)	46.5	34.4	61.8	0.095

Note: Dispersion index is a measure of statistical dispersion of a set of data. It is between one and zero. Zero stands for perfect dispersion, each township having an equal share of industrial output, or equal share of rural industrial labors. One denotes absolute agglomeration, one township having all industrial output, or all rural industrial labors.
Source: KSBS, 2004, 2011

urban apartments. Two additional urban apartments ensure housing for unmarried children, and the housing assets provide a safety net for village families who abandon farming and land and opt for urban living. It is the enhanced land rent from rural village housing lots that facilitates the voluntary agglomeration of dispersed rural village houses into compact urban residential quarters. By 2012 in Yushan, 81.1 percent of rural households were no longer engaged in farming at all, and 61.9 percent of rural households had moved to urban housing quarters in the town center, rising from 54.8 percent one year earlier (2011) (see http://news.ksgs.net/201212/28/newscon3812.html).

Subsidiarity: the appropriate level of coordination for high density urbanization

The decentralization and empowerment of local communities are essential for inclusive urbanization. However, a balance between rural autonomy and urban integrity has to be maintained so as to ensure sustainable urbanization in the high-density developing regions. Coordination of the bottom-up urbanization beyond the village and at a higher level of township seems appropriate for making a compact city and maintaining equality when rural villages are incorporated into urban communities.

Being a traditional social organization, villages are a basic unit of China's rural society. Determined by the nature of agricultural production, cooperation between village members is mutually beneficial and overall productive. Collectivity as social capital has been built up by members' lifelong attachment and affiliation as well as trust between each other. However, rural development is hampered by subsistence farming because of deficient arable land endowment in relation to its burgeoning peasant population. Nonagricultural development and economic productivity are pursued as an indispensable strategy, which induces the tension between collaboration managed by collective actions and pursuits based on individual initiatives.

Top-down collective farming imposed by the socialist revolution was disastrous both politically and economically. Kunshan was not an exception. Peasants were deprived of any chance of working by individual initiatives within the organization of People's Commune. Though household-based farming since the economic reform has increased agricultural productivity drastically because of the imbedded incentive structure, intensive farming on the basis of low arable landholding per capita is not a promising mode of production that can enhance the village well-being significantly. Rural collective industrialization came to the fore, saving the rural communities from disintegration. Phenomenal rise of rural industrialization has improved the life of numerous peasants significantly, evidenced by well-refurbished village houses with modern facilities. Peasants' integration into urbanization looked attainable. Nevertheless, the path to collective nonagricultural development was cut short as the ambiguous collective ownership over the village enterprises finally brought rural industrialization down.

The leading role in industrialization and urbanization has therefore shifted from rural villages to urban state. The municipal government–coordinated industrialization has been very successful in bringing in global and private firms and jobs to Kunshan, attracting an influx of migrant workers who even outnumber locals. Local villagers are in the open market, competing for jobs with usually more competent migrant workers, as migrants come to Kunshan by choice, while locals are pushed into urbanization without choice. It is not uncommon that some locals may not like or benefit from the drastic social and economic changes. Village communities can mitigate their predicament by offering collective cares and welfares. Interestingly, urbanization is what offers an opportunity for villages to retain their collectivity via enhanced collective land assets. Land shareholding cooperatives capture land rental incomes for the collective to continue its social services and social welfares. It is also the land rent that constitutes a significant part of municipal government's fiscal capacity. Uneven development of village nonagricultural economies induced by industrial agglomeration is dealt with by the municipal fiscal transfer, so that those villages in remote locations can equally enjoy the benefits of urbanization. Sooner or later, those less-developed regions in rural-urban transition will catch up with the coastal region. Kunshan can serve as a model to those regions of integration of rural villages into urban communities. Collective entitlements are gradually phased out and replaced by urban welfares.

Urbanization has changed the social equilibrium maintained by autonomous rural villages. Villages are no longer autonomous units in an era of industrialization and urbanization. Cities are made in an integrative manner. According to the principle of subsidiarity, decisions should be made at the lowest level possible and the highest level necessary. In a high-density developing region, autonomy at too low a level will lead to fragmented development, with farmland and built-up land spatially intermingled and excessively piecemealed. For the sake of equality during urbanization, the coordination for urban development has to go beyond the level of villages. Kunshan municipal government has been successfully building up its fiscal capacity along with the extraordinary industrialization. After municipal fiscal transfers to the villages in the names of farmland conservation and ecological protection, minimum and mean levels of village collective income rose significantly.[9]

With government investments, two striking landmarks are worth highlighting to demonstrate the achievement of a county-level city in its quality urbanization. The first is the Kunshan Industrial Technology Research Institute established in 2008. It is the first of its kind for a county-level city where its government is committed to scientific industrial research and technological development. The second is the Duke Kunshan University, which is jointly run by Duke University and Wuhan University with its campus provided by the Kunshan government. It is the first university in Kunshan to provide tertiary education to its young people.

Notes

1 Of course, the terms 'high' and 'low' are of relative nature.
2 Marcussen (1990: 23–124) elaborates on development and subdivision stages of a land plot of 527 square meters purchased by a migrant for his family in the 1940s in Jakarta, Indonesia. Fifty years later, ten households are living on the subdivisions. Mahtab-uz-Zaman and Lau (2000: 149) investigate a similar case in Dhaka, Bangladesh, where original 13 land parcels in 1920 became hundreds of tiny land lots in 1990 after incessant land subdivision.
3 ¥1 equals US$0.15 as of September 11, 2017.
4 Labor-intensive sectors include industries of food, beverages, paper products, textiles, garments, and wood products. The average output per labor in these sectors was ¥0.36 million during 2006–2010 (KSBS, 2006–2010).
5 Technology-intensive sectors are composed of industries of electronic and IT products as well as of instruments. The average output per labor in these sectors was ¥0.72 million during 2006–2010 (KSBS, 2006–2010).
6 Farmland shareholding cooperatives are created by consolidating farmland from villagers who no longer till the land and who work in nonagricultural sectors. Assembled land parcels are leased to a contractor as a farm, so that farming with economies of scale can be pursued instead of long-lasting small household farming.
7 Community property shareholding cooperatives are the trustees of the village assets built earlier, such as TVE premises and farmers' marketplaces. With urbanization, these properties have become income-yielding assets. The revenues are mainly used for social welfare for those senior, aging villagers who have contributed to the formation of village assets over their lifelong working in the village.
8 Real estate investment shareholding cooperatives are the schemes to engage villages in the investment of urban properties demanded by industrialization such as industrial premises and workers' dormitories, so that villages can hold investments with steady rental incomes. In order to distribute land rent equally, members of remote villages are invited to join and invest in the cooperatives that have investments in villages close to the city. Therefore, land rent is shared among the members across villages.
9 The municipal fiscal transfer accounted for 34.7 percent of the total collective income for 162 villages on average, the highest being 90.2 percent and the lowest being nil (ORW/KMG, 2013).

References

Amit, V. & Rapport, N. (2002) *The trouble with community: Anthropological reflections on movement, identity and collectivity.* London: Pluto Press.
Batty, M., Besussi, E. & Chin, N. (2003) *Traffic, urban growth and suburban sprawl.* Working Papers Series, Paper 70, UCL Centre for Advanced Spatial Analysis.

Buchanan, J. M. & Yoon, Y. J. (2000) Symmetric tragedies: Commons and anticommons. *Journal of Law and Economics*, 43: 1–13.
Burton, E. (2000) The potential of the compact city for promoting social equity, in K. Williams, E. Burton & M. Jenks (eds.) *Achieving sustainable urban form*, 19–29. London: E & FN Spon.
Buxton, M. (2000) Energy, transport and urban form in Australia, in K. Williams, E. Burton, & M. Jenks (eds.) *Achieving sustainable urban form*, 54–63. London: E & FN Spon.
Cervero, R. (1998) *The transit metropolis: A global inquiry*. Washington, DC: Island Press.
Chan, K. W. (1994) *Cities with invisible walls: Reinterpreting urbanization in post-1949 China*. Hong Kong: Oxford University Press.
Chan, K. W. (2009) The Chinese *hukou* system at 50. *Eurasian Geography and Economics*, 50(20): 197–221.
Chan, K. W. (2014) *Achieving comprehensive hukou reform in China*. Paulson Policy Memo.
Chan, K. W. & Buckingham, W. (2008) Is China abolishing the *hukou* system? *The China Quarterly*, 195: 582–606.
Che, J. & Qian, Y. Y. (1998) Insecure property rights and government ownership of firms. *Quarterly Journal of Economics*, 113(2): 467–496.
Cheng, T. & Selden, M. (1994) The origins and social consequences of China's *hukou* system. *The China Quarterly*, 139: 644–668.
Chien, S. S. (2007) Institutional innovations, asymmetric decentralization, and local economic development: A case study of Kunshan in post-Mao China. *Environment and Planning C: Government and Policy*, 25: 269–290.
Duany, A., Plater-Zyberk, E. & Speck, J. (2000) *Suburban nation: The rise of sprawl and the decline of the American dream*. New York: North Point Press.
Elkin, T., McLaren, D. & Hillman, M. (1991) *Reviving the city: Towards sustainable urban development*. London: Friends of the Earth.
Ewing, R. (1997) Is Los Angeles-style sprawl desirable? *Journal of the American Planning Association*, 63(1): 107–126.
Firman, T. (1997) Land conversion and urban development in the northern region of West Java, Indonesia. *Urban Studies*, 34(7): 1027–1046.
Friedmann, J. & Wolff, G. (1982) World city formation: An agenda for research and action. *International Journal of Urban and Regional Research*, 6(3): 309–343.
Fuerst, J. S. & Petty, R. (1991) High-rise housing for low-income families. *Public Interest*, 103: 118–131.
Gao, M. C. F. (1999) *Gao Village: A portrait of rural life in modern China*. Honolulu: University of Hawaii Press.
George, H. (1879/1938) *Progress and poverty: An inquiry into the cause of industrial depressions and of increase of want with increase of wealth – the remedy*. New York: The Modern Library.
Girard, G. & Lambot, I. (1993) *City of darkness – Life in Kowloon Walled City*. London: Watermark.
Gordon, P. & Richardson, H. W. (1997) Are compact cities a desirable planning goal? *Journal of the American Planning Association*, 63: 95–106.
Government of Guangzhou Municipality (2015) *On urban renewal of Guangzhou, Decree No. 134*. Retrieved from www.gz.gov.cn/gzgov/s8263/201512/48d975c888e344c1b b05df7b6ef618c4.shtml, accessed February 7, 2017. (In Chinese).
Hamnett, C. (2001) Social segregation and social polarization, in R. Paddison (ed.). *Handbook of urban studies*, 162–176. London: Sage.

Hardin, G. (1968) The tragedy of the commons. *Science*, 162: 1243–1248.
Heller, M. A. (1998) The tragedy of the anticommons: Property in the transition from Marx to markets. *Harvard Law Review*, 111: 621–688.
Jabareen, Y. R. (2006) Sustainable urban forms: Their typologies, models, and concepts. *Journal of Planning Education and Research*, 26(1): 38–52.
Jenks, M., Burton, E., & Williams, K. (1996) *The compact city: A sustainable urban form?* London: E & FN Spon.
Jiangsu Province Construction Department (JPCD) (2002–2007) *Jiangsu urban construction statistics yearbook*. Beijing: China Statistical Press. (in Chinese).
Jin, N. B. (ed.) (2010) *Kunshan's human development*. Beijing: China Population Press.
Knight, J. (1992) *Institutions and social conflict*. Cambridge: Cambridge University Press.
Kunshan Bureau of Statistics (KSBS) (1970–2012) *Kunshan statistical yearbook*. Beijing: China Statistics Press. (in Chinese).
Leaf, M. (1999) Vietnam's urban edge – The administration of urban development in Hanoi. *Third World Planning Review*, 21(3): 297–315.
Li, Z. & Wu, F. (2006) Socio-spatial differentiation and residential inequalities in Shanghai: A case study of three neighborhoods. *Housing Studies*, 21 (5): 695–717.
Li, Z. & Wu, F. (2008) Tenure-based residential segregation in post-reform Chinese cities: A case study of Shanghai. *Transactions of the Institute of British Geographers*, 33 (3): 404–19.
Liang, Y. N., Xie, Y. & Zhu, P. P. (2015) A survey of farming households in Dianshanhu Township, Kunshan, Jiangsu. *Agricultural Sciences*, 56(4): 544–546. (in Chinese).
Liang, Z. & Ma, Z. (2004) China's floating population: New evidence from the 2000 census. *Population and Development Review*, 30(3): 467–488.
Lin, Y. X. (2015) Rural industrialization in periurban areas from the perspective of rural governance: A comparative research of the Pearl River Delta region, South Jiangsu and Wenzhou. *Urban Planning Forum*, 3: 101–110. (in Chinese).
Maffesoli, M. (1996) *The time of the tribes: The decline of individualism in mass society*. London: SAGE.
Mahtab-uz-Zaman, Q. M. & Lau, S. S. Y. (2000) City expansion policy versus compact city demand: The case of Dhaka, in M. Jenks & R. Burgess (eds.) *Compact cities: Sustainable urban forms for developing countries*, 141–152. London: Spon Press.
Marcussen, L. (1990) *Third world housing in social and spatial development: The case of Jakarta*. Aldershot, Hants, England and Brookfield, VT, USA: Averbury.
Marton, A. M. (2000) *China's spatial economic development: Restless landscapes in the Lower Yangzi Delta*. London and New York: Routledge.
McGee, T. G. (1991) The emergence of *desakota* regions in Asia: expanding a hypothesis, in N. Ginsburg, B. Koppel & T. G. McGee (eds.) *The extended metropolis: Settlement transition in Asia*, 3–25. Honolulu: University of Hawaii Press.
Meng, X. & Zhang, J. (2001) The two-tier labour market in urban China: Occupational segregation and wage differentials between urban residents and rural migrants in Shanghai. *Journal of Comparative Economics*, 29(3): 485–504.
Ministry of Construction, People's Republic of China (2008) *The methods of housing registration*. unpublished official document.
Nanhai Archives Bureau (NHAB) (1982, 1990) The third and fourth Nanhai population census. Unpublished reports. (in Chinese).
Nanhai Bureau of Statistics (NHBS) (2011) *Nanhai's statistical yearbook*. Foshan: Nanhai Press. (in Chinese).
Nanhai Population Census Office (NHPCO) (2002) *The fifth Nanhai population census*. Foshan: Nanhai Press. (in Chinese).

Neuman, M. (2005) The compact city fallacy. *Journal of Planning Education and Research*, 25(1): 11–26.
Office of Rural Works/Kunshan Municipal Government (ORW/KMG) (2013) *Statistics of village economies, 2013*. Unpublished report. (in Chinese).
Ostrom, E. (1990) *Governing the commons: The evolution of institutions for collective action*. Cambridge: Cambridge University Press.
Ostrom, E. (2000) Collective action and the evolution of social norms. *The Journal of Economic Perspectives*, 14(3): 137–158.
Parsons, T. (2007) *American society: A theory of the societal community*. London: Paradigm Publishers.
Pullinger, J. (1989) *Hooked on the city: The life and death of Kowloon Walled City*. London: Hodder & Stoughton.
Qin, H. (1998) Great communes and traditional China's society. *Sociological Research*, 5: 14–23. (in Chinese).
Roy, A, & AlSayyad, N. (2004) *Urban informality – Transnational perspectives from the Middle East, Latin America, and South Asia*. Lanham, MD: Lexington.
Sassen, S. (1991) *Global city: New York, London and Tokyo*. Princeton, NJ: Princeton University Press.
Shen, J. F., Wong, K. Y. & Feng, Z. Q. (2002) State-sponsored and spontaneous urbanization in the Pearl River Delta of South China, 1980–1998. *Urban Geography*, 23(7): 674–694.
Shi, J. S. (2000) Rural community land shareholding cooperative system: review and prospect. *China Rural Economics*, 1: 63–7. (in Chinese).
Shishan Township Government (2013) *Statistics of Shishan village economies, 2013*. Unpublished report. (in Chinese).
Solinger, D. J. (1999) *Contesting citizenship in urban China: Peasant migrants, the state and the logic of the market*. Berkeley: University of California Press.
Sun, Z., Luo, W. & Zhao, K. (2010) A report on rural land shareholding cooperatives in Jiangsu Province. *Agricultural Economic Issues*, 8: 30–35. (in Chinese).
Swanwick, C., Dunnett, N. & Woolley, H. (2003) Nature, role and value of green space in towns and cities: An overview. *Built Environment*, 29(2): 94–106.
Tang, W. S. & Parish, W. (2000) *Chinese urban life under reform: The changing social contract*. Cambridge: Cambridge University Press.
Tian, L. & Zhu, J. M. (2013) Clarification of collective land rights and its impact on nonagricultural land use in the Pearl River Delta of China: A case of Shunde. *Cities*, 35: 190–199.
Tönnies, F. (1957) [1887] *Community and society*. East Lansing: Michigan State University Press.
Tsai, L. L. (2007) Solidary groups, informal accountability, and local public goods provision in rural China. *American Political Science Review*, 101(2): 355–372.
Wei, Y. H. D. (2010) Beyond new regionalism, beyond global production networks: Remaking the Sunan model, China. *Environment and Planning C: Government and Policy*, 28: 72–96.
White, P. (1998) Social inequalities and urban restructuring. *GeoJournal*, 46: 1–5.
Whyte, M. K. (2010) Social change and the urban-rural divide in China, in F. Hong & J. C. Gottwald (eds.). *The Irish Asia strategy and its China relations*, 45–60. Amsterdam: Rozenberg Publishers.
Wirth, L. (1938) Urbanism as a way of life. *American Journal of Sociology*, 44: 1–24.
Wong, C. P. W. (1997) Rural public finance, in C. P. W. Wong (ed.) *Financing local government in the People's Republic of China*, 167–212. Hong Kong: Oxford University Press.

World Bank (2008) *The growth report: Strategies for sustained growth and inclusive development*. Washington, DC: World Bank.

Wu, W. (2004) Sources of migrant housing disadvantage in urban China. *Environment and Planning A*, 36: 1285–304.

Yushan Town Government (2012) *Yushan town statistical yearbook, 2011*. Kunshan: Yushan Town Government.

Zhao, L., Develtere, P., Cui, Z. Y. & Wang, D. (2009) *New co-operatives in China: The emergence of an indigenous model of social enterprises*, Paper prepared for the EMES conference on Social Enterprises, Trento, Italy, 1st–4th July, 2009.

Zhou, X. H. (1998) *Tradition and transformation – The social psychology of Jiangsu and Zhejiang villages and the change since modern times*. Shanghai: SDX Joint Publishing Company. (in Chinese).

Zhu, J. M. & Guo, Y. (2014) Fragmented peri-urbanization led by autonomous village development under informal institution in high-density regions: The case of Nanhai, China. *Urban Studies*, 51(6): 1120–1145.

8 Conclusion
Land rights and sustainable urbanization in the future

China's rapid urbanization since the 1980s has been facilitated by institutional changes in land rights that also have profoundly impacted on the resultant urban physical forms. An initial land market regulated by the explicit land rights of leasehold is formulated as a result of three types of land rent dissipation, which leads to symmetric low-density suburban sprawl and over-compact central cities. It further complicates the future urban change by the fundamental issues of fairness and efficiency embedded in the spatial structure of land uses. The welfare of rural peasants has to be considered in the transition of collective land rights so as to promote urbanization inclusive to rural-urban migrants.

Land rights as an institution

Rapid industrialization since the launch of economic reforms in the late 1970s has been propelling urbanization drastically in China, where tremendous urban changes have occurred and a population of 620.5 million (1978–2016) and an area of 46,041.3 square kilometers (1981–2016) were urbanized (see Tables 1.1 and 1.2). Cities are built on land as an essential factor, and land rights as institutions are closely linked to economic systems and social norms. Land rights can be assigned by the state, transacted through the market, and maintained by the communities according to public, private, and social interests. Land rights have a profound impact on the urban built environment. The socioeconomic transition from plan to market provides a great opportunity to understand the formation of China's cities in the context of institutional change to land rights. Uncertainty and ambiguity generate land rent. Land rent seeking and consequent land rent dissipating have a profound impact on the built urban forms.

Based on the Marxist notion that land should be a means of production only, land was excluded from transaction determined by the equilibrium between demand and supply. Instead, land resources were assigned by the state to state-owned land users and the masses. It was meant to facilitate building proletarian producer cities and suppressing bourgeois consumer cities. Socialist urban structures with ostensible equality were created, where 'productive sectors' were prioritized over 'nonproductive sectors'. Collective farming was adopted along with the collective land ownership for the rural regions.

Inefficient modes of urbanization were questioned, which ushered in the economic reforms in the late 1970s. Old institutions of land rights were phased out gradually and incrementally toward the establishment of land leasehold. Two sets of dual land markets were hatched out as a result of gradualist institutional changes. Market mechanisms have unleashed tremendous pent-up demand for buildings, which is met by responsive supplies. Enormous land rent was also created, as ambiguous and transient land rights encouraged rent seeking. The role of the state as the third party for the emerging land markets was completely compromised, which made the market for land development the quasi-commons.

Though state-owned urban land has been transformed to land leasehold since 1988, collectively owned rural land remains a Marxist means of production, i.e. socialist land use rights only to the landholders. Substantial arbitrage opportunities between the two land regimes are irresistible to the rural stakeholders. Rural change occurs with two modes of collective land development that is either initiated by villages or coordinated by townships. Land development for the sake of land rent taking generates a fragmented built-up environment, where ecological integrity and land use efficiency are gravely compromised. Social equity is worsened as rural-rural divide appears on top of the extant rural-urban divide.

An initial structure of landed interests shaped by land rent dissipation

During the transition from land as 'a means of production' to land as an asset, emerging land rent is contested rigorously basically between two key stakeholders – the urban government and existing land users holding socialist land use rights. The former is the pro-growth local developmental state, whereas the latter are the status quo interests, intending to appropriate land rent as much as they could in the capacity of socialist land use right holders. Appropriation of land rent induces land rent dissipation. There are three types of rent dissipation that take place in the process of urbanization.

The first occurs in peri-urban areas, where ambiguous property rights over collective land induce disordered competition among the stakeholders for land rent. Consequent fragmented structure of land use without land use planning that ensures provision of public goods and facilities seriously compromises ecological integrity and optimal utilization of scarce land resources, a symptom of land rent dissipation (Zhu and Hu, 2009; Lai et al., 2014).

The second happens in the redevelopment of central cities constructed under the old institution of land as 'a means of production'. The *danwei* land users bargain for more land rent differentials than the density prescribed by zoning before they would relinquish their socialist land use right. Altering zoning regulations informally and covertly imposes social costs on the neighborhood, constituting an act of rent seeking. Gains to the existing land users are at the expense of losses to other land users in the neighborhood. As a result, physical density in the central cities grows much higher than what the capacity of infrastructure allows. Over-compaction in the central cities lowers the environmental quality, thus land rent dissipation.

The third occurs in the acquisition of farmland, where rent dissipation takes place in the form of a large quantity of vacant or underused greenfield land because of ambiguous delineation of property rights over land between the principal and agents – that is, between the people (represented by the central state) and local governments. Decentralization advocated by the economic reforms separates ownership from control, which gives decision-making power to agents that tend to pursue their own interests. Quantitative expansion of new urban districts and appropriation of land rent differentials suit the best interest of local governments (agents), whereas the interest of the people (principal) are undermined. A suboptimal spatial structure in the form of suburban sprawl ensues as a result.

Low-density suburban sprawl and over-compact central cities

Land rent grabbing is facilitated by imbedded ambiguity to the rural collective land in the context of arbitrage opportunities between the rural collective landownership and urban land leasehold (Zhu and Hu, 2009). The economic reforms continue the dominance of cities over the countryside. Under provincial governments that were the first-tier local governments below the central state, there were two parallel administrations of governance: prefectures, which governed counties (the basic agricultural units in the China's administration hierarchy), and cities, which were directly responsible to the provincial governments. The economic integration of towns and the countryside started with the abolition of prefectures and transfer of their subordinate counties to the leadership of cities. This structural change in administration is called *shidaixian*, literally meaning 'cities-leading-counties'. The leading role of the city has thus been explicitly established to usher in an epoch of urbanization for the first time in Chinese history. Conversion of rural land to urban uses has been legitimately chiefly led by the urban governments ever since.

In those less dynamic areas like the central and western regions, rural nonagricultural growth is far less progressive than that in the eastern region, and the regions become the main origins of sending out rural-urban migrants who amounted to 26.4 percent of the total rural population in 2013, rising from 1.5 percent in 1990 to 6.3 percent in 2000 (http://www.stats.gov.cn/tjsj/zxfb/201405/ t20140512_551585.html, accessed April 25, 2015; NBSC, 2014). Industrialization and urbanization in these areas are chiefly led by the urban governments. Land rent has become a significant source of municipal revenues, and capitalization on emerging land rent has become a forceful incentive, facilitating urban expansion. The strategic concept plan, a nonstatutory plan, was initiated firstly by some coastal cities that experienced dynamic growth in the early 1990s. It has been adopted ever since by many other cities that envision ambitious spatial expansion in the future. Whereas spatial expansion in some dynamic, growing cities is driven by the real demand of drastic economic growth, rapid increments of urban area in other cities are rather speculative and unjustifiable. The strategic concept plan is mainly to plan or expand a spatial structure so as to accommodate anticipated dynamic growth of urban economies ostensibly. Taking land rent from the conversion of rural land to urban uses is the real pursuit.

Equipped with the strategic concept plan, the local municipal government is legitimized to be bold in its large-scale appropriation of farmland with the objective of facilitating rapid urbanization. Many large-scale urban expansion projects are deemed out of proportion in relation to the actual demands. Driven by land rent taking, low-density urban sprawl appears in the peripheries of many cities. It was reported that about 50-odd cities had built new university districts[1] by 2005 (http://www.landscapecn.com/news/html/news/detail.asp?id=29730, accessed July 11, 2006), and 36 cities were pursuing new central business districts in 2003, instead of consolidating the existing city centers (http://news.soufun.com/2003-04-16/150448.htm, accessed July 11, 2006). In 2003, there were 174 cities with a population exceeding one million and 33 cities with a population over two million (NBSC, 2005). New CBDs and university districts are only justified for those large cities with millions of population. The amount of land (36,000 square kilometers) designated for 3,837 newly planned industrial development zones in the whole country (http://www.people.com.cn/GB/14857/22238/28463/28464/2015058.html, accessed June 21, 2004) even exceeds the total existing urban built-up area of 30,406 square kilometers in the country (2004) (NBSC, 2005). Many large underutilized or even vacant sites manifest wasteful sprawl in the suburbs. The most striking news is that reportedly urban new districts planned nationwide can accommodate 3.4 billion population (http://news.xinhuanet.com/politics/2014-04/20/c_1110319687.htm, accessed November 10, 2015), which is absurd as the total population in China is about 1.3 billion (2014).

If the physical density of cities is below 50 percent of the yardstick of urban population density at 10,000 persons per square kilometer, those cities are named 'ghost towns'. There were 33 cities that received the 'ghost town' title in 2015 (http://china.huanqiu.com/article/2015-11/8006492_2.html, accessed December 8, 2015). There were 12 cities only reaching 27–40 percent of the standard density, and 21 cities reaching 42–50 percent. There were 25 of those 'ghost towns' in the western and central regions. On average, urban physical density is only of 88 percent of the yardstick for the cities in the central region and 70 percent in the western region in 2013 (NBSC, 2014).

Many major and provincial capital cities fall into the category of over-compaction in their central areas by a yardstick of urban population density at 10,000 persons per square kilometer (indexed as 1.0), namely Guangzhou (Yuexiu) (3.3), Beijing (Xicheng) (2.6), Tianjin (Hedong) (2.5), Wuhan (Jianghan) (2.1), Hangzhou (Shangcheng) (2.0), and Shenzhen (Futian) (1.7) (NBSC, 2014). In Shenzhen, one of the prominently dynamic cities in the Pearl River Delta, the density of Luohu (its historical old quarter) measured by plot ratio was below 2.0 in the early 1980s. The 1989 master plan stipulated that the plot ratio should not exceed 3.0

for the redevelopment of Luohu. However, the subsequent redevelopment had substantially intensified land use to the extent where density stood at 4.3 by 2000 (Zhu, 2004). Guangzhou, the capital of Guangdong Province, saw its building density in its central city increased by 4.1 times during 1978–2001 and further by 0.9 time during 2002– 2013 (GMBS, 2014).

Implication of the structure of landed interests for progressive urban change

Continuous urban change in the future can be implicated by the landed interests structured under phased-out transitional land rights. As a result of rent seeking, vacant, undeveloped land parcels in the suburbs, because of underpriced land sales, amount to private land hoarding. Along with rapid urbanization, demand for land will sooner or later catch up and create windfall gains to those who hold lands. Entitlement to windfall gains in land rent becomes a disputable issue. Fragmented structure of land uses and over-compaction make further spatial change a strenuous endeavor in the suburbs and central cities, as delicate balance in landed interests is susceptible to slightest spatial change (Lin, Hao, and Geertman, 2015). Necessary installation of urban amenities and social facilities will either cause betterment (parks, mass rapid transit stations, etc.) or worsenment (substations, incinerators, etc.) in the urban neighborhoods, giving rise to inequity if externality issues are not addressed. Those affected negatively will resist change rigorously if their concerns are not dealt with, which stalls progressive urbanization. Holding out by a small minority of the status quo is a tragedy for progressive urbanization where rural-urban migration is still proceeding. Urban residents only account for about 50 percent of the total population right now.

Instruments for recouping betterment (unearned rent increment)[2] and mitigating worsenment (inflicted rent reduction)[3] are critical to ensure equity during continuous urbanization. A mechanism of windfalls for wipeouts can be useful to address unintended redistribution of land rent caused by public actions like government projects and regulations (Hagman and Misczynski, 1978; Healey, Purdue, and Ennis, 1995; Brown, 1999; Grant, 1999). Stiglitz (1977) demonstrates that under certain conditions, spending by the government on public goods (urban infrastructure and amenities) will increase aggregate land rent by an equal amount. It is dubbed as 'Henry George theorem', suggesting that unearned increment in land rent should be recouped by the state and used for financing public goods (George, [1881] 2009). It is advocated that betterment should be recouped by the state so as to benefit the general public, as well as to compensate for worsenment inflicted by some public projects. It is the principle of internalization of externalities, whether positive or negative.

If these two issues are unaddressed, the progressive urbanization that benefits numerous rural-urban migrants will be stalled. Optimal land utilization is necessary to maximize the provision of building spaces per unit area of land in high-density Asian cities (Glaeser, 2011). Suboptimal land utilization either exacerbates building shortages or consumes more land resources than would otherwise be the case to meet building needs driven by the rapid urbanization and thus worsens land scarcity. As limited land resources are made artificially scarcer by suboptimal land utilization, dramatic increase of land rent will result in significant political implications. Rising land prices push up urban living cost, which hits low-income groups particularly hard. Entitlement of the status quo to land rent as place-based exclusive benefits deteriorates social inequality between newcomers and existing residents. Rent dissipation compromises the capacity of urban governments to provide the economically disadvantaged with affordable social housing, which is already underprovided in many cities. Due to unregulated competition for land rent, rampant NIMBYism will make land development highly expensive and encourage speculative investment in the real estate.

Clarification of the collective land rights and fair distribution of land rent for inclusive urbanization

China has been progressing rapidly with drastic urbanization and economic growth, which have improved the welfare of its people tremendously. However, great economic development seems achieved at the expense of social equality when most rural peasants do not benefit equally from the urbanization at unprecedented scale and speed. Inclusive urbanization is meant to take up the challenge of rural-urban transition, where bottom-up rural development has been either feeble or interrupted by the unexpected demise of rural industrialization, while villages in those dynamic regions have seen ecological deterioration and fragmentation. Inclusive urbanization suggests a significant shift from the earlier mode of city-centered urbanization, where developers and urban governments were only interested in conversion of rural land to urban uses and urban spatial expansion. It is argued that rural peasants have not been socially and beneficially included in the process of urbanization. Huge social cost has been imposed on rural migrants during the transition.

Inclusive urbanization is a three-pronged strategy. Firstly, peasants' right to their collective land should be delineated clearly so that the village collective and peasant households have a clear idea of how much landed assets they can claim as their own. Secondly, rural development and village improvement, which have been ignored because of urban-rural divide, should be incorporated into municipal planning as one of the priorities. Thirdly, urban spatial expansion should be restricted so as to curb urban sprawl, to make cities compact and to save the countryside. Inward consolidation of the built-up areas should be pursued.

Clarification of entitlements to collective land as assets is a way allowing peasants to enjoy the benefits brought forward by urbanization. In high-density urbanizing regions, distribution of growing land rent derived from urbanization is an important matter for social justice. Non-agricultural land rent is highly unevenly distributed spatially. The convention of land rent taken by the village members only gives rise to contentious social inequality not only between locals and migrants but also between villages in urbanizing locations and those remaining in agricultural production.

Land rent enhanced by urbanization should be traded and shared in a large jurisdiction. Efficiency and fairness can be achieved by enlarging the size of markets for trading. This thinking has already been translated into practices. 'Chongqing Trading Platform of Rural Non-agricultural Land Entitlements' (*Chongqing Nongcun Tudi Jiaoyisuo*) has been established since December 4, 2008. One of the intended objectives is to establish a single market for transaction of legitimate rural collective non-agricultural land entitlements within the region of Chongqing municipality, so that those villages in the peripheral areas enjoy the same prices for giving up entitlements as those in the urbanizing areas. In other words, villages within the municipality share the urbanization benefits that are embedded in the entitlement prices, regardless of their location (https://m.baidu.com/paw/c/www.360doc.cn/mip/658183444.html, accessed April 8, 2018). The State Council recently issued a new policy in March 10, 2018, stating that some poor regions in the western provinces can transfer their collective nonagricultural land entitlements to the advanced provinces, so that these entitlements can fetch higher prices (because of advanced urbanization) than if traded within the same locales (http://www.gov.cn/zhengce/content/2018-03/26/content_5277477.htm, accessed April 8, 2018). It suggests that the poor regions could enjoy some urbanization benefits via this interprovince transfer of land entitlements.

Notes

1 The university district is a sizable zone in the urban periphery where a cluster of universities and student accommodation facilities is located. These universities are relocated from the cramped central area.
2 Although urban land can be made more productive by improved building services provided by the landowner than would otherwise be the case, provision of infrastructure and public facilities contribute significantly to the increase of land rent, or 'unearned increment' to the landowners as coined by John Stuart Mill (1878). Much of the rentals paid by land users to landowners in cities where land is scarce are the economic rent of land. Increasing demand for land derived from economic development and population growth associated with urbanization drives up land economic rent and thus 'unearned increment'. It is reported that the redevelopment of Liede Village near the new central business district of Guangzhou has benefited the villagers and collective tremendously. Land-related income has increased by 2.6 times for the village households and four times for the collective (G. C. S. Lin, 2015). It is a typical unearned rent increment.
3 'Inflicted rent reduction' is opposite to 'unearned rent increment', and it is caused by the negative externalities induced by some urban facilities such as highways and incinerators.

References

Brown, H. G. (1999) Land speculation and land-value taxation, in K. C. Wenzer (ed.) *Land-value taxation – The equitable and efficient source of public finance*, 46–57. Armonk, New York: ME Sharpe.

George, H. (1881/2009) *Progress and poverty: An inquiry into the cause of industrial depressions and of increase of want with increase of wealth: The remedy*. Cambridge: Cambridge University Press.

Glaeser, E. L. (2011) *Triumph of the city: How our greatest invention makes us richer, smarter, greener, healthier, and happier.* New York: Penguin Press.

Grant, M. (1999) Compensation and betterment, in J. B. Cullingworth (ed.) *British planning: 50 years of urban and regional policy*, 62–75. London: The Athlone Press.

Guangzhou Municipal Bureau of Statistics (GMBS) (2014) *Statistical yearbook of Guangzhou, 2013*. Beijing: China Statistics Press. (in Chinese).

Hagman, D. G. & Misczynski, D. J. (eds.) (1978) *Windfalls for wipeouts: Land value capture and compensation*. Chicago, IL: American Society of Planning Officials.

Healey, P., Purdue, M. & Ennis, F. (1995) *Negotiating development: Rationales and practice for development obligations and planning gain*. London: E & FN Spon.

Lai, Y. N., Peng, Y., Li, B. & Lin, Y. L. (2014) Industrial land development in urban villages in China: A property rights perspective. *Habitat International*, 41: 185–194.

Lin, G. C. S. (2015) The redevelopment of China's construction land: Practising land property rights in cities through renewals. *The China Quarterly*, 224: 865–887.

Lin, Y. L., Hao, P. & Geertman, S. (2015) A conceptual framework on modes of governance for the regeneration of Chinese 'villages in the city'. *Urban Studies*, 52(10): 1774–1790.

Mill, J. S. (1878) *Principles of political economy: With some of their applications to social philosophy*. London: Longmans, Green, Reader and Ryer.

National Bureau of Statistics, China (NBSC) (2005, 2014) *China urban construction statistical yearbook*. Beijing: China Statistics Press. (in Chinese).

Stiglitz, J. (1977) The theory of local public goods, in M. S. Feldstein & R. P. Inman (eds.) *The economics of public services*, 274–333. London: McMillan.

Zhu, J. M. (2004) Local developmental state and order in China's urban development during transition. *International Journal of Urban and Regional Research*, 28(2): 424–447.

Zhu, J. M. & Hu, T. T. (2009) Disordered land rent competition in China's peri-urbanization – Case study of Beiqijia Township, Beijing. *Environment & Planning A*, 41: 1639–1646.

Index

Ambiguous land rights iii, 14, 16, 154
Anticommons, the 10, 17, 167, 171, 172

Beiqijia 134–136, 148–150
Bourgeois consumer cities 11, 84, 199

Chengzhongcun 84–87, 91
Coase Theorem 6
Collective land ownership 47, 147, 173, 181, 199
Collective land rights 14, 17, 126, 140–143, 181, 183, 199, 204
Commons, the 7–9, 84, 86, 107, 117, 172
Community management 4, 180
Compact city 167–168, 186, 192
Cooperative 16, 31, 47, 141, 151–154, 176, 178, 189–190, 193–194

Danwei 14, 18, 43, 65–66, 68–69, 79–80, 91, 101–103, 105, 107, 117–118, 122, 200
Danwei-enterprises iii, 17, 71, 75, 80, 91, 118–120
De facto property rights 44, 101
Decentralization 43, 67, 73, 75, 77–78, 80–81, 105, 121–122, 186, 192, 201
Dual land market 17, 51, 64–65, 71, 89–90, 100, 200
Dualism 15, 17, 71, 73–75, 90, 120

Eight Key Industrial Cities 24

Fragmentation 47, 126, 133, 138, 150–151, 155, 181, 183, 204
Fragmented urbanization 140, 143–150

Gradualism 15, 17, 68, 71, 73–74, 90, 120
Growth coalition 17, 71, 73, 80, 97, 105–106, 117, 119–120

Henry George 180, 203
Household Production Responsibility Scheme 47, 127, 132, 141, 143, 150, 160
Housing commodification 67–68
Huaihai Road East 97, 112–115
Hukou 30, 139, 143, 153, 174–175, 177–179, 183

Inclusive urbanization 180, 192, 204
Informality 7–8, 16, 108, 152
In situ urbanization 17, 126, 129–130, 132
Institutional change 1, 11–12, 15–18, 51–52, 63, 73, 75, 97, 110, 116–118, 121, 126, 148, 151, 181–183, 199–200

Jing'an 44, 102–105, 108, 112–114

Kaihsienkung 45, 48
Kunshan 130–131, 134–138, 184–190, 192–194

Land development right 17, 97, 100, 102, 104, 150
Land leasehold 14, 17, 51, 63–65, 69, 71–72, 81, 100, 109, 118, 121–122, 200–201
Land marketization 54, 63, 67, 89
Land rent dissipation 16, 18, 159, 199–201
Local coalition 73, 80

Local developmental state 17, 71, 75, 78–80, 82, 84, 105, 101, 117–121, 147, 156, 200
Localism 77–78, 81–82

Market failures 3, 7, 121
Market provision of public goods 117
Means of production 11–12, 14, 16–17, 23–24, 31–33, 47, 54, 75, 97, 99–100, 108–109, 141, 143, 148, 161, 183, 199–200

Nanhai 134, 139, 140, 147, 153–154, 161, 176–178
Nanjing Road West 97, 112, 114
Nonproductive sectors 16, 23, 30–31, 199

Panyu 143–146, 154–155, 157, 159–161, 181
Pearl River Delta 17–18, 86, 126, 129–130, 138–139, 143–144, 151, 158, 167, 174, 180–182, 202
Private governance 16, 126, 156–157, 159
Productive sectors 11, 16, 27, 30–31, 36, 199
Proletarian producer cities 11, 23, 84, 199

Rent-seeking 3, 54, 92, 123
Renewal and Refurbishment Program (RRP) 18, 167, 181–183
Rentier class 18, 45, 126, 150, 167, 176, 180, 183

Rural development 17–18, 126–128, 130, 132, 167, 172–174, 176, 183–184, 192, 204
Rural industrialization 17, 126–127, 129, 132–133, 138, 141, 146, 150, 173, 175, 181–182, 184–185, 189, 193, 204
Rural-rural inequality 17, 167, 174

Shenzhen Special Economic Zone 51–52, 63, 87
Socialist land use right 11, 14, 17, 97–98, 100–101, 111, 117–118, 200
State-owned-enterprises (SOEs) 32, 53–57, 66, 71, 74–76, 79–80, 90–91, 98, 104, 118–121
State provision of private goods 117
Subsidiarity 18, 167, 175, 192–193

Township-village enterprises (TVEs) 126–127, 129, 132–133, 148, 176, 184, 187–190

Uncertainty 3, 6, 14–16, 90, 107, 116, 121, 151–152, 182, 199

Workers' New Villages 34–35

Yangtze River Delta 17–18, 45, 126–127, 129–130, 133, 136–137, 167, 174, 184, 187
Yonglian village 127–128

Zoning 4, 6–9, 86, 97, 108, 122, 154, 161, 172, 181, 200